BECOME A BETTER YOU

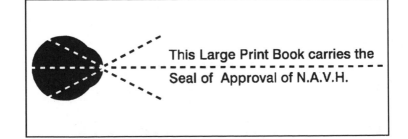

This Large Print Book carries the
Seal of Approval of N.A.V.H.

BECOME A BETTER YOU

7 KEYS TO IMPROVING
YOUR LIFE EVERY DAY

JOEL OSTEEN

WHEELER PUBLISHING
An imprint of Thomson Gale, a part of The Thomson Corporation

Detroit • New York • San Francisco • New Haven, Conn. • Waterville, Maine • London

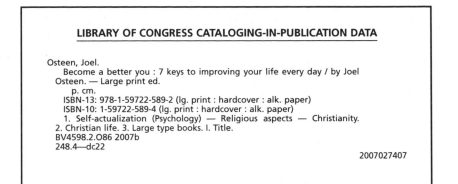

THOMSON
━━━━━★━━━━━ ™
GALE

LIBRARY OF CONGRESS CATALOGING-IN-PUBLICATION DATA

Osteen, Joel.
    Become a better you : 7 keys to improving your life every day / by Joel Osteen. — Large print ed.
    p. cm.
    ISBN-13: 978-1-59722-589-2 (lg. print : hardcover : alk. paper)
    ISBN-10: 1-59722-589-4 (lg. print : hardcover : alk. paper)
    1. Self-actualization (Psychology) — Religious aspects — Christianity. 2. Christian life. 3. Large type books. I. Title.
BV4598.2.O86 2007b
248.4—dc22

                    2007027407

Published in 2007 by arrangement with Free Press,
a division of Simon & Schuster, Inc.

Printed in the United States of America on permanent paper
10 9 8 7 6 5 4 3 2 1

To Victoria, the love of my life.
Thanks for believing in me and inspiring me to greater things. Your love, friendship, and your kind, gentle spirit make living with you each day a gift. I would not be who I am without the seeds you have sown in my life.

I respect you, admire you, and look forward to spending the rest of our lives together.

To Jonathan.
Thanks for being such an incredible son! You are kind, respectful, and have a great sense of humor. You amaze me with your wisdom, your insight, and your talent. I treasure the time we share together. You are going to make a significant impact on our world. I am proud to call you my son.

To Alexandra, my little jewel.
You are not only beautiful on the outside, but you are beautiful on the inside. You have such

a tender heart, filled with kindness and compassion. You are smart and funny, and have a voice like an angel. When you sing, we feel God's love. I am proud of you and I will always be your number one fan!

CONTENTS

ACKNOWLEDGMENTS

Writing a book is a bit like gathering some raw materials and through an extensive refining process, shaping them into a finely tuned, high performance automobile — it takes a great team of skilled and dedicated people to see a concept, and then turn it into reality. I've been blessed to have just such a team working with me on *Become a Better You,* and I appreciate each person who has contributed.

First, I want to thank the many people who have poured spiritual wisdom into my life. Growing up in a pastor's home as I did, I was privileged to meet and talk with a wide variety of "world-changers," individuals from around the world, ministers and their families, men and women who wanted their lives to count, to make a difference, and who believed that our best days were still ahead of us. Many of the people who visited with us or ministered to our community were humorous and interesting, and all possessed a wide repertoire of incredibly fascinating stories, laced with life principles and truth. To them, along with my mother and father, I am grateful for laying the strong foundations on which much that I do today is built.

Next, I want to thank the many great authors and speakers whose books and audio messages have helped shape my life, as well. These mentors "built the infrastructure," and contributed greatly to my continuing education, and I thank each one for the investment you have made in me. With every life that is touched through my books, speaking, audio or video ministries, you share the credit; any success I have known, and any eternal impact I may have is part of your legacy.

Special thanks to Carolyn Reidy, Dominick Anfuso, and Martha Levin of Simon & Schuster, for believing in this project and for going the extra mile to make sure it happened. Thanks, too, to Jason Madding, for a great cover design.

I am immensely grateful to Jan Miller and Shannon Marven, of Dupree/Miller, who caught the vision for what could be, and then patiently oversaw all our negotiations.

Special thanks to collaborator Ken Abraham, who provided key editorial assistance as well as valuable insights and perspectives to my material.

Thanks also to the Lakewood Church family — the thousands of faithful who attend each week as well as the those who watch our services on television, the internet, pod casts, or who listen on radio. I'm so grateful to the devoted staff of Lakewood Church, for facilitating much of the research and logistical details involved with this project. Michelle Trevino, my executive assistant, coordinated so many important aspects of the book-writing process. Paul Osteen, Kevin Comes, Don Iloff, and Duncan Dodds — my inner circle of mighty men — deserve great credit. These men smoothly manage the myriad aspects of the ministry while allowing me to do what I do best.

Heartfelt thanks to my mom, Dodie Osteen, who loves me, prays for me, and always encourages me. And to Georgine Iloff, the best mother-in-law a man could ever want! Thanks to my sister, Lisa Comes, whose excellence and integrity inspire me; to Gary and April Simons of High Point Church and Jim and Tamara Graff of Faith Family Church, my sisters and brothers-in-law. God has richly blessed me through each of you. Last, but certainly not least, thanks to my sisters-in-law, Jackelyn Iloff and Jennifer Osteen, for your constant support and encouragement.

INTRODUCTION

Whether life is going well for you or collapsing right before your eyes, we all want to be better. We want to be more effective in our lives. We want to know God better; we want to be better spouses and parents, better lovers, better encouragers, better community leaders, better employees, and better bosses and managers. God put something deep down inside us that evokes a desire to be more like Him. In our inner being, we hear a voice saying, "You were born for better than this; you are meant to live at a higher level than you are currently. Don't be satisfied with less. You can be better."

The question is: "How? What must I do to become a better me?"

In my first book, *Your Best Life Now,* I presented seven steps to living at your full potential. Today many people are developing a greater vision for their future and are experiencing more of God's blessings and favor.

But even if you are living your best life now, it is important that you do not become stagnant. God always wants to increase us, to do more in and through us. He always wants to take us deeper into self-discovery and then wants to raise us to a higher level of living. He didn't create us to be average. He doesn't want us to settle for "good enough." He wants us to keep stretching, to keep pressing forward into the next level.

Now, in *Become a Better You,* I want to help you do just that. I want to take you deeper; I'm hoping to help you look inside yourself and discover the priceless seeds of greatness that God has placed within you. In this book, I will reveal to you seven keys that you can use to unlock those seeds of greatness, allowing them to burst forth in an abundantly blessed life. These keys are not complicated or difficult; in fact, their sheer simplicity often causes them to elude many people's notice. Nevertheless, they are seven key principles that have helped shape me and continue to keep me expecting good things in my personal life, in my relationships, in my family, and in my career. I know these principles work, because I have experienced them firsthand in my own life.

Too many people settle for mediocrity in their thoughts, attitudes, or actions. It's time to put off those negative mind-sets and rise higher. Remember, God has put in you everything you need to live a victorious life. Now, it's up to you to draw it out. We can't let wrong mind-sets, a negative past, or other people's opinions discourage us or cause us to give up and quit pressing forward. People who want to live at their full potential have discovered that the good can often be the enemy of the best.

Have you ever noticed a person and thought, *What a great attitude! She's a great mother,* or *He's a tremendous employee.* Most likely, that person you admired was a walking, talking example of someone who is becoming a better person.

What does it mean to become a better you? First, you understand that God wants you to become all that He created you to be. Second, it is imperative that you realize that God will do His part, but you must do your part as well. To become a better you, you must:

1. Keep pressing forward.
2. Be positive toward yourself.
3. Develop better relationships.
4. Form better habits.
5. Embrace the place where you are.
6. Develop your inner life.
7. Stay passionate about life.

Most of us make some effort to improve in these areas, but to truly see the kind of marked improvement we want, we must start focusing on them in a more deliberate manner. In the pages ahead, I'll explain each of these principles in depth: how they work and how you can use them to improve your life and affect generations to come. I'll help you see where you are, where you have been, and where you are going. As we grow together, God will continue to pour good things into our lives, and He will indeed take us to places that we never dreamed possible.

If you are going through a tough time, take heart. There are better days ahead! God wants to bring you through, to bring you out even better, and to restore everything you have lost, plus give you more!

If you are thriving and enjoying life, you can use these principles to help guard your heart and mind, and to maintain an attitude and lifestyle that is pleasing to God. Be quick to acknowledge God's goodness in your life, keeping in mind that it is His blessing that you are enjoying and that you are blessed to be a blessing to someone else, and He will continue to fill your life with immeasurable love, joy, and peace.

Get ready! You are about to embark on an inner journey through which you will explore parts of yourself that perhaps you've rarely or never previously tested. Every step is about your head, your heart, and your soul, but you will be surprised to see how your inner journey influences your "outer" life, producing better quality relationships, a more productive use of your gifts and talents, and ultimately a totally better life.

I must warn you: Practicing the seven keys within this book could be a potentially life-changing process! And while I can't guarantee that you will become rich or famous, I can assure you that if you follow this plan, you will live a more fulfilled life.

Becoming a better you is all about growing, learning, and improving. The more you learn to trust God, the better you will be. He will continually expand your horizons, and you can become a better you!

PART ONE: KEEP PRESSING FORWARD

CHAPTER 1
STRETCHING TO THE NEXT LEVEL

The famous architect Frank Lloyd Wright designed many beautiful buildings, homes, and other magnificent structures. Toward the end of his career, a reporter asked him, "Of your many beautiful designs, which one is your favorite?"

Without missing a beat, Frank Lloyd Wright answered, "My next one."

Frank Lloyd Wright understood the principle of stretching, constantly pressing forward, never being satisfied simply with past successes. The entire world is waiting for your next adventure.

Too many people are living far below their potential. They have many gifts and talents, and so much more going for them. But they've gotten comfortable, settled where they are, and lately become too easily satisfied.

I often hear people making excuses for stagnating in their personal growth:

"I've achieved as much as most."

"Compared to other people, I'm doing pretty well in my career."

"I've gone as far as my parents did."

That's great, but God wants you to go further. He's a progressive God, and He wants every generation to be increasing in happiness, success, and significance. No matter where we are in life, God has more in store. He never wants us to quit growing. We should always be reaching for new heights in our abilities, in our spiritual walk, in our finances, careers, and personal relationships. We all have areas where we can come up higher. We may have achieved a certain level of success, but there are always new challenges, other mountains to climb. There are new dreams and goals that we can pursue.

No doubt, God has already done a lot in your past. He's opened doors for you that nobody else could open. Maybe He's given you a wonderful family and home. Perhaps He's caused you to be promoted, given you favor with your employer or supervisors. That is marvelous, and you should thank God for all that He has done for you. But be careful: Sometimes when you are enjoying life, it is easy to become complacent, to get satisfied, and think, *Yes, God's been good to me. I can't complain. I've achieved my goals;*

I've reached my limits. But God never performs His greatest feats in your yesterdays.

He may have done wonders in the past, but you haven't seen anything yet! The best is yet to come. Don't allow your life to become dull. Keep dreaming, hoping, and planning for new projects, experiences, and adventures with God.

I've discovered that God likes to outdo Himself. He wants to show His favor in your life in greater ways today than He did yesterday. He wants you to be more blessed tomorrow than you are today. He intends for you to have a greater impact on the world than you have had. That means if you're a teacher, you haven't taught your best lesson yet. If you're a builder, you haven't built your best home yet. If you're a businessperson, you haven't negotiated your best deal yet. It's time to get your hopes up; enlarge your vision, and get ready for the new things that God has on the horizon. Your best days are not behind you. They're in front of you.

But if this is going to happen, we have to keep pressing forward, stretching ourselves. Get rid of low expectations. Don't make little plans for your life. Don't have little dreams. Don't go around thinking, *Everybody gets good breaks except me. I've reached my limits. I'll probably never get this promotion. I don't know why I'm not as talented as that other person.*

No, get rid of that defeated mind-set. You are a child of the Most High God. God has breathed His life into you. He planted seeds of greatness in you. You have everything you need to fulfill your God-given destiny. God has already put in the talent, the creativity, the discipline, the wisdom, and the determination. It's all in you. You are full of potential. But you have to do your part and start tapping into it. You have to make better use of the gifts and talents that God has given you.

The Scripture teaches that we have a valuable treasure on the inside. You have a gift. You have something to offer that nobody else has. You didn't just show up on planet Earth by accident. You were handpicked by Almighty God. He saw you before you were formed in your mother's womb and placed you here for a reason. You have an assignment. There's something that God wants you to accomplish. Somebody needs your touch. Somebody needs what you have.

Don't live with that treasure undiscovered, and don't die with the treasure still in you. Press forward. Give birth to the dreams and desires that God has placed in your heart.

Neurologists have discovered that the average person uses less than 10 percent of his or her mind. That means more than 90 percent of the mind's capability lies dormant. It never gets tapped into. But if we could just understand what we have: God has deposited a part of Himself in you. When it came time for you to be born, God said, "Let Me give you some of this gift; some of this talent; some of this creativity." You have the seed of Almighty God on the inside of you. You were never created to be average. You were never created to reach a certain level and then plateau. You were created to excel. There's no limit to how high you can go in life. There's no limit to what you can accomplish, if you will just learn to shake off complacency and keep stretching into the next level.

But it all starts in our hearts and minds. We have to believe that we have what it takes. We have to believe that we have a gift, a treasure on the inside. People may have tried to push you down. Circumstances may have soured your outlook on life.

Maybe you've tried to succeed in life but have hit a brick wall again and again. Try again. Somebody may have told you "no" a thousand times; ask again. Keep asking until you get the "yes" that you've been waiting to hear. You've got to keep pressing. Too many people grow satisfied with far less than God's best for their lives. Sometimes they get discouraged, but all too often, they simply get comfortable. They stop stretching anymore; they are not exercising their faith, and like a once muscular, toned body that no longer exercises, they grow flabby. One of the main reasons for this sort of complacency is that people don't really understand what they have on the inside. They don't understand their God-given potential.

Years ago, a friend of mine and a passenger were in Europe driving on the Autobahn, the superhighway across Germany. Unlike American freeways, the Autobahn has no speed limits. You can travel as fast as you want to drive.

My friend was so excited as he pressed down on the accelerator and took the car up to 80 miles an hour, then 90, 100, 110. He felt like the king of the road, zooming past people left and right.

A few minutes later, another car streaked down the freeway. This car was the exact same model as my friend's car, but it blew by him like he was standing still. That second automobile must have been going 170 per hour.

The passenger traveling with my friend laughed and said, "See; you're not going as fast as you can. You're just going as fast as you will."

Think about that: My friend's car possessed tremendous potential. It too was capable of going 180 miles per hour. The manufacturer put in the potential. How fast my friend drove didn't have anything to do with the car's capability. In other words, the potential was not lessened just because he chose not to use it. And simply having the potential on board did not affect his future.

It's the same way with us. Our potential has been put in us by our Manufacturer, our Creator, Almighty God. Whether we use it or not does not diminish it, but it does impact our future. The events of your past do not reduce your potential. How somebody has treated you or what he or she said about you doesn't change your potential. Maybe you've been through some disappointments, or have had some unfair things happen in life. None of that affects your potential. It has been put in you permanently by the Creator of the Universe. When we believe, we take a step of faith and stretch ourselves; that's when we start to tap into it. That's when we'll rise higher.

The capability is in you. The real question is: Are you willing to break free from your self-imposed limitations and start stretching to the next level?

Too often, we allow experiences from the past to keep us from pressing forward. Perhaps a business partner, a coach, a relative, or a friend said, "Hey, do you really think you can do that? Maybe that opportunity is not right for you. What if you try and fail? What if it doesn't work out?"

These negative words may haunt you and stymie your progress in pressing forward. Understand that none of those statements can change your potential on the inside. It's still in you. Don't allow other people to talk you out of using what God has given you and doing what you know God wants you to do.

Many people have had negative comments spoken over them, such as "You don't have what it takes. You're not very talented. I don't think you'll ever be successful."

If we're not careful, we'll allow those negative words to play over and over in our minds. They can create a stronghold.

A young woman named Sherry came to me for advice. She had tolerated an abusive relationship for years in which she was repeatedly told, "You can't do anything right. You're so slow. You're not attractive." After hearing that for so long, it had totally beaten her down physically, emotionally, and spiritually. She had no joy, little confidence, and extremely low self-esteem.

I told her what I'm telling you: "Your value, your gifts, and talents have been put in you by Almighty God. And it doesn't matter what anyone else has spoken over you. The good news is God has the final authority. He says you have a treasure on the inside. He says you have a gift. He says you are valuable. You've got to quit playing that old tune and put on a new one. You need to be dwelling on thoughts like: I am creative. I am talented. I am valuable. I have a bright future. My best days are still out in front of me. You have to get your mind going in this new direction. Because dwelling on negative thoughts about yourself will keep you from becoming all God has created you to be."

Regardless of who has spoken negative words into your life — a parent, a spouse, a coach, or a teacher — you must cast those words down. Words are powerful. They can create barriers in your heart and mind. Sometimes one little phrase can hold us back for years.

A friend of mine used to travel as an assistant with a well-known minister. One day, a man came to the hotel and wanted the minister to pray for him. The associate told the man, "I'm sorry, but the minister can't be disturbed. He's resting and getting prepared for the meeting tonight."

But this man refused to take no for an answer. He was extremely aggressive and determined. My friend remained kind and courteous, trying to placate the unexpected visitor. But the caller continued to press.

Finally, my friend said, "How about this? I will pray for you. I work with the minister every day. I'll be glad to pray for you."

At that, the obnoxious man turned his nose up. He said, "I don't think so. *You* won't do."

The words stung: "You won't do." The implicit message was "You are not good enough. Your prayers can't get the job done."

My friend later told how those words seared through his heart and mind day after day. "You won't do." Lying in bed at night, he'd think, *You don't have what it takes. You're not anointed like the famous preacher. You can't help a soul.*

The young man already struggled with his confidence, but now he was allowing these negative words to play repeatedly in his subconscious mind. He couldn't shake them off, and instead allowed those negative words to hold him down for years.

Too many people don't have the confidence and the self-esteem they should because they're constantly dwelling on negative thoughts about themselves. I don't say this arrogantly, but in my mind, all day long I try to remind myself: *I am anointed. I am creative. I am talented. I am successful. I have the favor of God. People like me. I'm a victor and not a victim.*

Try it! If you go around thinking those kinds of thoughts, low self-esteem, lack of confidence, or inferiority won't have a chance with you. Throw your shoulders back, put a smile on your face, and be looking for opportunities to stretch into the next level.

Back in the Garden of Eden, after Adam and Eve ate the forbidden fruit, they hid. In the cool of the day, God came to them and said, "Adam, Eve, where are you?"

They said, "God, we're hiding because we are naked."

I love the way God answered them. He said, "Adam, who told you that you were naked?" In other words, "Who told you that something was wrong with you?" God immediately knew the enemy had been talking to them.

God is saying to you today, "Who told you that you don't have what it takes to succeed? Who told you that the best grades you could make in school would be C's rather than A's?

Who told you that you are not attractive enough to succeed in your personal relationships or talented enough to flourish in your career? Who told you that your marriage is never going to last?"

Those are lies from the enemy. You need to reject those ideas and discover what God says about you.

"Well, I don't think I could ever get this promotion, Joel."

Who told you that? God said, "No good thing will He withhold when you walk uprightly."

"Well, I don't think I'll ever get married, Joel. I haven't had a date in so long I don't think I'll ever find someone who would love me for who I am, and with whom I would be compatible."

Who told you that? God said, "When you delight yourself in Him, He will give you the desires of your heart."

"Well, I don't think I could ever be in management. I don't think I could be a leader."

Who told you that? God says, "You can do all things through Christ." The potential is inside you. It doesn't change just because you don't believe it or just because you've been through some negative experiences in the past. It has been deposited in you permanently by the Creator of the Universe. The

Scripture says, "God's gifts and His callings are irrevocable."[1] That means God is never going to take back the potential He has poured into you. He's never going to say, "I'm tired of dealing with you. You've tried and failed too many times. You've made so many mistakes. Let me just have the gifts back."

No, those gifts, and the calling on your life, will be with you till the day you leave this earth. But it is up to you to decide whether you tap into them and use them or not.

IF YOU ONLY KNEW

In John 4, Jesus met a woman at a well in Samaria, and He asked her for a drink of water. She was surprised, because back then, the Jews didn't have anything to do with the Samaritans. She said, "How can you ask me for a drink?"

Jesus said, "If you knew who I was, you would ask me for a drink, and I would give you living water."

The woman thought that Jesus was talking about literal water. She said, "Sir, you don't even have anything with which to draw water. You don't have a bucket, and the well is deep. How can you possibly give me water?"

I wonder how many times God tells us that

He wants to do something great in our lives, that we are going to be healthy and well; we are going to get out of debt. We feel it strongly, but like the woman at the well, we start thinking about what we don't have, and all the obstacles in our path, and before long, we've talked ourselves out of God's best.

"That could never happen for me. I don't have the education; I don't have the talent; I don't have the discipline. I'll never break this addiction; I'll never accomplish my dreams." No, you must quit looking at what you don't have, and start believing that all things are possible.

I never dreamed that I'd be doing what I am doing today, encouraging people around the world. For seventeen years, my father tried to get me to speak at our home church, but I had no desire. I'm naturally quiet and reserved and would much prefer working behind the scenes.

But when my father went to be with the Lord, I knew that I was supposed to step up. Although I had never preached before, never had been to seminary, and had no formal training, I said, "God, I'm not going to look at what I don't have. I'm looking unto you. I know in my weakness, you show up the strongest." I took that step of faith, and God has taken me places I never dreamed.

He can do the same for you. Don't get stuck in a rut in your attitude, your career, or your marriage. You have incredible potential within you — much more than you may realize! God is not limited to the laws of nature. He can do what human beings cannot. The key is to get your eyes off your problems and onto your God.

When God puts a dream in your heart, it may look impossible in the natural. Every voice may tell you it will never happen. "You'll never break that addiction. You'll never accomplish your dreams. You'll never be happy." But if you will believe and stay in faith, and expect good things, you too can defy the odds.

I talked to a famous tightrope walker, who comes from a family of seven generations of circus entertainers. I asked him, "What is the key to walking on the tightrope? You make it look so easy."

He said, "Joel, the secret is to keep your eyes fixed on where you are going. You never look down. Where your head goes, that's where your body is going, too. If you look down, there's a good chance you will fall. So you always have to look to where you want to be."

It's the same principle in life. Some people

are always looking back, focused on their hurts and pains. Other people are looking down, living in self-pity, and complaining that life is not fair. The key to rising higher is to keep looking to where you want to go. Dream big dreams! Don't focus on where you are today; keep a positive vision and see yourself accomplishing your goals and fulfilling your destiny.

As a young man, growing up, Pete loved playing baseball. That was his passion. But when he tried out for the team, the coach didn't even give him a chance. He said, "I'm sorry, son; you're just too small. You will never be able to play on this team."

Pete was devastated. His heart was set on playing baseball. His mom picked him up from school, and he and his best friend climbed into the backseat of the car. Poor Pete was doing all he could to keep his composure, trying not cry, and then his friend — who was much bigger than Pete — said, "Hey, did you tell your mom you didn't make the team because you're too little?"

The friend's words pierced Pete's heart. He hated being small. He went home feeling low and dejected. Later that week, though, the school made a special announcement: "Since so many boys tried out for the team, we are going to create a second team; a B team." Pete tried out and made the B team.

That season, those two teams ended up in a play-off for the championship, and the second team, the B team, beat the A team. Guess who the winning pitcher was. That's right; the B team won the championship thanks to Pete's great pitching ability.

Now, consider this question: How much potential did Pete have when he was rejected for the A team? Was his potential any different when he began pitching for the B team?

The point is: Other people's opinions do not determine your potential. What they said or what they think about you does not change what God has placed on the inside. Don't allow negative words or attitudes to take root and keep you from pressing forward. God may be asking you today, "Who told you that you were too small? Who told you that you aren't intelligent? Who told you that you don't have the necessary talent?"

God would not have put the dream in your heart if He had not already given you everything you need to fulfill it. That means if I have a dream or a desire, and I know it's from God, I don't have to worry whether I have what it takes to see that dream fulfilled. I know God doesn't make mistakes. He doesn't call us to do something without giving us the ability or the wherewithal to do it.

You have to realize that God has matched you with your world. In other words, even though at times you may not feel that you are able to accomplish your dreams, you have to get beyond those feelings and know deep inside, *I have the seed of Almighty God in me.* Understand, God will never put a dream in your heart without first equipping you with everything you need to accomplish it. If you feel that you don't have the necessary wisdom, talent, ability, or resources, simply remind yourself, *God has matched me with my world. He has already put in me what I need.*

A minister once handed a man a twenty-dollar bill and asked him to hide it secretly in his wife's Bible. "Be sure she doesn't see you do it," he emphasized.

Later, during the sermon, the minister asked the woman to stand up. "Do you trust me, ma'am?" he asked.

"Yes, of course," she replied.

"Will you do what I ask you to do?"

"Yes, I will," she answered.

"Good, then please open your Bible, and give me the twenty-dollar bill inside."

The woman cringed, as she said, "Oh, I'm sorry. I don't have a twenty-dollar bill."

"I thought you said that you trusted me?" the minister asked with feigned incredulity.

lives, fine; but that won't keep me from believing. I know the promises of God are in me."

That's the attitude we need to have as well. So what if other people say I can't succeed? So what if someone tries to pull me down; so what if a person doesn't believe? I am not going to allow their actions, attitudes, or comments to cause me to give up on my God-given dreams. I'll not allow their unbelief to influence my faith.

Don't Let Rejection Keep You Down

Too often, when we suffer some kind of rejection or disappointment, we get so discouraged that we settle right where we are. "I guess it wasn't meant to be," we rationalize. Or "I thought I could go out with that attractive person, but maybe I am not good-looking enough." Or "I thought I could get the promotion, but I tried and failed. Maybe I don't have the talent. It didn't work out."

When disappointment or rejection knocks you down, get back up and go again. We give up too easily on our dreams. We need to understand that just as God supernaturally opens doors, sometimes God supernaturally closes doors. And when God closes a door, it's always because He has something better in store. So just because you've come to a dead end, that's not the time to give up. Find a different route and keep pressing forward.

Often, out of our greatest rejection comes our greatest direction. When you come to a closed door, or something doesn't work out in your life, instead of seeing that as the end, regard that as God nudging you into a better direction. Yes, sometimes it's uncomfortable; sometimes we may not like it. But we cannot make the mistake of just sitting back and settling where we are.

Back in 1959, my father was the pastor of a successful church with a thriving congregation. They had just built a beautiful new sanctuary and my father had a bright future. About that time, my sister Lisa was born with something like cerebral palsy. Hungry for a fresh touch from God, my dad went away for a while and got alone with God. He searched the Scriptures in a new way, and he began to see how God was a good God, a healing God, and that God could still perform miracles today. My dad went back to his church and he preached with a new fire, a new enthusiasm. He thought everybody would be thrilled, but the congregation's reaction was just the opposite. They didn't like his new message. It didn't fit in with their tradition. After suffering much persecution, heartache, and pain, my father knew the best thing for him to do was to leave that church.

Naturally, my dad was disappointed. He didn't understand why such a thing should happen. But remember, out of rejection comes direction. When one door closes, God is about to open up a bigger and a better door.

My father went down the street to an abandoned feed store. There, he and ninety other people formed Lakewood Church on Mother's Day, 1959. The critics said it would never last, but today, nearly fifty years later, Lakewood Church has grown to become one of the largest churches in America and is still going strong.

I don't believe that my father would have enjoyed the ministry he had, and I don't believe he would have become all God created him to be, if he would have stayed in that limited environment. Here's a key: The dream in your heart may be bigger than the environment in which you find yourself. Sometimes you have to get out of that environment in order to see that dream fulfilled.

Consider an oak tree. If you plant it in a pot, its growth will be limited. Once its roots fill that pot, it can grow no further. The problem is not with the tree; it is with the environment. It is stifling growth. Perhaps you have bigger things in your heart than your present environment can facilitate. That's why, at times, God will stir you out of a comfortable situation. When you go through persecution and rejection, it's not always because somebody has it in for you. Sometimes, that's God's way of directing you into His perfect will. He's trying to get you to stretch to the next level. He knows you're not going to go without a push, so He'll make it uncomfortable for you to stay where you are currently. The mistake we make at times is getting negative and sour; we focus on what didn't work out. When we do that, we inhibit the opening of new doors.

A few years ago, Lakewood Church was trying to buy some property on which we could build a new sanctuary. We had looked for months, and finally had found a wonderful one-hundred-acre tract of land. We were so excited. However, the day we were to close the deal, the people sold the land right out from under us.

I was terribly disappointed, and I had to tell myself, "Joel, God has closed this door for a reason. He has something better in store." Sure, I was down, and I admit that I was discouraged, but I had to shake that off and say, "No, I'm not settling here. I'm going to keep pressing forward."

A few months later, we found another nice

piece of property. It would have worked as well, but a similar series of events transpired and the owner refused to sell it to us. Another disappointment. I didn't understand it, but I said, "God, I'm trusting you. I know your ways are not my ways. This doesn't seem right. It doesn't seem fair. But I'm going to stay in an attitude of faith and keep expecting good things."

Not long after that, the door to the Compaq Center, a sixteen-thousand-seat sports arena, opened up in downtown Houston, right in the middle of one of the busiest sections of the city. Then it became clear why God had closed the other doors. Had we purchased either of those properties, those choices might have kept us from God's best.

Throughout life, we're not always going to understand everything that happens along the way. But we've got to learn to trust God. We've got to believe that He has us in the palm of His hand, that He is leading and guiding us, that He always has our best interests at heart.

I know people who have experienced rejection in their personal relationships. Maybe their marriage didn't work out. They put all those years into it and now they're hurt, dejected, going around defeated and not expecting anything good.

I don't believe that divorce is God's best. Unfortunately, sometimes it is unavoidable. If you have been through a divorce, understand that God still has another plan for your life. Just because somebody rejected you or walked out of your life and left you hurt, that doesn't mean you should retreat and settle where you are. That rejection did not change what God put on the inside of you. It doesn't mean that you cannot yet be happy. When one door closes, if you will keep the right attitude, God will open another door. But you have to do your part and keep pressing forward. Too many people get bitter, they get angry, and they start to blame God. Instead, let that hurt go. You may not understand it, but trust God and move on with your life. Don't look at it as the end. Look at it as a new beginning. Somebody may have rejected you, but you can hold your head up high knowing this: God accepts you. God approves you. And He has something better in store.

Friend, don't die with the treasure still inside you. Keep pressing forward. Keep reaching for new heights. Give birth to what God has placed in your heart. Don't let other people talk you out of your dreams. Listen to what God says about you, not all the negative voices. When you face rejection and disappointment, don't stay there. Know that God has another plan. That closed door simply means God has something better in store. You may not have experienced God's favor in the past, but this is a new day. You have not seen, heard, or imagined the wonderful things God has in store for you. Don't be weighed down by the distractions and disappointments in life; instead, keep stretching to the next level, reaching for your highest potential. If you do that, I can tell you with confidence your best days are in front of you. God is going to show you more of His blessings and favor, and you will become a better *you,* better than you ever dreamed possible.

Chapter 2
Give Your Dreams
a New Beginning

Years ago, I went into a government building that had two sets of double doors spaced about fifteen feet apart. The doors opened automatically as I approached, but for security reasons, when I went through the first set of doors, I had to let them close tightly before the next set of doors would open in front of me. As long as I stayed at the first set of doors, the second set would not open.

In many ways, life operates in a manner similar to those automatic doors. You have to let go of your disappointments, let go of your failures, and let those doors totally close behind you. Step forward, into the future that God has for you, knowing there's nothing you can do about past disappointments. You cannot change the past, but you can do something about the future. What's in front of you is far more important than what is behind you. Where you are going is more significant than where you came from or where you have been.

If you will have the right attitude, you will give birth to more in the future than you've lost in the past. Quit looking back. This is a new day. It may seem like your dreams have died, but God can resurrect your dead dreams or give you brand-new ones. He is a supernatural God and when we believe, all things are possible.

God has not given up on you; He knows that He put seeds of greatness in you. You have something to offer that nobody else has. He's given you noble dreams and desires. Too often, however, we allow adversities, disappointments, and setbacks to deter us, and before long, we find that we're not pressing forward anymore. We're not stretching; we're not believing we will rise any higher in life.

Ironically, some of the most gifted, talented people go through some of the most unfair, unfortunate experiences: divorce, abuse, neglect. And it's easy for such a person to think, *Why is this happening to me? What did I do to deserve any of this?*

Unfortunately, the enemy knows something about what's on the inside of you, as well. He knows the potential you're carrying, so he does everything he can to keep that seed from taking root. He doesn't want your gifts and talents to flourish. He doesn't want you to accomplish your dreams. He wants you to live an average, mediocre life.

But understand this: God did not create any person without putting something extremely valuable on the inside. Life may have tried to push you down through disappointments or setbacks. In the natural, you don't know how you could rise any higher. You don't see how you're ever going to be happy. You need to dig your heels in and say, "I know what I have on the inside. I'm a child of the Most High God. I'm full of His 'can-do' power, and I'm going to rise up to become everything God has created me to be."

The Apostle Paul urged his young understudy, Timothy, "Stir up the gift within you." Similarly, you need to stir up your gifts, talents, dreams, and desires — in short, the potential within you. Maybe these qualities and traits are buried beneath depression and discouragement, negative voices of people telling you that you can't; beneath weaknesses; beneath failures or fears.

But the good things of God are still there. Now you've got to do your part and start digging them out.

You may have had more than your share of unfair, negative experiences. But know this:

God wants to do a new thing. He wants to give you a new beginning. Don't give up. Don't go around thinking that you've peaked; that you've reached your limits in life. "Well, Joel, you don't know my situation. I've gone as far as my education can take me. You don't know my struggles."

No, I may not know any of that. But I do know our God, and He is all-powerful. He has more in store for you. My question for you is: Can you perceive it? Can you make room for it? The first place it starts is in your thinking. If your thinking is limited, then your life is going to be limited.

"But, Joel, I've gone through bankruptcy. I've tried and failed."

Well, let it go. This is a new day.

"My marriage didn't work out. I'm so disappointed. I never thought that I'd be in this situation at this point in my life."

That's unfortunate, but it's not the end. When one door closes, God will always open another. If all the doors close, He'll open a window! God always wants to give you a fresh beginning. He still has a great plan for your life. Do you know when that's going to happen? It will commence the moment you quit looking back. Whenever you quit grieving over what you've lost. Nothing will keep you from the good things of God as much as living in the past.

You may feel that life has knocked you down through disappointments or other unfair situations. But whatever you do, don't stay down. Get back up again, dust yourself off. If you can't find anybody to encourage you, learn to encourage yourself. Get up in the morning, put your shoulders back, look in the mirror, and say, "I've come too far to stop now. I may be knocked down, but I'm not knocked out. I'm going to get back up again. I know I'm a victor, not a victim."

You must keep yourself stirred up if you're going to see these new doors open. I know too many people who are living in the land of "good enough."

"Joel, I don't like my job, but it's good enough." "My husband and I, we don't get along well, but it's good enough; we're surviving." "I'm not using my gifts. I'm not doing what I like, but it's good enough; at least I'm working."

No, don't ever let "good enough" be good enough. Keep pressing. Keep believing. You were not made to be average; you were made to excel. You were made to leave your mark on this generation. At the start of each new day, remind yourself: "I am talented. I am creative. I am greatly favored by God. I am equipped. I am well able. I will see my dreams come to pass." Declare those statements by faith and before long, you will begin to see them in reality.

Understand that throughout life we will always have forces opposing us, trying to keep us from becoming all God's created us to be. And many times, the adversities, the unfair situations are the results of the enemy's efforts, attempting to discourage us and to deceive us into giving up on our dreams. You may feel as if you're at an empty place in life today. Not much is going your way. You've been through severe difficulties. But God wants to restore you, to encourage you, to fill you with His hope. He wants to resurrect your dreams. He wants to do a new thing.

Continually remind yourself that you have a gift on the inside. You are talented. You are creative. That's exactly why the enemy is trying to push you down, to keep your gifts, your creativity, your joy, your smile, your personality, and your dreams from ever seeing the light of day. He would love for them to lie dormant your whole lifetime. Thank God, it's not up to your enemy: it's up to you.

Granted, you may have gotten off to a rough start in life. You may have had more than your share of unfair things happen. But it's not how you start that counts. It's how you finish. Shake off the past; shake off discouragement. Remind yourself that God is still in complete control of your life. If you'll keep your trust in Him, He promises that no weapon formed against you will prosper. Your situation may seem unfair, it may be difficult; it may seem that the forces working against you are winning momentarily, but God said He'd turn your circumstances around and use them to your advantage.

Don't get complacent. Don't let "good enough" be good enough. Keep yourself stirred up. The forces that are for you are greater than the forces that are against you. The Scripture says, "Weeping may endure for a night, but joy is coming in the morning."[2]

You've got to get your dreams back. Get your fire back. Don't just survive your marriage; get a new vision for it today. Don't just drag into work doing the same thing: start taking some steps of faith. You've got more in you. Push yourself a bit. What you are hoping for may not have happened in the past, but this is a new day. If you'll keep pressing, hoping, believing, not only will you rise higher, but also you'll see things begin to change in your favor.

"Joel, I tried and I failed. My dream was dashed."

Well, dream another dream.

"But I've suffered a big loss, a major set-back."

Get back up and go again. That's what we all have to do.

Imagine the disappointment and devastation Adam and Eve must have felt when they discovered that their son Cain had killed their son Abel. Despite their pain, they said in Genesis 4:25, "God has appointed another seed unto us." They were saying in effect, "We are horrified that something like this could happen in our family, and we feel wiped out. But we're not going to mourn forever, because we know God has another seed."

In your difficult times, when you feel like conditions couldn't get any worse, God still says, "Take heart. I'm going to appoint another seed. I'm going to do a new thing."

You may have received a bad report from the doctor; or perhaps a relationship didn't work out. For everything that you've lost, everything that's been stolen, everything that's been taken away, know this: God has another plan. He has another seed.

God uses the word *seed* because that hints at what is coming. Remember, if you will do your part to let go of the old, and start pressing forward, you will give birth to more in the future than you've lost in the past.

Many people have a tough time letting go of what lies behind. They're always focused on who hurt them or how unfairly they have been treated. "Why did this happen to me?" Meanwhile, their gifts, talents, and dreams are pressed down. All the potential is lying dormant.

That almost happened to my father. My dad was married at an early age, but, unfortunately, the relationship didn't work out. My father was devastated. He felt certain that his days of ministry were over and that he'd never have a family again. He thought sure that he had ruined his life and destroyed any future impact for good that he might hope to have. He spent long hours just sitting around depressed, defeated, and dejected.

Then one day, he did what I'm asking you to do. Instead of settling for good enough, instead of focusing on all his mistakes and dwelling on his failures, he decided to let it go. Years later, he told me the hardest thing for him to do was to receive God's mercy. But the Bible says that when we confess our sins, God not only forgives us, He chooses not to remember them anymore. If somebody keeps bringing up your past, you need to know it is not God. If God has let go of it, why don't you let go of it, too?

That's what my father did. One day, he got up, dusted himself off, and said, "Yes, I've made some mistakes. I've made some poor choices. But I know God has another seed. I know He has another plan." Shortly after that, he met my mother. Eventually, they got married and over the years, God blessed them with five children!

Many people who, like my father, have experienced hurt and pain are sitting around wallowing in their mistakes, feeling guilty, condemned, and frustrated. Feeling like they're washed up in life, they allow their gifts and talents to waste away; they place their dreams on hold.

Please, don't let that be you. If you've made mistakes, know this: God is the God of a second chance, a third chance, a fourth, and more. I'm not saying to take the easy path and bail out of a marriage. No, if at all possible, stick with that marriage and make it work. However, if you're already past that point, don't sit around thinking that life is over and that you're never going to be happy. No, God has another seed. He wants to give you a new beginning.

Let the door close completely and step forward into the future God has for you. Quit looking back. Instead, receive God's mercy and start pressing forward in life.

The car you drive has a large windshield, but only a relatively small rearview mirror. The implication is obvious: What happened in your past is not nearly as important as what is in your future. Where you are going is much more important than where you've been. If you stay focused on the past, you're liable to miss numerous excellent opportunities ahead.

How do we let go of the past? First, discipline your thoughts to stop thinking about it. Quit talking about it. Quit reliving every negative experience.

If you have been through a loss or one of your dreams has died, of course there's a proper time for grieving. But at some point, you need to get up, dust yourself off, put on a fresh attitude, and start pressing forward in life. Don't let disappointment become the central theme of your life. Quit mourning over something you can't change. God wants to give you a new beginning, but you have to let go of the old before you'll ever see the new. Let that door close behind you and step through the door in front of you.

Maybe you've allowed other people to convince you that you're never going to rise higher, that you will never see your dreams come to pass. It's been too long. You've messed up too severely.

Don't believe those lies. Instead, take courage from the Old Testament character Caleb. When Caleb was a young man, he and Joshua were part of an exploratory spy mission to determine the strength of the enemy before God's people moved into the land that God had promised them. Of the twelve spies, only Caleb and Joshua presented a positive report to Moses. They said, "We are well able to take the land." The other ten spies said, "No, Moses, there are giants in the land; the opposition is too formidable; the obstacles to overcome are too large." And the majority tried to talk Moses and the rest of the children of Israel out of pressing forward into the blessings that God promised them. They were all too willing to settle for second best, to dwell for the rest of their lives right where they were. Unfortunately, that group of negative thinkers never did make it into the Promised Land. They spent the next forty years spinning their wheels and wandering around aimlessly in a desert. Eventually, most of them died with their dream still in them, as God raised up an entire new generation of people.

By then, Caleb was eighty-five years old, but he hadn't given up on the dream God had placed in his heart. A lot of people that age would be sitting back in a rocking chair, thinking about the good old days, but not Caleb. He kept himself stirred up, and he kept himself in shape as well. He told Joshua that he was still as strong as he was when the promise first came to him.

Caleb went back to the exact same place; the same mountain that the others had feared to climb. He said, "God, give me this mountain." Caleb was saying in effect "I don't want another place to live. I still have this dream in my heart."

Interestingly, Caleb did not ask for an easy inheritance. In fact, the mountain he claimed had five giants living on it. Surely, he could have found a place less fortified, more accessible, or more easily occupied. But Caleb said, "No, I don't care how many obstacles are there. God promised me this place. Although it is forty years later, I'm going to keep pressing; I'm going to keep believing until I see that promise fulfilled."

That's the kind of attitude we need to have. We give up too easily. "Well, I didn't get the promotion I wanted; I guess it's not going to happen."

"My husband and I can't get along. I guess it's over."

No, keep pressing forward and keep believing. Keep yourself stirred up. You've got the gifts, the talents, and the dreams. Don't allow complacency to keep you from seeing God's promises fulfilled in your life.

STAY IN A HEALTHY ENVIRONMENT

Another important key to reaching your full potential is putting yourself in an environment where the seed can grow. I know people who are extremely talented. They have incredible potential. But they insist on hanging around the wrong sort of people. If you are close friends with people who are lazy and undisciplined, people who don't have great dreams, people who are negative and critical, they will rub off on you. Moreover, that environment in which you place yourself will prevent you from rising any higher. You cannot hang out with negative people and expect to live a positive life. If all your friends are depressed and defeated and have given up on their dreams, make some changes. Let's be honest: You're probably not going to pull them up; more likely, if you continue to spend too much time in their presence, they will pull you down.

Certainly, you love your friends; you can pray for them and try to encourage them to make positive changes in their lives, but sometimes the best thing you can do is break away from negative people and put yourself in a healthy, positive, faith-filled environment. This is extremely critical, because it doesn't matter how great the potential in the seed, if you don't put it in good soil, it will not take root and grow.

Natalie was living in an extremely negative environment, complete with physical, emotional, and verbal abuse. Although her husband Thomas was domineering and controlling, and refused to seek help, Natalie remained in that marriage year after year. She was afraid to leave; afraid she'd be lonely, afraid she couldn't support herself and her two daughters, afraid she'd never meet another man who would be willing to love and accept her, let alone her children.

When Natalie asked me if I thought she should stay in that abusive relationship, I replied, "I don't believe that's God's best. I'm all for sticking together and trying to make things work out, Natalie. But understand that God did not create you to be mistreated and abused. Your mother was in an abusive relationship, and now you are, and unless you make some changes, your daughters will be as well."

It was heartrending for her, but Natalie finally mustered her courage and let the door close on that relationship. She made a fresh start, went back to school, and graduated with honors. She found a good job and met a man who fell in love not only with her but with her children as well. Today, Natalie is happily married and is thriving. Yet none of that would have happened had she not let one door close and walked through another.

I've had people tell me, "Joel, I don't know why I'm drawn to abusive people like that. I get out of one bad relationship and I get into another one that's twice as bad. I know I should get out. I know it's not good for me. But I just can't leave. I'd feel guilty."

I usually answer, "No, you have a responsibility to keep yourself healthy and whole. You have a gift. God has entrusted you with His talents, with His dreams. And it may be painful, but the best thing you can do is get away from somebody that is a constant drag on your spirit. Don't allow somebody to treat you that way. You are extremely valuable. You are made in the image of Almighty God."

"Joel, if I take a stand and set some boundaries, that person may leave; he or she may walk away." In truth, that would be the best thing that could ever happen. I heard somebody say there's something called "the gift of good-bye." That means when somebody who is pulling you down chooses to leave, you may not realize it, but he just did you a great favor. Don't look back; instead keep looking forward. Get ready for the new thing God wants to do in your life.

At times, all of us will have people who leave our lives. They may not be bad people. It's just that the season for that relationship is over. We may not understand it, but God knows what He's doing. Maybe that person is holding you back. Maybe she's keeping you from spreading your wings. Maybe he is not a good influence. You may discover that, sometimes, if you don't keep things stirred up, God will stir things for you. When somebody leaves your life or a relationship is over — whether it is a business partner, a friend, a neighbor, or a coworker who parts company — don't get upset. Don't try to talk them into staying. Let God do the new thing. Understand that your destiny is not tied to the people who walk away from you.

You may think, "But I need that person in my life. He's a great friend. I depend on her to be there for me. She's a great business partner."

No, that person is not the key to you becoming a better you. When God is finished with something, there's no amount of glue that can hold it together. You might as well let it go and get ready for something new that God wants to do in and through your life.

Keep yourself in a healthy physical environment. If you tend to struggle with discouragement and depression, don't sit around in a dark house all day long thinking about your problems. Open the windows; let the sun shine in. Put on some good uplifting music. Create a positive environment. When you're tempted to get discouraged, don't you dare go find five other friends who are discouraged and sit around discussing your problems. Find somebody happy to cheer you up. Get around people who will inspire you to rise higher. Be careful with whom you associate, especially when you feel emotionally vulnerable, because negative people can steal the dream right out of your heart.

When I first considered the move of Lakewood Church to our present location in the former Compaq Center in downtown Houston, numerous people told me that we'd never move into that facility. Business leaders and other "experts" said, "Joel, don't waste your time and money. It's not going to happen."

I could have easily given up and thought, *They're probably much smarter than I am in this area. They have much better business acumen than I have. Maybe I should just let it go.*

But I said, "No. I believe God put this

dream in my heart, and I'm not going to look up fifty years from now and say, 'I wonder what would have happened if I'd have just believed? I wonder what would have happened if I hadn't let them talk me out of that dream?' "

I can't think of anything worse than coming to the end of your life and having a bunch of regrets: What could have happened? What might have happened? What should have happened?

Beware of the negative influences around you as you pursue your dreams. I remember one consultant we hired during our quest to secure the Compaq Center. Every time we met, he told us all the reasons why it wasn't going to work out. He always had a negative report. When I finally realized the profound impact that consultant was having, I said, "We don't need that man on our team. He is contaminating our environment. He's pulling everybody down."

Surround yourself with people who encourage you, people who will build you up. Certainly, you need people who will be honest enough to tell you when you are making a poor choice or a bad decision. Don't surround yourself with a bunch of "yes-men." On the other hand, don't tolerate a bunch of negative, critical, "can't do it" people. Sometimes the people who will discourage you the most are the people who are closest to you.

Remember King David? When he was just a boy, he told his older brother Eliab that he wanted to fight the huge Philistine giant, Goliath. Eliab tried to discourage David by putting him down. He said, "David, what are you doing out here on the battlefield? You're supposed to be at home taking care of our father's few sheep." He was really saying, "David, you're never going to do anything great. You don't have what it takes."

Right there, David had to make a crucial choice: Would he believe that negative assessment from his brother, or would he believe what God had put in his heart? He could have said, "Well, maybe my brother is right. He's older than I am, more experienced, more knowledgeable about the obstacles we're facing. I'm just a kid. I don't feel too talented. Maybe I will get killed out there."

But no, David said, "Eliab, I don't care what you say about me. I know who I am. I know what God has placed inside me. I'm going to step out and fulfill my God-given destiny." He did just that, facing and felling the giant with a few pebbles from the brook.

Isn't it interesting that even Jesus had to leave His hometown of Nazareth because the people there were so filled with unbelief? Jesus knew that if he stayed in that negative environment, it would hold Him back.

You, too, may have family members or relatives who lack vision and can't imagine you achieving greatness. Don't get angry with them. Most likely, they're good people. You love them and treat them with respect, but understand that you cannot be around them on a daily basis. You have to love them from a distance. Life is too short for you to be pulled down by negative, jealous, cynical people. It doesn't matter how great your gift is or how much potential is locked inside your seeds of greatness, if you don't put that seed in an environment conducive to growth, it will not take root. It will be nearly impossible for your dream to flourish.

You need to hang around other dreamers — not daydreamers, but people with big goals, people who plan to do something significant with their lives. Hang around people who are going to help you become all God created you to be.

God is saying this is a time of new beginnings. Get your fire back. Get your passion back. You may have been sick a long time, but this is your day to get well. You may have struggled with depression and discouragement, but this is the time to break free. You may come from a family of defeat, failure, and negativism, but this is your time to rise above that morass.

Start stretching your faith once again. Get up each morning expecting good things to happen. And remember, God is on your side. He loves you. He's for you. The Scripture says, "If you put your trust in him, you will not be disappointed."[3]

My father often quoted a simple yet profound statement by Edwin Markham (1852–1940) that sums up the attitude we need: "Ah, great it is to believe the dream as we stand in youth by the starry stream; but a greater thing is to fight life through and say at the end, the dream is true!"

Don't settle for mediocrity; never let good enough be good enough. You too will discover that the dream is true!

CHAPTER 3
THE POWER OF YOUR
BLOODLINE

I read recently about some famous race-horses, the kind you might see at the Kentucky Derby or other prestigious horse races. I never realized how much time, effort, and resources went into the making of one of those championship horses. I had always thought that somebody was out riding and one day, he or she discovered that a certain horse was fast and gifted. So they decided to enter the horse in some races. Of course, the development of a champion racehorse takes much more than that.

These are not ordinary horses; these are thoroughbreds. They have generation after generation of winners on the inside. These horses have been carefully studied and bred for generations. The breeders, trainers, and veterinarians may search data and statistics for the past fifty or sixty years to check the animal's bloodline. It's no coincidence that a horse raced in the Kentucky Derby.

In horse racing, the "blood stock agent" focuses his attention on the animal's bloodline. He or she will spend months studying a particular line of horses, researching the lineage. The blood stock agent will examine how the horse's father fared as a racer, how long his stride was, how fast he could run, what size he was, and on and on. The breeders understand that winners don't randomly happen. Winning is in the blood.

Simply to breed one of these world champion thoroughbreds can cost up to half a million dollars. And there's no guarantee that the colt will win. In fact, when that newborn colt is born, his legs are all wobbly, he can barely stand up, and his eyes are glazed. The uninformed observer might say, "Those poor owners wasted their money. That horse couldn't win anything. He looks like an average, ordinary horse."

But the owners know that on the inside, in his blood, that colt has a legacy of championship genes. In fact, he may have a dozen world champions on the inside. It's all in the blood. That's why the owners are not necessarily concerned about the colt's initial weakness. They don't really care what color he is, how pretty he is, or even how large he is. They know that deep down on the inside, that colt has the blood of a winner.

Friend, that is how God looks at you and me. Our external appearance is irrelevant. It doesn't matter what color your skin is or what your ethnic background is. It doesn't matter how many weaknesses or flaws you have. You have the DNA of Almighty God. You come from a long line of champions.

Consider this: Your Heavenly Father spoke the galaxies into existence. Your elder brother defeated the enemy. Think about some of your natural ancestors:

Moses parted the Red Sea. There's great faith in your bloodline.

David, a shepherd boy, defeated Goliath with only a few pebbles he picked up from a brook. That is courage in your bloodline.

Samson toppled a building. There's supernatural strength in your bloodline.

Daniel spent an entire night in a lion's den and wasn't harmed. Divine protection flows through your bloodline.

Nehemiah rebuilt the walls of Jerusalem when all the odds were against him. Determination and persistence pulsate through your bloodline.

Queen Esther put her life on the line to save God's people. Sacrifice and heroism are in your bloodline.

Do you understand? You come from a bloodline of champions. You are not ordinary; you are a thoroughbred. It doesn't matter what your present condition looks like; you need to know that inside you flows the blood of a winner. On the inside of you are seeds of greatness. Take a better look at your bloodline. On the inside of you is champion after champion. You are the seed of Almighty God.

That's why you must quit focusing on your weaknesses and get a bigger vision for your life. Understand that God sees you already at the Winner's Circle. He's already seen them putting the roses around your neck. That's what David was talking about when he said, "God, all of my days you ordained before one of them came to be." [4] In other words, you may be a mere thirty, forty, or fifty years of age, but God has been working on you for a long time. He had you planned long before you were born. You are extremely valuable; you are not ordinary; you come from great stock. You've been destined to live in victory, destined to overcome, destined to leave your mark on this generation.

Sometimes you hear people say, "Well, he's just got good genes. He just comes from good stock." Let me tell you, you come from superior stock. God brought you out of His best.

Interestingly, to most people, the famous

racehorses don't look much different from ordinary horses. Certainly, they are beautiful animals, but the average person couldn't ascertain the champion from the merely well-bred horse. The difference is in the blood. That's what makes them extremely valuable.

It's the same way with us. The Scripture says we overcome by the blood of the Lamb, the Word of our testimony, and a willingness to lay down our lives.[5] Because of what God has done, every one of us is a thoroughbred.

"But you don't know the life I've led," I hear you saying. "I've failed here and I've made mistakes over there, and I still have this addiction."

That doesn't change your bloodline; it doesn't change what's in you. You may never have realized how valuable you are. Perhaps you never realized the price God paid for you. You need to recognize what you have on the inside. It says in First Corinthians that you were bought with a high price. God gave His very best for you, His only Son. So please don't go around thinking that you are worthless, that you don't have a future. You are a champion on the inside. It's in your blood.

One time, years ago, my father went to a meeting at a friend's church. My father arrived a little late, so he simply sat down on the back row. A few minutes later, a young man came in and sat down not too far from my father. Daddy noticed that the young man looked extremely distraught. My father's heart went out to the young man; he was deeply concerned about him. Daddy thought to himself that after the service he would speak to the young man and try to encourage him in some way. In the middle of the meeting, however, the young man got up and left.

My father felt compelled to follow him; Daddy got up from where he was sitting and went looking for him. He looked all over the front lobby of the church but couldn't find him. My dad searched the parking lot and still couldn't find him. He came back in and was about to give up, but he decided to check the restroom. A few other people were in there, so my father just waited. Sure enough, a few minutes later, the young man came out.

He looked surprised to see my father, so Daddy said, "I know you don't know me, and I don't mean to get in your business, but I'm very concerned about you. And I want you to know that God loves you and you are extremely valuable to Him."

The young man stared back at my father, and suddenly tears began to flow down his face. He said, "My life is so messed up. I'm addicted to so many drugs that I can't take it anymore. I decided to come to church one last time, and then I was going home to take every pill that I could find and end it all."

Later, he told how he had seen my father sitting down the row from him. He didn't know who Daddy was, but he was impressed by the dress shoes my father wore. Those shoes left an impression in his mind, and when he went out there, he knew Daddy was coming after him. He said, "I tried everything to get away, but everywhere I looked, those same shoes kept following me."

My father told him, "It doesn't matter where you are right now. You may have made mistakes. You may have failed a thousand times, but understand that it does not change your value in God's eyes. You are not here on earth by accident. God has a plan and a purpose for your life. He has an assignment for you. And it's not just to drift around in mediocrity."

My father and the young man prayed together, and that night was a turning point in his life. Today, more than thirty years later, that man is a pastor of a church, and he has helped thousands of other people to make a difference in our world.

Maybe you are like that young man. Perhaps you have never fully considered what you have on the inside. You may have made mistakes, but don't let your mistakes keep you down. Get back up and go again. Your errors or wrong choices do not change your bloodline. They don't change what's in you. Oftentimes, society will write a person off when he or she fails or makes poor choices, but God is not that way. God sees your potential. He knows what you're capable of being. He's the one who designed you, and He knows that you can still do great things. It's in your blood.

He has programmed you with everything you need for victory. That's why every day you can say things like, "I have what it takes. I am more than a conqueror. I am intelligent; I am talented. I am successful; I am attractive; I am an overcomer." God put all those things in your bloodline.

Granted, you may have to overcome some negative elements in your family's natural bloodline, but always remember your spiritual bloodline is more powerful than your natural bloodline. You have been handpicked by Almighty God. You have His royal blood flowing through your veins. Put your shoulders back and hold your head up high knowing that you have been chosen. You've been set apart before the foundation of the world.

Understand your value and shake off inferiority or insecurity. The "champion" is already within you, just waiting to be discovered. It's in your blood.

WHAT ABOUT BAD BLOOD?

Where I grew up, folks often described a troublemaker by saying, "Well, he's just got bad blood." Really, there's some truth to that. What's in our bloodline is extremely important. We all have a natural bloodline flowing from our parents, grandparents, great-grandparents, and other family members in our family tree.

But we also have a spiritual bloodline. The good news is that our spiritual bloodline can override our natural bloodline. The Scripture talks about all things becoming new. The old is passed away.[6] In other words, we have entered into a new bloodline. When you really understand all God has done for you, and you begin to act on it, then you can rise up out of any adversity; you can overcome anything negative from your past. There's power in your spiritual bloodline.

David said in Psalm 139:13, "God, you created my inmost being; you knit me together in my mother's womb." Verse 16 of that psalm says, "All the days ordained for me were written in your book before one of

80

them came to be." Notice, David is saying that God saw us before we were born. Before Adam and Eve, before Abraham, before Moses or your grandparents, God knew you. In other words, your parents didn't simply get together and decide to have a child. You were preordained to be here before the foundation of the world.

God is the great architect of the universe. He planned everything, and prearranged for you to be here at this particular time in history. That's one reason why we should feel a sense of destiny and value.

Understand that your value is not based on how somebody else has treated you or on how perfect of a life you have lived, or even how successful you are. Your value is based solely on the fact that you are a child of the Most High God. No, we're not perfect, we make mistakes; we all have weaknesses. But that doesn't change our value in God's eyes. We are still the apple of His eye. We are still His most prized possession.

Sometimes "religion" tries to beat people down and make them feel bad about themselves. "You've done this and you failed here, and you didn't treat this person right, and you didn't raise your kids as well as you should have." Many people wallow in that condemnation and they go around with low self-esteem and a sense of unworthiness. Their attitude is *God could never bless me. I've made too many mistakes. I blew it.*

No, God knew you weren't going to be perfect. Why don't you lighten up and give yourself a break? Quit beating yourself up over everything you've done wrong. After all, you can't change the past. If you've made mistakes, just say, "God, I'm sorry; I repent. Help me to do better next time." Then let it go and move on. If you hold on to it, you open the door to guilt and condemnation. Before long, you'll be going around with a "poor old me" mentality.

"I don't deserve anything. I'm just a weak worm of the dust," I hear people say. No, you're not a weak worm of the dust; you are a child of the Most High God. Hold your head up high, put your shoulders back, and start acting like a child of Almighty God.

Friend, you've got to believe in yourself and believe that you have something to offer this world that nobody else has. You've been made in the image of Almighty God. That means you're not like another animal — a dog, a cat, a horse. No, the Scripture says that God breathed His life into you.[7] You are a person of destiny. You didn't just happen to show up. God was thinking about you before you were even born. The Bible says that He has meticulously made everything about you.

Some people are always finding fault with themselves. "I wish I didn't look like this. I wish had her personality, and I wish I had his talent."

No, God designed you as you are on purpose. You are an original. Quit being negative and critical toward yourself and start enjoying yourself as the unique creation of God.

I hope you take this in the right sense, but I like being me. I know I'm not perfect, and I have areas in which I need to improve. Overall, though, I enjoy being myself. I realize I am valuable to God.

You, too, may have some things you wish you could change, but rather than focus on those areas, take what God has given you and make the most of it. You are valuable to God. I heard somebody put it like this: If God had a refrigerator, your picture would be on it. If God carried a wallet, your photo would be in it.

You may say, "Joel, I haven't gotten good breaks in life, and my parents struggled with these same problems. I think this is my lot in life."

No, your lot in life is to be a victor and not a victim. Your lot in life is to be happy, healthy, and whole. Sure, you may have some things to overcome in that natural bloodline, but your spiritual bloodline looks very good. Your Father spoke the worlds into existence. He could have chosen anybody, but He chose you. He equipped you and approved you.

I love the Scripture that says, "If we belong to Christ, we are Abraham's seed, and heirs according to the promise."[8] That means we can all experience the blessings of Abraham. If you study Abraham's record, you'll discover that he was prosperous, healthy, and lived a long, productive life. Even though he didn't always make the best choices, he enjoyed God's blessings and favor.

No matter how many mistakes you've made, you need to know that on the inside, you have the seed of Almighty God. Your attitude should be, "I may have a lot to overcome, people may have tried to push me down, maybe I didn't get the best breaks, but that does not change who I am. I know I can fulfill my destiny." You should go out each day expecting good things, anticipating God's blessings and favor. God has planned all of your days for good, not evil.

"I don't really see that happening in my life," you say. "I've endured so much adversity."

Maybe so, but if you will keep pressing forward, if you'll keep believing, God says He'll take those negative experiences, turn them around, and He will use them to your advantage.

Remember, we are called overcomers. That means we're going to have obstacles to overcome. You can't have great victories without having difficult battles. You'll never have a great *testimony* without going through a few *tests*. The enemy always fights the hardest when he knows God has something great in store for you.

If you've had unfair things happen to you, or people have robbed or cheated you, the Scripture says that God will bring you out with twice what you had before.[9] If you are struggling through tough times, start declaring, "I'm coming out of this experience with twice the joy, twice the peace, twice the honor, twice the promotion." Every day when you get up, declare, "This is going to be a day of victory in my life. I'm expecting God's unprecedented favor. Promotion, favor, increase, they're all on the way."

TAP INTO GOD'S POWER

I've had people tell me, "Joel, I know that someday I'll be happy. I know one day I'll enjoy my life in the sweet by and by."

I appreciate what they are saying, but God wants us to enjoy our lives right here in the nasty now and now. He wants us to have a little heaven on earth, right where we are. One of the reasons Christ came was that we might live an abundant life. You can be happy and free in this life, not simply in heaven one of these days; you can accomplish your dreams before you go to heaven!

How can you do that? By tapping into God's power inside of you.

The Bible says, "Christ has redeemed us from the curse of the law." [10] The curse is behind any kind of defeat — sin, mistakes, wrong choices, fear, worry, constant sickness, unhealthy relationships, or bad attitudes. Please understand that those are all things from which you have already been set free. But here's the catch: If you don't appreciate and take advantage of your freedom, if you don't get your thoughts, your words, your attitudes going in the right direction, it won't do you any good.

You may be sitting back waiting on God to do something supernatural in your life, but the truth is, God is waiting on you. You must rise up in your authority, have a little backbone and determination, and say, "I am not going to live my life in mediocrity, bound by addictions, negative and defeated. No, I'm going to do like the Apostle Paul and start pressing forward. I'm going to take hold of everything God has in store for me."

I heard a story about a little dog that had been kept on a twenty-foot leash for years, tied to a tree. He had his home there and the owner came out to feed him and play with him occasionally. But the dog remained on the leash. He would see the other dogs, and he would run right out to the end of his leash. He knew exactly how far he could go. He wanted to chase them. He wanted to go play, but he knew he was limited. If he went too far, the leash jerked him back into place.

One day, the owner felt sorry for the dog, so he decided to let him off that leash. Instead of removing the whole leash, however, the owner simply unfastened the leash from the dog's collar. The collar remained around the dog's neck, but it wasn't buckled anymore. The owner thought sure the dog would take off running, happy and free. Another dog came along, and sure enough, his dog got up and took off running. Much to the owner's surprise, when his dog got to where the leash would have ended, he stopped right where he always did.

A few minutes later, a cat came strutting by. This cat had tormented the dog for years. But that cat knew where to walk — just a couple of feet outside of the leash's range. Again the dog took off running but stopped right where he normally did.

The dog was free; he just didn't realize it. The leash was loosed. All he had to do was go one step farther than he was used to going and he could have walked right out of it.

Many times, that's similar to what we are doing. God has loosed our chains of addictions, of personal defeats, of bad attitudes. The problem is we're not walking out of them.

"I've always been this way. I've always had a problem with my temper. I've always had this addiction," some people lament.

No, you need to realize you have already been set free. Two thousand years ago, God loosened your collar. Now, it's up to you to start walking out of it.

How do you do it? Change your attitude. Quit saying, "I can't do it; I'll never be well; I'll always be in debt. I've got too much to overcome."

Every enemy in your life has already been defeated — enemies of worry, depression, addiction, financial lack — and you have power over all of them. The same power that raised Christ from the dead is inside you. There is nothing in your life that you cannot overcome; no hurt is too deep that you cannot forgive. You have the power to let go of the negative things of your past. You may have been knocked down a thousand times, but you have the power to get back up again. The medical report may not look good, but you have the power to stand strong.

Refuse to sit back and accept things that are less than God's best. Your attitude should be, "I know my chains have been removed; I know the price has been paid, and even if I have to believe my whole lifetime, even if I have to stand in faith till the day I die, I'm not going to sit back and accept a life of mediocrity. I'm going to keep pressing forward."

Too many people learn to function in their dysfunction. They embrace all kinds of things that are not God's best. They're argumentative, bitter, and resentful; they allow strife in their home, and they're critical and judgmental. Instead of dealing with it and being willing to change, they merely put a bandage on it and continue living in bondage, functioning in their dysfunction.

You can never change what you tolerate. As long as you accept it and accommodate it, you're going to stay right where you are. But you don't have to live that way. You are learning to function in your dysfunction. I encourage you to go one step further. Try giving up one cigarette a day. Forgive one person who has offended you. Strive to be just a little more disciplined today than you were yesterday.

"Well," you say, "Joel, I've been this way so long. I don't see how I could ever change." No, your freedom has already been purchased, but you have to rid yourself of that defeated mentality and start thinking power thoughts. Start saying, "I'm free. This addiction does not control me. Greater is He who is in me than he that's in the world." Don't ever say, "I'll never see my dreams come to pass; I'll probably never get married." Or "My bills are so high, and my income is so low, I don't think I'll ever get out of debt." No, turn that around. You need to be saying, "I am more than a conqueror. I will fulfill my destiny. God is supplying all of my needs."

You must press in if you're going to take hold of everything God has in store for you. It's easy to get passive, to say, "That's a lot of work; that's hard. I don't want to change that much. I know I'm prone to be negative, but I don't feel like having a good attitude. I know I shouldn't eat this junk food, but I enjoy it. I know I need to quit smoking, but I'm tired of trying."

Those kinds of attitudes will keep you from becoming a better you. You *can* rise higher. You *can* be a better person, a better parent, spouse, coworker, or a better leader. God has more in store for you.

You may have had many negative things in your family line for generations. They just keep being passed down from one generation to the next: sicknesses, bad attitudes, addictions, financial stress, low self-esteem, and other chronic conditions. Please understand those are some of the things from which you have been redeemed. Those things are under the curse, and that curse has been broken.

No doubt, the people who went before you — your parents, family members, your ancestors — were good people. But when a person doesn't understand what God has done for him or her, it's easy just to accept a life of mediocrity.

A young man named Eric told me, "Joel, my grandfather was an alcoholic and my dad was an alcoholic. Now, I've got the same problem. I just can't beat it."

"No, you can beat it," I encouraged him. "The power in you is greater than that addiction. But you've got to change your attitude. You've got to start saying, 'I'm free.' Declare that every day. Don't talk about the

91

way you are, talk about the way you want to be."

Often you hear people say, "Once you're addicted, you're always addicted." "Once an alcoholic, always an alcoholic." People may spout such nonsense, but God's Word says, "Whom the Son sets free is free indeed."[11] God's help can overcome any evil in your life. You can break any bad habit. You can overcome any obstacle.

"Well, Joel, my grandmother had diabetes. My mother has diabetes. It looks like I'm going to have it, too."

When you think like that, you're planning to be diabetic. You're inviting that malady into your life. You need to put your foot down and say, "Grandmother may have had it. Mother may have had it. But as for me and my house, we're redeemed from diabetes. I'm going to live under the blessing and not the curse." Don't make plans for negative things.

In my family, on my father's side, as far back as we can trace, there has been a history of heart disease — people in my family dying early deaths because of heart problems. But I'm not planning to have heart disease. I'm planning to live a long, healthy life. I do my part to stay healthy; I try to eat right and exercise regularly. And I declare every day, "I will fulfill my destiny in good health."

Maybe Alzheimer's disease runs in your family genes, but don't succumb to it. Instead, say every day, "My mind is alert. I have clarity of thought. I have a good memory. Every cell in my body is increasing and getting healthier." If you'll rise up in your authority, you can be the one to put a stop to the negative things in your family line.

Vanessa is a medical doctor who attends Lakewood Church. In 1995, she was practicing medicine in Washington, DC, when she began to feel terrible pain in her joints. The pain intensified to the point where she could hardly stand it. She came to Houston to have an operation on her knees, hoping the surgical procedure would fix the problem, but, unfortunately, it grew worse. Her body continued to decline. Although she was not yet thirty years of age, Vanessa walked with a cane. She told us that she felt and looked like a ninety-year-old woman.

Interestingly, Vanessa's father had the same disease in his early twenties, and he ended up dying from it at the age of forty-three. Her grandmother had the exact same ailment and lived as a paraplegic. It looked as though Vanessa was headed down that same path.

When she attended church at the old

Lakewood campus, it took her forty-five minutes to get from her car to her seat inside the sanctuary. It took most other people about two or three minutes. After the service, she usually waited until the crowd cleared out, so nobody could see how bad her condition was. During the week, she would get up at three in the morning to start getting dressed, and start getting her joints loosened up so she could be at the hospital by seven.

The easy thing for her to do was to just sit back and think, *Too bad for me. Daddy had it. Grandmother had it. I guess this is my lot in life.*

But Vanessa didn't do that. She was a warrior.

She said, "I'm going to rise up and take hold of everything that God has in store for me." She started praying, believing, and declaring every day: "I'm getting better and better. God is restoring health unto me. I will live and not die." For three years, she didn't see any sign of change. It didn't look as though anything was happening. That didn't deter Vanessa; she just kept on believing.

Sometimes you have to show the enemy that you're more determined than he is. That's what Vanessa was doing.

One day, out of the clear blue, she noticed the pain wasn't quite as bad. She could move her joints a little easier. The next day, she felt slightly better. The following day, she moved a bit easier. It didn't happen overnight, but over that next three months, Vanessa got better and better, and today she's totally free. Dr. Vanessa is happy, healthy, and whole.

She took a stand and she broke the curse of that sickness. Now, her children, her grandchildren, generations to come will benefit because she made a decision to live under the blessing and not the curse.

"Well, Joel, I don't know if that would happen for me. You don't know my circumstances."

You're right. It's not going to happen if you are negative and doubtful. This type of blessing is for believers, not doubters. You need to rise up like Dr. Vanessa, look that obstacle in the eye, and say, "I will defeat you. I am a child of the Most High God, and I am going to become all that He has created me to be."

Get rid of that weakness mentality. Start thinking powerful thoughts, such as *I can do all things through Christ. I am a victor and not a victim.* Remember, the same power that raised Christ from the dead is inside you. Your collar has already been loosed. The price has already been paid. It's up to you to rise up and walk in your authority.

What's holding you back in life? Addictions, bad attitudes, low self-esteem? Recognize what it is. Don't just learn to function in your dysfunction. Be willing to make some changes. The Old Testament prophet Joel said, "Wake up the mighty men." You are a mighty man or woman; don't settle for anything less than God's best. Stir up the gift on the inside. Keep your dreams alive. Make a decision today that from now on, you are going to live under the blessing and not the curse. As you do, you'll discover that Almighty God has already loosened the leash in your life and has given you the power to break free from things that have held you back in the past.

CHAPTER 4
BREAKING FREE FROM
THE STRONGHOLDS
OF YOUR PAST

It is startling but true: The decisions we make today don't simply affect ourselves; they affect our children and our children's children for multiplied generations. The Bible talks about how the iniquity of the fathers can be passed down for three or four generations. That means bad habits, addictions, negativity, wrong mind-sets and other types of iniquities can be passed down.

Perhaps you are struggling in certain areas right now because people who came before you made poor choices. Many times, you can look back and see the results of those choices somewhere in your family line. It is important that we recognize what has happened and that we not passively accept these negative patterns. "Well, this is just the way I am. This poverty and sickness has been in my family for years."

No, you need to rise up and do something about it. It may have been there for years, but the good news is it doesn't have to stay there. You can be the one to put a stop to it. You can be the one to choose the blessing and not the curse.

Recent research seeks to identify specific genes and determine how genes for traits such as addiction, eating disorders, even depression, are passed down. The researchers can see definite patterns, but they cannot conclusively determine whether the cause is genetic, environmental, or hereditary, or some combination of those factors.

Certainly, all those things can be factors, but I believe the root cause is spiritual. The Bible calls it an *iniquity*.

We have to understand that just as the strong physical characteristics can be inherited, the negative things in our family's bloodline will continue from generation to generation until somebody rises up and puts a stop to it. For example, when Adam and Eve disobeyed God, that decision didn't just affect them; it affected their children. Do you know who the first murderer was in the Bible? It was Adam's son Cain. The second murderer was one of Cain's descendants, a man by the name of Lamech. That iniquity kept getting passed down through generations of Cain's offspring. It was in their family line.

Similarly, many of the things we struggle with today may be traced to somebody in our family line who gave in to it, and now we have to deal with it. We shouldn't use that as an excuse or a rationalization for continuing that pattern, but we must recognize what has happened, and we need to be more determined than ever that we are going to be the ones to put a stop to it.

A beautiful young woman named Betsy struggles with anorexia. She explained to me how her mother had succumbed to it, several of her aunts had it, her sisters had it, and several cousins did too. This one sickness was practically tearing this family apart. That was not just a coincidence; that's a negative, destructive spirit that keeps getting passed down in that family. It probably would have continued to decimate the family had Betsy not made a choice to live under the blessings of God rather than a curse. Betsy realized that her struggle against anorexia was not merely a physical battle; it was a spiritual battle as well. As she took authority over those issues in the name of Jesus, Betsy broke free from the bondage she had inherited.

Examine the areas in your life where you constantly struggle, in the areas where it seems as though something is trying to drag your family down. Maybe it's a pattern of divorce, poverty, addictions, abuse, depression, even sicknesses.

Nearly every male in Tim's family has had a heart attack and died by the time he was fifty years old. Tim is currently forty-eight, so you can imagine how concerned and worried he is. "Tim, you can be the one to break that curse," I told him. "Don't start planning your funeral. Don't assume that you will have a heart attack. Take a stand against it."

I said, "Eat right, exercise regularly, and every day, declare, 'With long life, God is satisfying me and showing me His salvation.' "

Friend, you have to make the choice whether you will receive the blessing and not the curse. If these negative patterns exist in your family line, recognize what's happening and do something about it. Don't just keep passing it down. The pattern may not have been initiated from any horrible wrong that was done. Sometimes these things are a result of somebody opening the door to the enemy. Perhaps one of your ancestors opened the door to fear, anxiety, or worry, and everyone else has picked up on it for years. Regardless of how the negative pattern began, you can be the one to stop it.

Stephen and Susan's son Bradley started

first grade, and he was so excited about it. He was outgoing and energetic and met many new friends. After a couple of months, however, Bradley began having intense panic attacks at school. He would get so upset and afraid that his parents weren't going to come back and pick him up. Bradley's teacher tried to calm him down by getting Stephen or Susan on the phone, so one of them could tell him how much they loved him and, of course, that they'd be back to pick him up as soon as school was over. But nothing his parents said calmed Bradley. Time after time, the parents would have to rush to the school and assure their child that everything was okay.

There was no reason for Bradley's unexplainable fear. Stephen and Susan were loving parents, and they had never before left him anyplace. Nevertheless, the panic attacks continued month after month. The situation got so bad that when Bradley was at home, he would not leave Susan's side. He'd follow her from room to room. If she went outside, he was right there. If for some reason he couldn't find her, he would burst into another panic attack.

The couple was frustrated and heartbroken, wondering what they had done to cause this awful condition, and what they could do to help Bradley. Then one day, Stephen was talking with his father, the child's grandfather, and as he explained the situation, it was as though a light turned on in the grandfather's mind. "Stephen, I know exactly what's wrong with Bradley," the grandfather said. "When I was a little boy in the first grade, my father died suddenly. I was so afraid that when my mother would try to walk me to school, I would cry so hard, thinking that she may not come back. Many times, she would just turn around and take me back home. I believe that somehow Bradley's fear is connected to mine."

Stephen and Susan realized that Bradley's fear didn't originate with him; it was passed down because of that traumatic event in the grandfather's life. They began to understand that things could get passed down from one generation to the next, things that they didn't have anything to do with. You can't simply deal with such conditions medically, psychologically, or in any other physical sense. You can't merely apply sheer willpower to overcome this condition; it is a spiritual battle. Stephen and Susan began to pray; daily they bound the stronghold of fear in their family's line, and they stood against that curse. Today, Bradley is a young man and is completely free, living a normal, healthy life.

Some people are living under a spirit of depression that gets passed from generation to generation. Their lives are characterized by a lack of joy and little enthusiasm. I've seen it even in little children. Other kids can be out laughing, playing, having a good time, but the child from the depressed family languishes in the doldrums, so serious and solemn, not even enjoying his childhood. That's a spirit of depression.

I've known men that have everything in the world going for them. They have great families, they make plenty of money, they're successful in their careers, yet they're never really happy or fulfilled. It's as though something is always gnawing at them, stealing their joy, peace, and victory. Friend, that is not normal. That is a spirit of defeat, a spirit of discouragement. And you have to deal with it in a manner similar to what Stephen and Susan did — rise up and stand against it through prayer and positive, biblically based affirmations.

You can be the one to break the curse in your family. Don't just sit back and say, "Well, we've always been negative." "I've always had this addiction." "Everybody in my family gets married and divorced three or four different times."

103

No, be the one to say, "Enough is enough. I'm sick and tired of being sick and tired. As for my family and me, we're choosing the blessing and not the curse."

You can be the one to stand against the forces of darkness and to break those strongholds that are keeping you and your family in bondage. The Scripture says, "The curse does not come without a cause."[12] That means when we are dealing with issues such as addictions, bad habits, and dysfunctions, either we've made bad choices or somebody in our family line has made some bad choices. There's a reason a child grows up to become an alcoholic. There's a reason a child becomes an abusive parent. There's a reason a young man commits crimes until he is sent off to prison, and when he is released, he goes right back to a life of crime. Certainly, societal issues may have an impact, but these things don't randomly happen in the spirit realm. Somebody, somewhere, opened the door to the enemy.

OVERCOMING NEGATIVE HISTORY

Understand, if you are struggling with one or more of these things, that does not make you a bad person. You need not mope around guilty and condemned because you have some obstacles to overcome. Many times, it may not even be your fault. Somebody else made the poor choices, and now you have to deal with the repercussions. Nevertheless, be careful that you don't use that as an excuse to perpetuate negative lifestyle patterns. You have to dig your heels in and do something about it.

One of the first steps to overcoming these generational curses is to recognize what you're dealing with. Identify it. Don't ignore it. Don't try to sweep it under the rug and hope that it will go away. It won't.

If you're lazy and undisciplined, don't make excuses; just admit it and say, "I'm going to deal with this." If you have an anger problem, or if you don't treat other people with honor and respect, don't try to convince yourself that everything is okay. Admit it and deal with it.

The Bible says, "Confess your faults one to another and pray for one another that you may be healed." [13] Notice, you must be honest enough with yourself to confess your faults. Notice, too, that you're going to have to find a good mature friend and say, "I need your help. I'm struggling in this area, and I need you to pray with me."

Too often, we do just the opposite. We think, *I'm not going to tell anybody about this problem. What would they think of me? I'd be embarrassed.*

Instead, swallow your pride, confess your weakness, and get the help you need so you can be free. It is not easy to admit that we need help, but it is necessary, and it is liberating.

Robert grew up in a violent, angry home. As a young man, he got hooked on drugs and began selling them to support his habit. He lived dangerously, in a perpetual self-destruct mode, following his family's pattern of violence and anger.

Then, in his mid-twenties, Robert gave his life to the Lord. As he studied the Bible, he began sharing the good news with others and eventually became a pastor. He was doing great personally, and the church grew in strength and numbers. Robert became one of the most respected citizens in the community as well as traveling and sharing his story of how God had changed his life.

People did not know that he still had a serious anger problem. God had delivered him from all sorts of other bad habits, addictions, drugs, and alcoholism, but Robert still struggled with this anger. He would never show it in public, but if something went wrong at home, he'd fly into a violent fit of uncontrollable rage. Many times, something insignificant would set him off and he would erupt. He was extremely abusive to his wife physically and verbally. He would throw things and treat her horribly, often placing her in physical danger. Then when he finally calmed down, he begged for her forgiveness, which she readily granted. She would say to him, "Honey, we have got to go get some help. We've got to go talk to somebody about this problem."

"I'm too embarrassed," he told her. "I'm the pastor of the church. I'm supposed to be the example. How could I ever tell anybody I have this terrible problem?"

His wife drew up every bit of courage she could muster and said, "But the Scripture says, 'Confess your faults so you can be healed.' Robert, you will never overcome what you're struggling with all by yourself. You've got to find a friend, a mentor, a pastor, a counselor. Find somebody that will stand with you. Find somebody that will pray with you. Find somebody that will hold you accountable."

Robert's wife was absolutely right. Just because you are dealing with some tough things doesn't mean that you're a bad person. We have to get past the misconception that because we love God and people look up to us, we're supposed to be perfect. It doesn't always work that way.

If you have an anger problem or a problem with alcohol, or some other kind of hidden addiction, don't try to beat that problem on your own. Don't hide it because you're too embarrassed. Find a godly person that will stand in faith with you. I'm not saying that you have to announce it to the world. But you need to find one person that you can really trust. As you do your part, God will help you to overcome the negative patterns in your life.

Pastor Robert later admitted that he wouldn't tell anybody about his anger problem because he thought that something was wrong with him. He couldn't understand how God had delivered him from all the other bad addictions, but he still had this serious anger problem. Robert later confided that even when he was enraged and out of control, deep down on the inside, he would be saying to himself, "Why am I doing this? Why can't I stop? What is wrong with me?"

The problem was that anger had been in his family line a long time. It wasn't as easy to overcome as some of those other habits were. Beyond that, he had to get past his fears of what everybody was going to think of him. Finally, Pastor Robert went for help. As he confessed his faults and stood against the forces of darkness, God set him free completely. Today he's one of the kindest, gentlest men you would ever want to meet.

In the same way, you can beat anything that's come against you. No addiction is too difficult for our God. No stronghold is impenetrable to Him. It doesn't matter how long you've had it, or how many times you've tried and failed, today is a new day. If you will be honest with yourself, recognize what you're dealing with, and find somebody to hold you accountable, then you too can start living under the blessing and not the curse. You can free yourself from those negative generational patterns, and start a new pattern of goodness and love for your descendants.

Take responsibility for your actions. God has given you free will. You can choose to change. You can choose to set a new standard. Every right choice you make will overturn the wrong patterns that other people in your family's lineage have made. Every time you resist a temptation, you are one step closer to your victory. You may have a negative history, but you don't have to perpetuate it. We can't change the past, but we can change the future by making right choices today.

Sadly, hurting people end up hurting other

people. You might think that when we come out of a negative environment, we would be quick to change. You hear people say it all the time: "Well, I'm never going to raise my kids like that." Or "I'll never treat my wife the way my father treated my mother." The truth is, more often than not, they end up doing exactly what they said they would never do. That spirit is passed down.

If you grew up in a negative environment, unless you break that spiritual pattern, there's a high probability that you will treat your children the same way you were treated. I know people that were abused physically and verbally growing up. You would think that since they suffered so much and went through all that pain, they would stay far away from it. However, studies confirm the opposite. People who have been abused are the most likely to become abusers. Why is that? It's not because they want to. They know how destructive it is. It's because that negative spirit keeps being passed down.

Thank God, you and I can do something about it. The Scripture says in Ephesians that our fight is not against flesh and blood, but we fight in the spiritual realm.[14] You have to rise up and say, "I'm taking authority over this thing and I am not going to live this way any longer." God will give you the power to do what you need to do. Don't just sit back and accept the status quo. Do something about it.

Many people play the blame game today. "It's his fault or her fault." "Well, I'm depressed because my mother was depressed." Or "I can't break these addictions because everybody in my family has these addictions." Or "I'm angry because you made me angry."

Avoid that mess. Take responsibility for your own actions. You may have experienced some unfair things in the past that have made life more difficult for you, but your attitude should be, "I'm not going to sit around and moan and complain about how I was raised or about how somebody mistreated me. No, this is the life God gave me, and I'm going to make the most of it. I'm going to make good choices starting today."

We've heard a lot about the generational curse, but equally as important is our generational choice. We don't have to stay the way we are.

Put a stop to any of the negative patterns in your family's bloodline. It may have been there for years, but you can be the one to make a difference. Remember, this is a spiritual battle. You must take authority over all the strongholds that are keeping you in bondage. One of the first things you must do is recognize what it is, identify it, get it out in the open, and deal with it. As you do, you will see God's blessings and favor in your life, and you will pass down those good things to the generations to follow. In the next chapter, I'll show you how you can leave a lasting positive legacy.

CHAPTER 5
THE GENERATIONAL
BLESSING

Most of us don't give much thought to the plethora of decisions we make as we go through each day. Yet the decisions we make today will affect our children, our grandchildren, and the generations to come.

Too often, we think only about the here and now. "Well, Joel, it's my life. I know I have some bad habits. I know I'm kind of hot-tempered. I know I don't treat everybody right. But that's okay; I can handle it."

The problem with that kind of thinking is it's not just hurting you; it's making life more difficult on those who come after you. The things that we don't overcome, the issues we leave on the table, so to speak, will be passed down for the next generation to deal with. None of us lives or dies to ourselves. A person's good habits as well as their poor choices — the addictions, bad attitudes, and wrong mind-sets — all are passed down.

But the good news is: Every right decision

we make, every time we resist temptation, every time we honor God, when we do the right thing, not only are we going to come up higher ourselves, but we're making it a little easier on the generations that will come after us.

Think of it like this: Each of us has a spiritual bank account. By the way we live, we're either storing up equity or storing up iniquity. Equity would be anything good: our integrity, our determination, our godliness. That's storing up blessings. On the other hand, iniquity includes our bad habits, addictions, selfishness, lack of discipline. All of these things, either good or bad, will be passed down to future generations.

I like to look at my life as a few laps in the marathon that our family line is running. When my life is done, I'm going to hand the baton to my children. Contained in that baton will be my physical DNA, my traits, hair color, size, and weight. It will also hold my spiritual and emotional DNA. It will include my tendencies, attitudes, habits, and mind-sets. My children will take the baton, run a few laps, and hand it to their children, and on and on. Every lap that we run with purpose, passion, and integrity is one more lap that can be used for good by those that come after us. In a sense, the laps we run well put future generations further down the road toward significance and success.

We need to think about the big picture. I want to leave my family line better off than they were before. I don't want selfishness, addictions, or bad habits to diminish my life. I want everything about my life now to make it easier on those who will come after me.

Even if you don't have children, you're going to live on through the people you influence. Your habits, attitudes, and what you stand for will all be passed down to somebody.

I read of an interesting study done in 1993 by the United States military. They were curious about what traits get passed down from one generation to the next. We know that our physical traits do. What about emotional, mental, and spiritual characteristics? What about bad attitudes and addictions? Or what about good qualities such as integrity, compassion, and godliness? Can they be passed down as well?

The researchers extracted some white blood cells from a volunteer and they carefully placed them in a test tube. They then put a probe from a lie detector machine down in that test tube, to measure the person's emotional response.

Next, they instructed this same volunteer

to go a couple of doors down and watch some violent scenes from an old war movie on television. When this man watched the scenes, even though the blood that was being tested was in another room, when he got all uptight and tense, that lie detector test shot off the page. It was detecting his emotional response even though the blood was no longer in his body.

The experimenters did this with person after person with the same results. They concluded that the blood cells seem to "remember" where they came from.

Now, if sicknesses and addictions and wrong mind-sets can be passed down, how much more can God's blessings, favor, and good habits be passed down through our blood?

As important as it may be to understand the generational curse, it is vital that we understand the generational blessings we can obtain. I know that much of the favor and blessing on my life did not come to me by my own effort; I didn't accumulate all that I am currently enjoying on my own. It was because my father and mother passed it down to me. They left me not just a physical inheritance; they imparted a spiritual inheritance to me as well.

We can build on the past. My father put

me forty years down the road when he passed the baton, handing over the ministry of Lakewood Church. My dream is to place my children far, far down the road. And I'm not talking financially; I'm talking about their attitudes, helping them along in their work habits, in their character, and in their walk with God.

We need to understand that the generations are connected. You are sowing seeds for future generations. Whether you realize it or not, everything you do counts. Every time you persevere, every time you are faithful, every time you serve others, you are making a difference; you're storing up equity in your "generational account."

It's easy in life to think, "Well, I'm just a businessman." Or "I'm just a housewife." Or "I'm just a single mom raising my kids, going to work. I'm not going to do anything great. Be realistic."

No, you've got to learn to think more generationally. The fact that you're a hard worker, faithful to your spouse and family, giving it your all — you are sowing seeds for those to come after you. You may not see it *all* happen in your lifetime. You may very well be sowing a seed for a child or for a grandchild to do something great. But don't get discouraged. It's your family legacy. It's not just your life you are changing; you are literally changing your family tree!

My grandmother on my father's side worked extremely hard most of her life. My grandparents were cotton farmers and they lost everything they had in the Great Depression. They didn't have much money, had little food, and no future to speak of. My grandmother worked twelve hours a day earning ten cents an hour washing people's clothes: a dollar-twenty a day.

But Grandmother never complained about her plight. She didn't go around with a "poor-me" mentality; she just kept doing her best, giving it her all. She was determined and persistent. She may not have realized it, but she was sowing seeds for her children. She passed down hard work, determination, and persistence, which my father built upon. Because Grandmother laid the foundation, Daddy was able to break out of poverty and depression and raise our family to a completely new level.

My grandmother never really enjoyed the blessings and the favor that her descendants did. Had she not been willing to pay the price, my father may never have escaped poverty, and I might not be enjoying the season of usefulness that I am experiencing today.

These days, Victoria and I tend to get a lot of credit for the successful lives we are leading, but we have learned to look back and give credit to whom credit is due: our forefathers and -mothers. Many people in our family lines gave us some help along the way.

My grandmother never received a lot of fanfare during her lifetime. She didn't get a lot of glory, but she ran some important laps in our family's race. When she passed that baton down, it contained determination, persistence, a never-give-up attitude, and a can-do mentality. Now those traits are instilled in our family's legacy. I believe that four or five generations from now, people in my family line will be better off because of Grandmother Osteen.

In the same way, when you get up early, work hard, and have a spirit of excellence, you are making a difference in your family's future. Don't be shortsighted and so ingrown that if it doesn't happen right now, you're not going to be happy. No, you are sowing seeds that will reap a great harvest for generations to come.

"But, Joel, I'm working hard," one single mom told me. "I'm trying to send my kid to college and I'm so tired."

I could sympathize with that dear single mom and many more like her. Nobody said it would be easy, but keep being faithful. You don't know how God may use that child to impact the world. Somebody in your family line may become a great businessman, leader, teacher, minister, statesman, or author. It may be in this generation or it may be four or five generations down the line. But it will happen partly because you were willing to pay the price.

Any time you see somebody who's successful or has accomplished something great, you can be sure they didn't do it all by themselves. Somebody else helped pay the price along the way. Somebody passed down those qualities that they needed.

When you live your life with excellence, going the extra mile, nobody else may notice. It may seem as though you are not reaping any of the benefits, but know this: In the bloodline being formed in your DNA are that fortitude, strength, and excellent spirit. They will be passed down to future generations. You are making a difference.

I have a friend who pastors a large church in another state. He and his wife established it fourteen or fifteen years ago, and today several thousand people attend services there regularly. It's a strong, healthy church.

But my friend has big dreams in his heart. He wants to see that church grow to thousands and thousands of people. Moreover, he has a dream of writing books that will affect the world.

After a few years of working at the church, he became extremely discouraged. The energy and enthusiasm had leveled off, not too much exciting was happening; the church's numerical growth had slowed. On top of that, when my friend drives to work each morning, he passes by another large church. This congregation numbers between fifteen thousand to twenty thousand people, and has a big, beautiful campus with many new buildings, exactly what my friend has been dreaming about and working toward.

On one particular day, my friend was sitting in traffic, staring at the big church's beautiful campus, and he felt as though salt were being rubbed in a wound. He was so discouraged, he said, "God, it's just not fair. I poured my heart and soul into the dream that You gave me, but I don't think I'll ever measure up to this man's success. Why won't my church grow?"

He honestly expressed his feelings as he continued. "God, I feel like I'm being laughed at. I don't even know if I should stay in the race."

Just then, God spoke to him, not aloud, but down inside his heart and mind. He said, "Son, what would you think if your son saw your dream come to pass? What if your daughter wrote a book that influenced the world? How would you feel if your children were to enjoy the success for which you are longing?"

My friend's eyes lit up. He said, "God, that would be great. That would be a dream come true." My friend later told me that this experience changed his perspective. He began to think more about investing in the future generations. "Maybe I'm sowing the seeds for my children," he said. "Maybe I'm laying the groundwork for my grandchildren to do something great."

Remember, every lap we run is one less lap for those who come after us. Every day you stay faithful, every test you pass or obstacle you overcome, you are storing up equity and blessings for future generations. You're making it easier on your children, and on your grandchildren. Your dreams may not come to pass exactly as you would hope, but the seeds you sow may be harvested by your sons and your daughters.

Interestingly, the pastor of the big church that my friend passed every day was a fourth-generation pastor. His father, his grandfather, and his great-grandfather had faithfully led smaller congregations of a few hundred people. Why did this man have such a large church, making such a tremendous impact?

Somebody paid the price. Yes, that pastor is talented and gifted. But his forefathers, those that went before him, are the ones who stored up the equity. Now the favor is being released on this generation.

Let me ask you: Are you willing to pay the price so your children and their children as well as future generations can rise higher and accomplish more? If you're like me, nothing would make you happier than to see your children go further and achieve more than you thought possible for yourself. Or to see your grandchildren go further than you ever dreamed.

YOUR CHILDREN WILL DO EVEN MORE!

Oftentimes, you may see further than you're going to go personally. God may put something bigger in you than you can accomplish on your own. Don't be surprised if your children or your grandchildren come along and finish what you started. I heard somebody say, "Nothing truly great can ever be accomplished in just one lifetime." At the time, I didn't understand that saying, because obviously, every generation can do something great. But I've learned since that sometimes

God's plans span more than one generation.

Many times, I heard my father say, "One day we're going to build an auditorium to hold twenty thousand people. One day, we're going to have a big place where we can all come together and worship." My father had the vision, but God used his children to complete it. Nevertheless, had he not stayed faithful — had he not stayed determined and kept that excellent spirit — I don't believe the fulfillment would have come to pass. Daddy sowed the seeds; he paved the way, and my family members — as well as millions of other people — have enjoyed the blessings as a result.

You may have a big dream in your heart. Keep in mind that God may have put that seed in you to get it started. Your children and your grandchildren may take it further than you ever thought possible.

In the Old Testament, King David had a dream to build a permanent temple where God's people could worship. David gathered the supplies, brought in huge cedar trees from Lebanon, amassed a fortune in gold and other precious metals. But God never allowed David to build the temple. Instead, God instructed David's son Solomon to construct His house of worship.

If not everything is happening in your timing the way you want, keep doing your best. God is still in control. In addition, as you continue sowing seeds and living with excellence, know this: You are making a difference. In God's perfect timing, the fruit of your labor will be seen.

The Scripture says that God's people left the place better off than it was when they found it.[15] That should be our goal as well: I'm going to leave my family with more integrity, more joy, more faith, more favor, and with more victory. I'm going to leave my loved ones free from bondage and closer to God.

Maybe you weren't raised by parents who set you up for success by planting positive characteristics in your family line. Possibly you've inherited attitudes of defeat, mediocrity, addictions, and negativity. But thank God, you can start a new family line. You can be the one to set a new standard.

Somebody has to be willing to pay the price. Somebody has to step up and clear the leftovers off the table. Negative things may have been in your bloodline, but they don't have to stay in your bloodline. All it takes is for one person to rise up and start making better choices. Every right choice you make begins to overturn the wrong choices of those who have gone before you.

Nobody else may have done so, but if you'll make positive changes, one day, people in your family line will look back and say, "It was because of this man. It was because of that woman. They were the turning point. We were defeated up till then. We were addicted up to that point. However, look what happened when they came along. Everything changed. We came up higher."

What happened? The curse was broken and the blessings began. That's what you can do for your family.

I know I am where I am today because somebody in my family line prayed. Somebody took a stand for righteousness. Somebody stuck with his or her commitments. Somebody lived a life of integrity. My forefathers, most of whom I have never met, have sown seeds into my life.

"Oh, Joel, you just got some lucky breaks," somebody might say.

Luck had nothing to do with it. My life is blessed today because somebody in my family line was praying, persevering even when times were tough, and honoring God through it all.

If you have godly parents, godly grandparents, you should be extremely grateful because you have innumerable advantages today. You have more of God's favor, more of

His blessings because of what they've done. They've paid the price to invest in your future.

Moreover, when you have this godly heritage, you will sometimes stumble into blessings. Great things will happen, and you won't even be able to figure out why. Seemingly impenetrable doors will open supernaturally. You'll get the promotion, and you know you didn't deserve it. That's not a lucky break. It's because that grandmother was praying. It's because your parents lived lives marked by excellence. Or your great-grandparents sowed seeds of integrity and success.

Certainly, each of us is responsible for our own actions, and you and I must work diligently to make use of the opportunities afforded us. But the Bible also indicates that when we have this heritage of faith, we will live in houses that we did not build. We will enjoy vineyards that we didn't plant. God's blessings will chase us down and overtake us. I thank God every day for my parents and my grandparents. Because of the way they lived and what they've done, I know I'm not living under a generational curse; I'm living under a generational blessing.

You can do something similar for your family. Money, houses, cars, or other material possessions may be part of your legacy to your children — if you leave those things to your heirs, that's great. Living a life of integrity and excellence that honors God is worth more than all of that. To pass on the favor and blessings of God to your future generations is worth more than anything else in this world.

Don't take the easy way out. Keep doing your best even when it's difficult. Keep loving, giving, and serving. Your faithfulness is noticed in heaven. You are storing up equity for both yourself and generations to come.

First Samuel, chapter 25, relates how David and his men protected the family and the workers of a man by the name of Nabel from their enemies. One day, David sent his men to ask Nabel for some food and supplies. David thought that Nabel would be grateful and that he would freely give David's troops the supplies for which they asked. But when David's men arrived, Nabel treated them rudely and disrespectfully. He said, "I don't even know who you are. I never asked you to do any of this, so just be on your way. Don't bother me."

When those men got back and told David how insolently they had been treated, David was furious. He said, "All right, men. Get your swords. We're going to go take care of

Nabel. We're going to wipe him out."

But on the way there, Nabel's wife, Abigail, stopped David. She had heard about her husband's insulting behavior, so she brought a bountiful supply of gifts and food, hoping to reduce David's anger. She said, "David, my husband is a rude and ungrateful man. He shouldn't have treated you like that." In verse 28, she said, "But David, if you will forgive this wrong, I know that God will give you an enduring house."

I like that phrase "an enduring house." Abigail was saying, "David, I know you have a right to be angry. I know my husband paid you back evil for your good, but if you can overlook it, take the high road, and let it go, I know God will bless you for generations to come. I know He will give you an enduring house."

David swallowed his pride, walked away, and overlooked the offense. He let it go, and God did indeed bless him and his future children as a result.

Throughout life, we're all going to have situations where we can find some excuse to be angry, some rationale to be bitter. You may say, "Joel, I've got a good reason to walk out of my marriage. I've been horribly mistreated." Or "I have every right to live with a chip on my shoulder. I've been forced to endure so much pain and unfairness."

Indeed, you may have good reason for feeling the way you do and for responding to life negatively. Still, I'm asking you to take the high road; don't give in to it. That stuff can get into your blood; it can be passed down. Your children and grandchildren already have enough to overcome without you adding to it.

It may be difficult, but you have the power to overcome the wrong choices made by your family members in previous generations. Beyond that, you can make life better for the generations that follow you. Every offense that you forgive, every bad habit you break, every victory you win is one less lap for those who come after you. Even if you don't do it for yourself, do it for your children, do it for your grandchildren. Do it so you can have an enduring house.

I heard somebody say, "Your blood always speaks." What they meant is your blood is charged with your experiences. It remembers, as was illustrated by that military study I mentioned earlier, where it has come from. A hundred years from now, your blood will still speak to future generations. In some way, either positively or negatively, your bloodline will affect others in your family line.

What will your blood say? Defeat. Mediocrity. Unforgiveness. Bitterness.

No, I believe your blood will speak Determination. Persistence. Integrity. Godliness. Generosity. Favor. Faith and victory!

Determine that you will pass down a godly heritage. Leave your family a legacy of good things. You may have inherited negative input from the past, but thank God, today is a new day. Draw a line in the sand and declare, "I am done with the generational curse. As for me and my family, we're going to live under the generational blessing."

Get up every day and give it your best effort. If you will do that, not only will you rise higher and accomplish more, but God has promised that your seed, your family line for up to a thousand generations, is going to have the blessings and the favor of God — all because of the life that you've lived.

Chapter 6
Discovering
Your Destiny

Before you were born, God saw you, and He endowed you with gifts and talents uniquely designed for you. He's given you ideas and creativity, as well as specific areas in which you can excel.

Why, then, do so many people today feel unfulfilled in their lives, merely going to work at some mundane job, trying to earn a living, stuck in a career they don't even like? The answer is simple: They are not pursuing the dreams and desires God has placed within their hearts.

If we are not moving toward our God-given destiny, tension and dissatisfaction will always exist in our inner being. It won't go away with time; it will be there as long as you live. I can't think of anything more tragic than to come to the end of life on earth and realize that you have not really "lived," that you have not become what God created you to be. You simply endured an average, mediocre life. You got by, but you lived without passion or enthusiasm, allowing your inner potential to lie dormant and untapped.

I heard somebody say the wealthiest place on earth is not Fort Knox or the oil fields of the Middle East. Nor is it the gold and diamond mines in South Africa. Ironically, the wealthiest places on earth are the cemeteries, because lying in those graves are all kinds of dreams and desires that will never be fulfilled. Buried beneath the ground are books that will never be written, businesses that will never be started, and relationships that will never be formed. Sadly, the incredible power of potential is lying in those graves.

A major reason why so many people are unhappy and lacking enthusiasm is that they are not fulfilling their destiny. Understand, God deposited a gift, a treasure inside you, but you have to do your part to bring it forth.

How can you do that? Simple: Determine that you are going to start focusing on your divine destiny and taking steps toward the dreams and desires that God has placed in your heart. Our goal should be that we're going to live life to the fullest, pursuing our passions and dreams, and when it comes our time to go, we will have used as much of our potential as possible. We're not going to bury our treasures; instead, we're going to spend our lives well.

How do you discover your sense of divine destiny? It's not complicated. Your destiny has to do with what excites you. What are you passionate about? What do you really love doing? Your destiny will be a part of the dreams and desires that are in your heart — part of your very nature. Because God made you and He is the One who put those desires within you in the first place, it shouldn't surprise you that your destiny will involve something that you enjoy. For instance, if you really love children, your destiny will probably be connected to something that has to do with kids — teaching, coaching, caring for them, mentoring them.

Or maybe you love seeing things built or renovated. Most likely, your destiny will probably fall into the fields of construction, design, or architecture. I know people who are extremely helpful, so compassionate, and caring. No doubt, their destiny will probably push them toward some field of social work, or possibly even a medical field, as a doctor, a nurse, a caregiver, minister, or counselor. Your destiny will usually follow the dream about which you are most passionate.

From the time I was ten or eleven years

old, I was fascinated with television production. I loved the cameras, editing, and the production of television shows and movies. Every part of the process excited me. As a young man, I spent most of my weekends at Lakewood Church, where my father was the senior pastor. At the time, the church owned some small industrial cameras, and I'd spend all day Saturday playing with the television equipment. I didn't really know how to run it, but I was fascinated by it. I'd turn the camera on and off, unplug it, plug it back in, coil the cables, and get the equipment ready for Sunday. I was passionate about it because it was what came naturally to me.

When I got old enough — maybe thirteen or fourteen years of age — I began helping to run the camera during the services; I became pretty good at it, too. In fact, I soon became one of the best cameramen that we had. It wasn't hard for me; quite the contrary, I loved it; to me working behind the camera seemed almost like a hobby.

Looking back, I see now that my love for television production was part of my God-given destiny. God had hardwired that into me before the foundation of the world.

I went to college and studied broadcasting for a year, returned home, and started a full-fledged television ministry at Lakewood

Church. Today, I am on the other side of the cameras, and I can see how God was guiding my steps and preparing me for the fulfillment of my destiny.

Maybe you don't like the field in which you are working; you awaken each morning dreading going to your job. The work is meaningless and mundane.

If that sounds like you, it may be time to reexamine what you are doing. You are not meant to live a miserable and unfulfilled life. Make sure that you are in a field that is a part of your destiny. Don't spend twenty-five years in a meaningless existence, doing something you dislike, staying there simply because it is convenient and you don't want to rock the boat. No, step into your divine destiny.

We should love what we're doing. We should go to work every day with enthusiasm, passionate about what we do. I'm not saying we don't have to work hard, or there are not going to be some frustrating days, and some people with whom we'd rather not deal. That's all a part of life. Ultimately, we should enjoy what we're doing. When you get home at night, you should feel that you've accomplished something, that you've helped to make the world a better place. I believe that when you discover your destiny, and start working in some realm associated with it, you will thrive.

Think about a good hunting dog — it's natural for that breed of dog to hunt. Put a hunting dog in a cooped-up area, and he'll lie around the yard all day long, lazy, unmotivated, with no enthusiasm, just dragging through the day. But when the owner comes home and opens up the bed of his pickup truck, and the dog realizes he is about to go hunting, he comes alive. He'll start barking, jumping, and running around the yard in excitement. It's a night-and-day difference.

Why? Because God designed hunting dogs that way. He put that passion inside them, so there's a natural excitement and enthusiasm. They don't have to get themselves all worked up to be happy. They don't have to say, "Well, let me go listen to a sermon or a motivational message. I need to work up some zest and zeal to go hunting today."

No, when those dogs know they're going hunting, they're excited about it. The Creator of the universe hardwired that desire into them.

I really believe when we get into our destiny and we are doing what we know we're called to do, enthusiasm and excitement will exude from us naturally. We may not jump up and down every day, but deep within, we're going to know: This is what I was called to do. This is why I was born. This is my destiny.

You have a sense of destiny hardwired into you, a divine purpose installed by the Creator of the universe. It is a part of your nature, who you really are.

I like to think of it like this: God made all sorts of animals and He's given each one unique characteristics and personality traits. For instance, the owl is nocturnal — it likes to be out at night. God has given the owl eyes that can see as well in the dark as human beings can see in the daylight. But if that owl decided that he wanted to start sleeping at night and staying out during the day, he would be working against his God-given destiny, and problems would certainly follow him. For one thing, he'd have a hard time finding food. He'd struggle all day, not enjoying his life, because he'd not be doing what God created him to do. He would have stepped outside his destiny.

On the other hand, when you're really in line with your destiny, many things come naturally to you. Continuing my analogy, nobody has to tell the owl to stay up at night. God made it nocturnal, so it is natural for an owl to operate in the darkness, and it has the equipment to do so.

In a similar fashion, God has installed certain traits in every one of us. If we can discover our destiny and do what we're good at naturally, life becomes much more enjoyable. It won't be a struggle or a headache.

If you have ever heard great singers, their performance sounds effortless. Why is that? Because they are doing what they are good at naturally.

On the other hand, if you're doing something that is not natural, it's always a struggle. If you try, train, practice, and push, and you still can't seem to get a skill down, recognize that's not in your nature.

Of course, at times we must persevere even though success doesn't come quickly or easily. Sometimes you must push through and learn things that are hard, and those lessons are often extremely beneficial. In general, though, life should not be a constant struggle. When you're living within your purpose, one of the most noticeable results will be how natural it feels. Learn to appreciate and use the skills, gifts, or abilities at which you are naturally talented.

Two friends of mine went to Bible school together, both young men planning to become pastors. When they graduated, Craig started a church, and he asked his friend Ron to come along and help. Ron was set on starting his own church, but since no opportunity had opened for him, he decided to help Craig for a while. Ron was a phenomenal musician, a tremendous piano player, songwriter, and singer.

Craig put Ron in charge of the music ministry at the church, and for several years, he excelled in that area. The church was known around the countryside for its outstanding music. The crowds grew larger, and the congregation thrived.

Nevertheless, Ron kept telling himself, "I've got to get out there and start my church."

Both Craig and Ron's wife recognized how his music was positively affecting people, but Ron wouldn't hear it. To him, music was too easy. He had always done that. It came naturally to him, and he excelled in that area. Ron felt sure he had to get out and try something more challenging, more difficult — something new.

One day, he realized that everything he hoped to impart to people, he was giving them through his music. He began to feel a sense of destiny about what he was already doing. In fact, when Ron really thought about being a pastor, he acknowledged that many aspects of that position weren't appealing to him at all.

Ron decided he would stay right where he was and continue using his God-given gifts and talents. He and his family have been blessed as a result, and many people have been encouraged and inspired through his music. But he almost missed his divine destiny because he was too close to it. It seemed too "normal" for him.

Similarly, God has given you certain talents, gifts, or skills that you can do well, specific areas in which you excel. Don't take them for granted. It may be in sales or communications, or in encouraging people or in athletics or in marketing; whatever it is, don't denigrate it simply because it comes naturally to you. That may well be precisely what God has hardwired into you. It may be an important part of your destiny. Make sure that you explore it to the fullest, keeping in mind that what seems boring to one person may be exhilarating to another for whom that area is part of his or her destiny.

My brother-in-law Kevin is the administrator at Lakewood Church, and he is a tremendous help to our entire staff. Kevin is a "detail person," extremely organized and efficient. He plans wisely and uses his time well. It is not merely something he learned at a time-management seminar; it is a God-given gift. (In my opinion, it is not normal to be that organized! But I'm glad that Kevin is.)

When we were overseeing the $100 million renovation of the Compaq Center into Lakewood Church, Kevin knew every detail of the construction project. He knew where every penny was spent, and he could explain why it was spent. Beyond that, he could tell you three other ways that we tried to accomplish the same thing while saving money. Kevin is a detail person.

When Victoria, I, and our children go on vacation with Kevin and Lisa's family, Kevin sends me an advance itinerary. He'll send me my tickets as well as a weather report. He'll send me rental car information and traffic instructions. He reminds me to bring my driver's license. The morning of our flight, he calls to tell me where traffic is backed up on the freeway.

One time I got to the airport and realized that I had forgotten my driver's license, so now Kevin sends me instructions — in writing — regarding matters that I never even think about. He is gifted in being detail oriented.

Kevin stays in his area of strength. He excels as our administrator. Kevin could think in the back of his mind, *Well, if I could get up there and preach, I'd really be making a differ-*

ence. But no. If Kevin got up and preached, we might not need the Compaq Center! He can't preach, and I can't administrate. He's doing what he's good at naturally. He's often told me, "Joel, this job is a dream come true." Kevin loves coming to work every day. He's passionate about it. It's what he's good at. It's a part of his destiny.

You need to be aware of your natural strengths as well and to use them to your best advantage and to the benefit of others. It says in Romans 12, verse 6, in *The Living Bible,* "God has given each of us the ability to do certain things well." You can't do everything well, but you can do *something* well. Focus on your strengths and make sure that you are not missing out on your destiny because you are always getting involved in something that doesn't come naturally. When you are truly in your destiny, it is not a constant struggle. It just feels right.

YOUR DESTINY WILL FIT YOU

My father loved traveling to India. That was one of his main passions. Two or three times a year, Victoria and I would travel with him. Oftentimes, after we landed in one of India's major cities, we would travel for four or five more hours, deep into the country, to one of the little villages. Of course, there weren't any nice hotels — or often, any hotels at all — back in there. Nor was there any food that we might want to eat. Added to that, the weather was usually hot and sticky, and within minutes after our arrival, we felt dirty and uncomfortable. But my father had a great love for the people of India, so we went year after year.

We sometimes stayed at this old, run-down Indian army barracks. It was nothing more than four concrete walls, with no inside bathroom, no air-conditioning, no sheets on the bed — in fact, it had no beds, just dingy, narrow, uncomfortable cots. At night, all sorts of bugs and other bothersome insects seemed to take over. Victoria and I never complained about the conditions, but we could not wait until we got out of there.

On one of Victoria's first trips to India, shortly after she and I had married, we were staying at those army barracks. Early one morning, my father and I were out on the front lawn eating breakfast. Suddenly, we heard Victoria screaming at the top of her lungs. I'd never heard a woman scream like that before.

Daddy and I dropped our breakfast plates and ran toward the building. As we approached, we saw Victoria running outside and down the stairs violently shaking her long blond hair just as hard and rapidly as she could. About that time, we saw the problem: A large iguanalike lizard was hanging in Victoria's hair. Noble newlywed husband that I was, all I could think of was, *Girl, just keep on shaking! If you're looking at me to get that thing off you, you're looking at the wrong person!*

Finally, much to my relief, my lovely Victoria shook that lizard out of her hair. I thought I was going to have to resuscitate her.

But my father barely seemed to notice the uncomfortable surroundings. Daddy acted as though he were staying in a fancy hotel. He didn't smell the smells. He didn't feel the heat. He didn't see the bugs. He was as happy as he could be. In fact, I had never seen my father any happier than when he was in the villages of India.

He told me one time, "Joel, if I didn't know I was supposed to pastor Lakewood Church, I'd live right here."

Why was that? Why wasn't he uncomfortable? It's because it was a part of his destiny. He was passionate about it. Just as God had hardwired television production into me, God had hardwired missionary work into him.

Proverbs 18:16 says that your gift will

make room for you. I'm convinced if you'll get into your destiny, no matter where you are, you won't have any problem getting hired or getting happy. You won't have any problem finding work, friends, or opportunity. In fact, if you'll focus on your strengths and do what you're gifted to do, you'll probably have to turn down opportunities.

If you are not fulfilled, it may well be because you are not pursuing your destiny. Make sure that you are fulfilling the dreams that God has placed in your heart. Are you tapping into the potential that's on the inside? Have you discovered what you do best, what comes naturally? Are you excelling in that area?

If you are called to be a stay-at-home mom and raise your children, do it to the best of your ability. Don't allow society to pressure you into some career simply because your friends are doing it. Recognize your purpose and do it well.

If you are gifted in the area of sales, don't sit behind a desk all day long in a room by yourself. Get into the area of your gifting and do it to the best of your ability. If you're going to fulfill your destiny, you must do what God hardwired you to do. Make sure you operate in a realm where you are passionate.

One of my favorite old movies is *Chariots of Fire.* In this film, Eric Liddell is a gifted runner whose dream is to compete in the Olympics, but he feels called to be a missionary in China. Yet he knows that God has given him his gift of running. When he runs, he feels that he is dedicating himself to God. In one of the classic lines from the movie, Liddell says, "When I run, I feel God's pleasure." He was saying, when I do what I know I'm called to do, when I'm using my gifts and talents, when I'm pursuing my destiny, I can feel God smiling down on me.

Another of my favorite lines in the film is when Liddell says, "To win is to honor God." I believe we should live by that same philosophy, striving to excel, pursuing our destiny, becoming the best that we can possibly be, and as we do, we will honor God. If you're called to be a businessman, excel at it and you honor God. If you're called to teach children, excel in it and you honor God. Whatever you are called to do, if you'll do it to the best of your ability and excel at it, you are honoring God.

You may not have yet stepped into your divine destiny. You're still doing many things for which you have little passion and no enthusiasm. It is time to become a better you.

Certainly, you can't just snap your fingers

and change careers, but at least examine your life and be aware of how you're spending your time. Are you pursuing your passion? Are you doing what you are good at naturally? If not, why don't you make some changes? Time is short. Find one thing that you're passionate about and start giving yourself to it. And God will lead you one step at a time.

I mentioned earlier how God put the desire in me for television production as a young man. I followed that passion, then when my father went to be with the Lord, I had the desire to step up and pastor the church and I followed that passion. I can honestly say today that I believe I've stepped into my God-given destiny. I know this is why God put me here; this is why I was born.

My desire for you is that you will follow God's divine destiny for your life, discover your calling, and stay in your purpose. Make a decision to keep pressing forward, keep believing, and keep stretching until you see your dreams fulfilled. Then one day, you will look back and say with confidence, "This is why God put me here."

1. Today I will meditate on thoughts such as these:

   "I have everything I need to fulfill my destiny."

   "God accepts me; He approves me; I know God has good things in store for me."

   "I am valuable; I have royal blood in my bloodline; I have a bright future!"

   "My best days are ahead of me."

2. I will take time this week to examine my life carefully, identifying any negative patterns that have been part of my family's past. I have decided that I will be the one to set a new standard; I will shake off negative mind-sets and begin living under the blessings of God rather than under the curse.

3. With God's help, I will overcome any challenges I face that might inhibit my growth as I stretch toward the next level in specific areas of my life.

4. I will be more aware that the decisions I make today will affect future genera-

tions as well as my own life. I will be more careful and deliberate about making wise decisions. I will pray, search the Scripture for guidance, seek godly advice, and take time to think before making major decisions. I will make choices based on my desire to leave my family better off than they were previously.

■ ■ ■ ■

PART TWO:
BE POSITIVE
TOWARD YOURSELF

■ ■ ■ ■

CHAPTER 7
STOP LISTENING
TO ACCUSING VOICES

If you truly want to become a better you, it is imperative that you learn to feel good about yourself. Too many people live under condemnation, constantly listening to the wrong voices. The Bible refers to the enemy as "the accuser of the brethren" who would love for us to live our lives guilty and condemned. He constantly brings accusations against us, telling us what we didn't do or what we should have done. He'll remind us of all our past mistakes and failures.

"You lost your temper last week."

"You should have spent more time with your family."

"You went to church, but you arrived late."

"You gave, but you didn't give enough."

Many people swallow these lines with little or no defense. Consequently, they walk around feeling guilty, condemned, and extremely discontented with themselves. They go through the day without joy, without confidence, expecting the worst and often receiving it.

Granted, no human being is perfect. We've all sinned, failed, and made mistakes. But many people don't know they can receive God's mercy and forgiveness. Instead, they allow themselves to be beaten up on the inside. They tune in to that voice telling them, "You blew it. You messed up." They are so hard on themselves. Instead of believing that they're growing and improving, they believe that voice telling them, "You can't do anything right. You'll never break this habit. You're just a failure." When they wake up in the morning, a voice is telling them what they did wrong yesterday and how they'll probably do something wrong today. As a result, they become extremely critical toward themselves, and that usually spills over to other people as well.

If we're going to live in peace with ourselves, we must learn to put our foot down and say, "I may not be perfect, but I know I'm growing. I may have made mistakes, but I know I am forgiven. I have received God's mercy."

Sure, we all want to be better human beings, but we needn't beat ourselves up over our shortcomings. I may not have a perfect performance, but I know my heart is right.

Other people may not always be pleased with me, but I'm confident that God is.

Similarly, as long as you're doing your best and desire to do what's right according to God's Word, you can be assured God is pleased with you. Certainly, He wants you to improve, but He knows that we all have weaknesses. We all do things that we know in our hearts we shouldn't do. When our human foibles and imperfections poke through our idealism, it's normal to get down on ourselves. *After all,* we tend to think, *we don't deserve to be happy; we have to prove that we're really sorry.*

But no, we should learn to receive God's forgiveness and mercy. Don't allow those condemning voices to play repeatedly in your mind. That will only accentuate a negative attitude toward yourself. If you have a bad attitude toward you, it will hinder every area of your life.

Negative accusations take various forms: "You're not as spiritual as you should be." "You didn't work hard enough last week." Or "God can't bless you because of your past."

Those are all lies. Don't make the mistake of dwelling on that rubbish, not for a moment. Sometimes when I walk off the platform, having spoken at Lakewood and around the world by means of television, the first thought that comes to my mind is, *Joel, that message just wasn't good today. Nobody got anything out of that. You practically put them to sleep.*

I've learned to shake that off. I turn it around and say, "No, I believe it was good! I did my best. I know that at least one person really got something out of it. I did. I thought it was good."

As long as we're doing our best, we don't have to live condemned, even when we make mistakes or fail. There's a time to repent, but there's also a time to shake it off and press forward. Don't live with regrets. Don't go around saying, "Well, I should have done this or that. I should have gone back to college." Or "I should have spent more time with my family." "I should have taken better care of myself."

No, quit condemning yourself. Your analysis and observations may be true, but it doesn't do you any good to put yourself down. Let the past be the past. You cannot change it, and if you make the mistake of living in guilt today because of something that happened yesterday, you won't have the strength you need to live this day in victory.

The Apostle Paul once said, "The things I know I should do, I don't. The things I know

I shouldn't do, I end up doing."[16] Even this great man of God who wrote half the New Testament struggled in this regard. That tells me God does not disqualify me merely because I don't perform perfectly, 100 percent of the time. I wish I did, and I'm constantly striving to do better. I don't do wrong on purpose, but like anyone else, I too have weaknesses. Sometimes I make mistakes or wrong choices, but I have learned not to beat myself up over those things. I don't wallow in condemnation; I refuse to listen to the accusing voice. I know God is still working on me, that I'm growing, learning, and becoming a better me. I have made up my mind that I'm not going to live condemned during the process.

That accusing voice will come to you and tell you, "You lost your temper last week in traffic."

Your attitude should be, "That's okay. I'm growing."

"Well, you said some things yesterday you shouldn't have."

"Yes, that's true. I wish I wouldn't have spoken like that, but I have repented. Now, I know I'm forgiven. I'm going to do better next time."

"Well, what about that failure you went through two years ago in your relationship and in your business?"

"That's in the past. I've received God's mercy. This is a new day. I'm not looking back, I'm looking forward."

When we have that kind of attitude, we take away the lethal power of the accuser. He can't control us when we don't believe his lies.

Perhaps you need to shake off that old guilty feeling. You need to quit listening to the voice that's telling you, "God is not pleased with you. You have too many weaknesses. You've made too many mistakes."

No, as long as you have asked God to forgive you, and you are pressing forward in the direction He wants you to go, you can know with confidence God is pleased with you. When that accusing voice taunts, "You've blown it; you don't have a future; you're so undisciplined . . ." don't sit back and agree, *Yeah, that's right.*

No, you need to start talking back to the accuser. You need to rise up in your authority and say, "Wait a minute. I am the righteousness of God. God has made me worthy. I may have made mistakes, but I know I am forgiven. I know I am the apple of God's eye. I know God has great things in store for me."

Scripture tells us to "put on the breastplate

of God's approval."[17] That's one of the most important pieces of our armor. Think about what the breastplate covers. It covers your heart, the center of your being, the way you think and feel about yourself deep inside. If you're going around with that gnawing feeling, thinking, *I don't have much of a future. I've blown it too many times. God couldn't be pleased with me,* I can tell you this: You're listening to the wrong voice. That's the accuser.

You need to start getting up every morning and saying with confidence: "God is pleased with me. God approves me. God accepts me just the way I am."

Understand that you are not a surprise to God. God is not up in the heavens scratching His head saying, "What did I get myself into? I never dreamed he'd have that problem. I never dreamed she'd have that many weaknesses."

God made us. He knows everything about you, and He still approves you. He is pleased with you. You may have faults, but you are still the apple of God's eye. You may not be where you should be, but at least you're not where you used to be. Quit condemning yourself.

The Bible tells us, "He that began a good work in you will continue to perform it until the day of Jesus Christ."[18] God is still working on us.

Take the pressure off yourself; give yourself the right to have some weaknesses and not to perform perfectly 100 percent of the time. When you make a mistake, don't sit around guilty for two or three weeks. Immediately go to God and say, "Father, I'm sorry. I repent. Help me to do better next time."

Here's the key: Then you have to receive God's forgiveness and mercy.

Sam asks God to forgive him every day for something he did three years ago. He has asked for forgiveness more than five hundred times for the same thing. Sam fails to grasp the fact that God forgave him the first time he asked. The problem is, Sam didn't receive the forgiveness and mercy. He continues listening to the accusing voices. "You blew it. God can't bless you. You know what you did a few years ago."

Instead, Sam needs to get up every morning and say something like, "Father, thank You that Your mercy endures forever. I may have made mistakes in the past, but I know nothing I've done is too much for Your mercy. I may have even made mistakes yesterday. But I know Your mercy is fresh and new every single morning. So I receive it by faith today."

If you get ahold of this truth, it will break the bondage that has held you back for years. Quit listening to the accusing voices. Quit going around feeling wrong about yourself. If you're living your life condemned, that's telling me you're not receiving God's mercy. At times, you may think, *I don't feel like I deserve it. I don't feel like I'm worthy.*

But that's what grace is all about. None of us deserves it. It's a free gift. We're not worthy in ourselves. The good news is, God has made us worthy. You are not a weak worm of the dust. You are a child of the Most High God. Refuse to listen to accusing voices anymore.

"Well, Joel, I've got a lot of things to overcome."

Who doesn't? We all have areas in which we need to improve. However, God does not focus on what's wrong with you. He focuses on what's right with you. He's not looking at all your faults and weaknesses. He's looking at how far you've come, and how much you're growing. You need to put your foot down today and say, "I'm not living condemned anymore. I'm not going through life feeling guilty and unworthy. No mistake I've made is too horrible. I've repented. I've asked for forgiveness. Now, I'm going to take it one step further and start receiving God's mercy."

As a parent, I don't focus on what our children do wrong. Our child can strike out a thousand times at the Little League field, but we'll go around bragging about the one hit he got all year long. As I write these words, our son Jonathan is twelve years old. If somebody asks me about him, I immediately think of all the things I love about Jonathan. I'll tell you he's smart, talented, and funny. He has a quick sense of wit.

I once mentioned in a sermon that most people use only 10 percent of their minds. Jonathan leaned over to Victoria and said, "Mom, I'm above average. I use eleven percent!"

Jonathan is not perfect. He makes mistakes, and it is my joy to teach him, to train him, to help him come up higher. That's the way God is with us. He loves us unconditionally.

What if Jonathan came in one day and said, "Daddy, I just don't feel like I deserve your blessings anymore. I don't feel like I'm worthy of your love. You know, back when I was three years old, I told that lie. Back when I was four, I hit my baby sister."

If he said something like that, I would check his temperature. Jonathan knows how to receive. He knows he's loved. He knows Victoria and I want to bless him.

A couple of years ago, we bought him a guitar, and he couldn't wait till we got home and set up the amplifier. A few minutes later, Jonathan came over and gave me a big hug. He said, "Daddy, thank you so much for this new guitar. And by the way, when do you think we can get my new keyboard?" My son certainly is not shy!

It would do us all good to have some of that boldness. The Scripture urges, "Let us come boldly to the throne of grace."[19] Why?

"To receive mercy for our failures."

Don't pray, "Oh, God, I blew it again. I'm a miserable failure as a parent. I lost my temper. I yelled at my kids. I know I don't deserve anything good in life."

No, if you want to receive something good from God, come to Him humbly and with reverence, but come to Him with boldness. "God, I've made mistakes, but I know You love me, and I'm asking for forgiveness; I'm receiving Your mercy." Then go out expecting God's blessings and favor.

I am bold enough to believe that I am a friend of Almighty God, and that He is smiling down on me right now. I've accepted the fact that I don't perform perfectly all the time, but I know my heart is right. To the best of my ability, I'm doing what pleases Him. That means I don't have to listen to the accusers. I don't have to live my life condemned. When I make mistakes, all I have to do is go to God, ask for forgiveness, then receive His mercy and keep pressing forward.

Maybe you are beaten down because of negative experiences. Perhaps it wasn't even your fault; somebody mistreated you, or somebody rejected you.

The enemy loves to twist that around, insinuating there's something wrong with you. I've seen it with people who were mistreated during their childhood. They weren't even old enough to know what was going on, but the enemy taunts them, "You brought this on yourself. It's your fault." Especially in relationships that don't work out, you may hear that voice telling you, "You are to blame. You're not good enough. You're not attractive enough. You didn't try hard enough."

Have you ever thought that perhaps that other person may have had some problems? Quit receiving all the accusations. Quit allowing the condemning voices to take root, crowding out the good things of God in your life. Some people are practically addicted to guilt. They don't know what it's like to feel good about themselves, to believe they are loved, forgiven, or to believe that they have a bright future.

"Joel, you don't know what I've done in my past," Regan told me. "You don't know what I've been through."

"Maybe not, Regan," I said, "but there's no need for you to internalize all the guilt, shame, and blame. You need to understand that when you came to Christ, when you received His forgiveness, God cleaned out all of your closets. He chooses not to remember your mistakes, your sins, your failures. My question is, Why don't you quit remembering them? Why don't you quit listening to the voice of the accuser?"

I love the story Jesus told about the prodigal son. This young man made a lot of mistakes. He told his dad that he wanted his share of the inheritance. When the father gave the son his money, the boy left home, went out, and lived a wild life. Eventually, those poor choices caught up to him. When his money ran out, so did his friends. He didn't have anything to eat, any place to stay, and he ended up working in a hog pen feeding the pigs. He got so desperate and low, he had to eat the hog food just to stay alive.

One day, sitting in that filth and shame, he said to himself, "I will arise and go back to my father's." That was the best decision that he ever made. When you make mistakes, when you go through failures and disappointments, don't sit around in self-pity. Don't go month after month condemning yourself, rejecting yourself. The first step to victory is to get back up again and go back to your Heavenly Father's loving arms.

The young man headed home, and I'm sure in the back of his mind, he thought, *I'm just wasting my time. My father is never going to receive me back. He's going to be so put out with me. I've made so many terrible choices.* I can imagine that he tried to talk himself out of it three or four times along the way. No doubt, he told himself, "I'm such a failure. My father will never forgive me."

The Scripture says, "When the father saw him a long way off." [20] That tells me the father must have been looking for him. The father must have gotten up every morning and said to himself, "Maybe today will be the day my son comes back home." Morning, noon, and night, the father was on the lookout. When he saw his son, he took off running toward him. He couldn't wait to see him. The parallels in the story are obvious, with the father representing God.

That intrigues me, since this is the only picture of God running in the Bible. To whom or what was God running? One of the disciples? One of the apostles? A famous religious leader? No, the Father is running to a young man that needs mercy. He's running to a person who has made grievous mistakes, a person who has failed miserably.

When the father got there, he embraced his son; he hugged him. He was so happy to see him, but the son just hung his head in shame. He started to say, "Dad, I've really blown it. I've made some terrible decisions. And I know I don't deserve any of this, but maybe you could take me back as one of your hired servants. I'll work out in the fields for you."

The father would have nothing to do with that. He said, "What are you talking about? You are my son. I want to celebrate the fact that you are home."

Perhaps you think that God could never forgive you. You've made too many mistakes, blown it too many times. But let me assure you, nothing that you've done is too much for the mercy of God. Your heavenly Father is not looking for ways to condemn you or to chew you out. He stands before you with His arms held open wide. If you are far from where you know you ought to be, you need to know that God is waiting for you, and the moment you take one step toward Him, your Father will come running to you.

Maybe you have been away for a long time, living in guilt and condemnation, feeling that God could never make anything out of your life.

Today can be a new beginning. God has mercy for any mistake that you've ever made.

The father said to one of his servants, "Go get the best robe and put it on my son." One translation says, "Put the robe of honor on him."

Similarly, you may have made foolish mistakes and suffered some severe setbacks. However, God doesn't simply want to restore you. He doesn't merely want to give you a new beginning. He wants to put the robe of honor on you. That's just the way our God is. In other words, even when we make mistakes, even when we bring the trouble on ourselves, God is so good, when we return to Him, He will not hold that against us. He will receive us back and make something great out of our lives.

The only way this can happen, though, is if we have the right attitude. We cannot continue wallowing in the dirt and expect to have God's best. You may not be where you should be in life, but don't sit around in self-pity. Do as that prodigal son did and say, "I'm going to arise and go back to my father." In other words, "I'm done with living in guilt, shame, and condemnation. I'm going to get up out of this mess, and start receiving God's mercy."

Sure, it will take faith, because everything in you will say, "You know what you've done. You know the mistakes you've made. Do you really think God is going to bless you?"

Precisely at that point, put your shoulders back and say, "I don't think so, I know so. I know God is a good God. I know His mercy is bigger than any mistake I've made. So, I'm going to start receiving His mercy and expecting good things in my life."

A lot of people think God is mad at them, that He's keeping a record of everything they have ever done wrong, and they may have blown it one too many times. When they make poor choices, they wouldn't dare go to God and ask Him for forgiveness and help. They assume they must pay for their own mistakes. Unfortunately, the way most people attempt to do so is by giving up on their dreams; they perpetually feel disqualified, depressed, and defeated, thinking they are paying God back by living at a much lower level than He intended them to enjoy.

But the good news is that the debt has already been paid. Why not accept God's mercy? Why don't you believe that God still has great things in store for you? Yes, you may have made mistakes, but nothing you have done is too much for the mercy of God.

Imagine that I hear my son Jonathan calling out to me, "Daddy! Come help me!"

I look out the window and I see my son hanging on to a tree limb high off the ground, and he looks as though he is about to fall. I instantly recognize that Jonathan could get hurt badly if he should hit the ground from that height.

How do you think I would respond?

I wouldn't say, "Mmm, let me think about this. How good has he been lately?"

I wouldn't ask, "Victoria? Has Jonathan been keeping up with his chores? Let me go check on his bedroom to see if everything is as neat and clean as we expect."

Meanwhile, Jonathan is hanging tenuously from the tree limb, crying out to me, "Daddy, please! Please help me, I'm in trouble."

"Just hang on a while longer, Jonathan; I want to go check your report card."

No, of course I wouldn't say or do such a thing. Jonathan is my son, and I love him (as I do our daughter Alexandra). If one of Victoria's and my children needs me, I'm going to do all I can to help.

That's the way God looks at you. He does

not focus on your mistakes or your failures. He does not desire to make your life miserable or to see how much frustration you can take. God wants you to succeed; He created you to live abundantly.

You needn't go through life with that nagging feeling, *God is not pleased with me. I'd be a hypocrite to ask for His help after all the mistakes I've made.*

Quite the contrary, you are the apple of God's eye. You are His prized possession. Nothing you have ever done, or will ever do, can keep God from loving you and wanting to be good to you.

Dare to believe that. Shake off those feelings of guilt and unworthiness. It doesn't please God for us to drag through life feeling like miserable failures, trying to show God how sorry we are for our wrong choices. Instead, recognize that you are His child, that He loves you and would do almost anything to help you. Dust yourself off, straighten up, and throw your shoulders back, knowing that you are forgiven. Declare, "I may have made some mistakes; I may have blown it badly, but I know God is full of mercy and He still has a great plan for my life."

Develop this new attitude free from guilt and condemnation, and — most of all — free from the accusing voice. No matter how long it has been lying to you, telling you that you're washed up, that you've made too many mistakes, God still has a great plan for your life. You may have missed Plan A, but the good news is that God has a Plan B, a Plan C, and a Plan D. You can turn your face toward Him, knowing that He has already turned His face toward you.

My parents often told our family members a poignant story of when my oldest brother Paul was just a small boy, before any of us siblings were born. Mother and Dad would put Paul in bed at night and then they'd go get in their own bed. Their room was just a few feet down the hall, and every night, my parents would say, "Good night, Paul."

Paul would answer, "Good night, Mother. Good night, Daddy." One night for some reason, Paul was afraid. After they had said their good nights, a few minutes later, Paul said, "Daddy, are you still in there?"

My father said, "Yes, Paul. I'm still in here."

Then Paul said, "Daddy, is your face turned toward me?"

Somehow, the assurance that Daddy was looking in his direction made Paul feel more secure. He could sleep peacefully knowing that my father's face was turned toward him.

"Yes, Paul, my face is turned toward you."

Paul soon drifted off to sleep, knowing that he was under Daddy's watchful care and protection.

Friend, please know your heavenly Father's face is turned toward you. The good news is that God's face will always be turned toward you, regardless of what you have done, where you have been, or how many mistakes you've made. He loves you and is turned in your direction, looking for you.

Maybe you used to be excited about your life, but along the way, you experienced failures, disappointments, and setbacks. Perhaps those accusatory voices have been nagging at you, keeping you down, discouraged, guilty, condemned. You need to know today that God is running toward you. His face is turned in your direction. He is not an angry, condemning God. He is a loving, merciful, forgiving God. He's your heavenly Father and He still has a great plan for your life.

Moreover, God can restore anything that's been stolen from you. You may have failed a thousand times or lost everything you once held dear. But God has not run out of mercy. You can receive it today. It all starts by changing your attitude. Quit being negative toward yourself. Stop accepting the accusations and start receiving God's mercy. Stop dwelling on your past and quit listening to condemning voices. Instead, start putting on God's approval, knowing that He is pleased with you, knowing that you are forgiven and that He has a bright future in store for you. When you do that, you will diffuse the power of the accuser and you will experience a new sense of freedom. You can even learn to like yourself and begin feeling good about yourself. In the chapters ahead, I'll show you how.

CHAPTER 8
LEARNING TO
LIKE YOURSELF

We all have areas that we need to improve, but as long as we're pressing forward, getting up each day and doing our very best, we can be assured that God is pleased with us. He may not be pleased with every decision we make, but He is pleased with us. I know it is difficult for some people to believe, but God wants us to feel good about ourselves. He wants us to be secure and to have healthy self-images, but so many people focus on their faults and weaknesses. When they make mistakes, they're extremely critical of themselves. They live with that nagging feeling that chides, "You're not what you're supposed to be. You don't measure up. You've blown it too many times."

Guess what. God knew that you were not going to be perfect. He knew that you were going to have weaknesses, faults, and wrong desires — He knew all that before you were even born — and He still loves you!

One of the worst things you could do is to go through life being against yourself. This is a major problem today. Many people have a war going on inside themselves. They don't really like who they are. "Well, I'm slow, I'm undisciplined, I'm unattractive, and I'm not as smart as other people." They focus on their weaknesses, not realizing that this negative introspection is a root cause of many of their difficulties. They can't get along in relationships, they're insecure, they don't enjoy their life, and it's largely because they're not at peace with who they are.

Jesus said, "Love your neighbor as you love yourself."[21] Notice, the prerequisite to loving others is to love yourself. If you don't have a healthy respect for who you are, and if you don't learn to accept yourself faults and all, you will never be able to properly love other people. Unfortunately, self-loathing destroys many relationships nowadays.

I've met many people who think their spouse is the reason they can't get along in their marriage. Or they're sure that it's their coworker's fault, but the fact is they have a civil war raging on the inside. They don't like their looks, they don't like where they are in life, they're upset because they haven't broken a bad habit, and that poison spills out into their other relationships.

Understand, you can't give away what you don't have. If you don't love yourself, you're not going to be able to love others. If you're at strife on the inside, feeling angry or insecure about yourself, feeling unattractive, feeling condemned, then that's all you can give away. On the other hand, if you'll recognize that God is working on you, and in spite of your flaws and weaknesses, you can learn to accept yourself. Then you can give that love away and have healthy relationships.

This basic principle could save your marriage; it could change your relationships with the people around you. You think everybody else is the problem, but before you can make significant progress in life, you must come to peace with who you are. Please recognize that if you're negative toward yourself, it's not only affecting you; it is influencing every relationship you have, and it will affect your relationship with God.

That's why it's so important that you feel good about who you are. You may have some faults. You may have some things you wish you could change about yourself. Well, join the crowd. We all do. But lighten up and quit being so hard on yourself. Interestingly, we might never criticize another person or tell him or her, "You are really dumb; you're unattractive, you're undisciplined. I don't like you." Yet we don't have any problem saying it to ourselves. But understand that when you criticize yourself, you are criticizing God's ultimate creation.

"I'm trying to live right," Pete said, "but, Joel, I'm so impatient. I can't control my temper and I get upset so easily."

"Obviously, losing your temper never helps matters, Pete," I told him. "But remember, God is still working on you. You're not a finished product. It's okay to like yourself while God is in the process of changing you. I don't know one person who's arrived just yet, who doesn't need to change in some area of his or her life. But as long as you are negative and critical toward yourself, the process slows down; you make matters worse."

I'm not talking about living a sloppy life, or having a flippant, unconcerned attitude toward sin and mistakes. The fact that you are reading this book indicates that you want to be better, that you are striving for excellence, and that you have a heart to please God. If that's you, don't live under mounds of condemnation merely because you are still struggling in some areas. When you make mistakes, simply go to God and say, "Father, I'm sorry. I repent. Help me to do better next time." Then let it go. Don't beat yourself up for two weeks, or two months, or two years. Shake it off and move on.

Many people are their own worst enemies. "Well, I'm so overweight. I've blown my diet. I don't spend enough time with my children. I'm so undisciplined I didn't even clean my house last week. Surely, God is not pleased with me."

Don't step into that trap. The Scripture indicates that God has already approved and accepted you. It doesn't say God approves you as long as you live a perfect life. No, it says God approves you unconditionally, just as you are. Frankly, it's not because of what you have or haven't done; God loves you because of who you are and because of who he is. God *is* love. You are a child of the Most High God. If God approves you, why don't you start approving yourself? Shake off guilt, condemnation, inadequacies, and a sense that you can't measure up, and start feeling good about who you are.

"Well, Joel, I don't know if I believe that," a dear, well-meaning man told me. "We're just poor old sinners."

No, we used to be poor old sinners, but when we came to Christ, He washed away our sins. He made us new creatures. Now, we are no longer poor old sinners, we are sons and daughters of the Most High God.

Instead of crawling around the floor with that "poor old me" mentality, you can step up to the dinner table. God has an incredible banquet prepared for you. He has an abundant life for you. No matter how many mistakes you've made in the past, or what sort of difficulties you struggle with right now, you have been destined to live in victory. You may not be all you want to be, but at least you can look back and say, "Thank You, God; I'm not what I used to be."

The enemy doesn't want you to understand that you have been made righteous. He much prefers you to have a sin consciousness, but God wants you to have a righteousness consciousness. Start dwelling on the fact that you've been chosen, set apart, approved, and accepted in heaven — and that you have been made righteous on earth.

Every morning, no matter how we feel, we need to get out of bed and boldly declare, "Father, I thank You that You have approved me. Thank You that You are pleased with me. Thank You that I am forgiven. I know that I am a friend of God."

Just as you put on your clothes, consciously put on the breastplate of God's approval. All through the day, everywhere you go, imagine big bold letters right across your chest saying "Approved by Almighty God." When those condemning voices attempt to pummel your self-image with comments such as "You're not this, you're not that, you blew it over here," simply look in the mirror and see that affirmation: Approved by Almighty God.

I know my children aren't perfect. They have faults and weaknesses, and they sometimes make mistakes. But I also know that they're growing. They're learning. Imagine you asking me, "Joel, are you pleased with your children?"

How do you think I would answer?

I would not list all their faults. I wouldn't think about what they have done wrong over their young lives or even the time they may have disobeyed last week. No, without hesitation, I would tell you, "Yes, I am pleased with them. They are great children." Then I'd tell you everything I like about them. I'd tell you they are loving, caring, attractive, talented. I mean, they're just like their father!

Seriously, that's exactly the way God sees you. He's not focused on your faults. He's not keeping a list of your shortcomings. God is not looking at everything you've done wrong over your entire life or your disobedience last week. He's looking at what you're doing right. He's looking at the fact that you have made a conscious decision to be better, to live right, and to trust Him. He is pleased that you are kind and courteous to people. He's looking at the fact that you have a desire to know Him better.

It's time for you to get in agreement with God and start feeling good about who you are. Certainly, you may have some areas in which you need to improve, and you will because you're growing. You're making progress. You can live free from the heaviness that has weighed you down in the past.

Keep in mind, the enemy accuses that you're never doing enough. "You're not working hard enough, not being a good enough marriage partner or parent; you did fairly well on your diet yesterday, but you shouldn't have eaten that dessert late last night."

Don't take that stuff. You have a multitude of good qualities to every one negative quality.

"But, Joel, I'm so impatient."

Well, that may be true, but have you ever thought about the fact that you're always on time? You're persistent. You're determined.

"I don't think I'm as good a mom as I should be."

Maybe not, but have you noticed that your

children are doing great in school? Your children never miss a meal. They are healthy, well rounded socially, and busy in sports, school, and church activities.

"Well, I'm not a very good husband, Joel."

Okay, maybe you work too much, but you've never missed a house payment. You provide a great living for your family.

"But I've made a lot of mistakes in life."

Yes, but you picked up this book and began reading, learning, seeking to change for the better. That's a pretty great choice. Give yourself the benefit of the doubt. Take off those rags of condemnation and start putting on your robe of righteousness. Put on the breastplate of God's approval.

You can, you should feel good about yourself. When you regard yourself positively, you are in agreement with God.

"What about that mistake I made last week? What about that time I failed last year?"

The moment you repented, God not only forgave you, He forgot about it. He chooses not to remember it anymore. Quit bringing up what God has already forgotten; let it go and start feeling good about who you are. We tend to think God is keeping a list of all of our mistakes. In your mind, you can see Him up there in heaven. "Oops! They failed there, let me get that down." And "Uh-oh, I heard that comment. Gabriel, make a special note of that one."

That's not God's heart at all. God is for you; He is on your side. He is the best friend you could ever have. God is not looking at what you've done wrong; He's looking at what you've done right. He's not focused on what you are; He's focused on what you can become.

You can be assured that God is pleased with you. He's in the process of changing you. That's why I can get up every morning and even though I make mistakes, I can boldly say, "God, I know you approve me, so I feel good about who I am."

"Joel, you're making it too easy," an older man complained. "You're giving people a license to sin."

No, you don't need a license. If you want to sin, you can sin. I sin all I want to. The good news is that I don't want to. I want to live a life that's pleasing to God. I want to live a life of excellence and integrity.

Stop dwelling on everything that's wrong with you and taking an inventory of what you're not. The Scripture says in Hebrews, "To look away from everything that distracts."[22] If you constantly pick yourself apart, you're bound to be depressed and defeated. Look away from that; recognize that you are changing, that you're making progress. Accept the truth that spiritual growth is a process, not an overnight flash. The Bible says God changes us little by little.

"But, Joel, I've got all these weaknesses," I hear you saying. "If you only knew me . . ."

Here's some good news: God's power shows up the greatest in our weaknesses. When we are weak, He is strong. You can learn to lean on God, and instead of being negative and critical toward yourself, say, "Father, I'm leaning on You. I'm asking You to help me to beat this bad habit. God, I know I'm weak in this area, but I believe You are strong in and through me. I'm asking You to help me have a better opinion about myself."

In your weaknesses, whatever they may be, instead of getting down on yourself, simply ask God to help you, and you'll see His power show up like never before.

I believe God allows us to have some weaknesses so we'll always have to trust Him. If you're waiting until you get rid of everything you struggle with and until you feel like you're perfect, before you begin to like yourself, you're going to be waiting your whole lifetime.

"Well, Joel, I'd feel good about myself if I could drop twenty pounds. I'd feel good about myself if I would be a little more patient, if I'd be a little more understanding."

No, you can start feeling good about yourself right now. You're not perfect, but you are trying to live better, and God looks at your heart. He sees the inside, and He is changing you little by little.

We're all at different stages in our spiritual maturity. That's why each of our attitudes can be, "God, I know I have these areas I need to improve, but I'm doing my best. I also know that You have already accepted and approved me, so I'm going to start accepting myself. I'm making up my mind that I am going to go through this day feeling good about me."

I heard a story about a man and his small son who were hiking up a mountain. Suddenly, the little boy slipped and slid about thirty yards down the mountainside, getting caught in some brush. Unhurt but frightened, he called out, "Somebody, help me!"

A voice called back, "Somebody, help me!"

The youngster looked surprised and confused. He said, "Who are you?"

The voice shouted back, "Who are you?"

The boy began to get aggravated. "You're a coward!" he yelled.

The voice shouted back, "You're a coward!"

The boy shot back, "You're a fool."

The voice repeated, "You're a fool."

By then, the boy's father had reached him and helped extricate his son from the brush. The boy looked up and said, "Dad, who is that?"

The father chuckled and said, "Son, that's called an echo, but it's also called life." He said, "Son, let me show you something." The dad shouted out, "You're a winner!"

The voice shouted back, "You're a winner!"

The dad's voice boomed, "You've got what it takes."

The voice boomed back, "You've got what it takes."

The dad shouted, "You can make it."

The voice shouted back, "You can make it."

"Son, that's exactly how it is in life," the father explained. "Whatever you send out always comes back to you."

Let me ask: What messages are you sending out about yourself?

"I'm a failure, I'm unattractive. I'm undisciplined. I'm broke. I've got a terrible temper. Nobody likes to be around me."

Start sending out "I'm approved, I'm accepted, I am the righteousness of God. I am creative. I am talented. I am more than a conqueror." Make sure you are transmitting good messages about yourself.

When Jesus was baptized, He came up out of the water and a voice boomed out of the heavens, saying, "This is my beloved son in whom I am well pleased." [23] Of course, Jesus was uniquely God's Son, but I believe God is saying that to you, too. He is well pleased with you.

"Oh, God couldn't say that to me. You can't imagine the life I've lived. You don't know the things I struggle with right now."

No, let this sink deep down into your heart, mind, and soul: God is pleased with you. He has already accepted and approved you. He may not be pleased with every decision you make, but if you have entrusted your life to Him, God is pleased with you.

What a tragedy to go through life being against yourself, especially when there is no rational reason to do so. Understand that it is not that God will be pleased with you one of these days, when you finally get your stuff together. No, God is pleased with you right now. The war within is over; God has won! That's why it's okay to feel good about who you are today, right now, this very moment.

Chapter 9
Making Your Words Work for You

God didn't create any of us to be average. He didn't make us to barely get by. We were created to excel. The Scripture teaches that before the foundation of the world, God not only chose us, but He equipped us with everything we need to live His abundant life.[24] You have seeds of greatness inside of you, but it is up to you to believe and act on them.

I see too many people today going around with low self-esteem, feeling inferior, as if they don't have what it takes. As long as we have that poor self-image, we're not going to experience God's best. You will never rise above the image that you have of yourself. That's why it is so important that we see ourselves as God sees us.

You need to have an image of a champion on the inside. You may not be there yet; you may have some areas to overcome, but you need to know deep down inside that you are a victor and not a victim.

One of the best ways that we can improve our self-image is with our words. Words are like seeds. They have creative power. It says in Isaiah that "We will eat the fruit of our words." That's amazing when you stop to consider that truth: Our words tend to produce what we're saying.

Every day, we should make positive declarations over our lives. We should say things such as, "I am blessed. I am prosperous. I am healthy. I am talented. I am creative. I am wise." When we do that, we are building up our self-image. As those words permeate your heart and mind, and especially your subconscious mind, eventually they will begin to change the way you see yourself.

The Scripture says, "With our tongue, we can either bless our life or we can curse our life." [25]

Some individuals curse their own future by saying things such as, "I don't have what it takes. I'm so clumsy I can't get anything right. I'm so undisciplined. I'll probably never lose this weight."

We must be extremely careful what we allow out of our mouth. Our words set the direction for our lives.

Which direction are you going? Are you declaring good things? Are you blessing your life, speaking words of faith over your future and your children's future? Or are you prone to saying negative things? "Nothing good ever happens to me. I'll probably never get out of debt. I'll never break this addiction."

When you talk like that, you are setting the limits for your life.

Many people suffer a poor self-image because of their own words. They've gone around for years putting themselves down, and now they've developed these wrong mind-sets that prevent them from rising higher in their careers or in their personal lives.

"Joel, I've made so many mistakes I don't see how God could bless me," Catherine said through her tears. "I just don't feel like I deserve it."

"No, we don't deserve God's blessings," I told her. "They are part of the free gift of God's salvation. The best thing you could do is to accept His offer, and all through the day start saying to yourself, 'I am a new creation. I am forgiven. I am valuable to God. He has made me worthy.' If you keep saying that long enough, you're going to start believing it. And you will begin expecting good things."

You may be lonely, but you shouldn't go around talking about it all the time. "Well,

I'm so lonely. I'm discouraged. Nobody likes to be around me. I'll probably never get married."

No, get up every day and say, "I am fun to be around; I am attractive and friendly; I have a good personality, I'm an engaging person; people are drawn to me." As you speak such positive statements day after day, you will soon discover your self-image is changing for the better. You'll feel better about yourself, and you'll not only have more confidence, you'll be friendlier; you will attract other positive people to yourself.

Maybe you have had other people speak negative, destructive words over you. Perhaps a parent, coach, or teacher said things like, "You don't have what it takes, you're never going to be successful, you can't go to that college; you're not smart enough." Now those words have taken root and they are setting the limits for your life. Unfortunately, you've heard those comments for so long they have seeped down into your self-image. The only way you can change the effects of those words is for you to get on the offensive and start speaking these faith-filled words over your own life. Moreover, the best eraser you can ever find is God's Word. Start speaking out of your own mouth what God says about you: "I am anointed; I am approved; I am equipped; I've been chosen, set apart, destined to live in victory."

When you speak such faith-filled words, you will bless your life. Furthermore, your self-image will begin to improve.

Positively or negatively, creative power resides in your words, because you believe your words more than you believe anybody else's. Think about it. Your words go out of your mouth and they come right back into your own ears. If you hear those comments long enough, they will drop down into your spirit, and those words will produce exactly what you're saying.

That's why it is so important that we get in a habit of declaring good things over our lives every day. When you get up in the morning, instead of looking at that mirror and saying, "Oh, I can't believe I look like this. I'm getting so old, so wrinkled," you need to smile and say, "Good morning, you good-looking thing!" No matter how you feel, look at yourself in that mirror, and say, "I am strong. I am healthy. God is renewing my strength like the eagles. And I am excited about this day."

In the natural, physical realm, those statements may not seem to be true. You may not feel up to par that day. Or you may have many obstacles to overcome. The Scripture

193

tells us that we are to "call the things that are not as if they already were." [26]

In other words, don't talk about the way you are; talk about the way you want to be. That's what faith is all about. In the physical realm, you have to see it to believe it, but God says you have to believe it, and then you'll see it.

For instance, you may be undisciplined in a certain area, but instead of complaining about it and talking badly about yourself, start calling in what you need.

Change the way you speak about yourself and you can change your life. Start each day with saying things such as, "I am disciplined. I have self-control. I make good decisions. I'm an overcomer. This problem didn't come to stay; it came to pass." All through the day — as you're driving to work, taking a shower, or cooking dinner — under your breath, declare positive, biblically accurate statements about yourself: "I am more than a conqueror. I can do what I need to do. I'm a child of the Most High God."

As you speak affirmatively about yourself, you'll be amazed to discover that you are getting stronger emotionally and spiritually, and that image on the inside is changing for the better.

Jacqueline is a bright young high school

student, but she did not believe that she could ever make good grades. "I'm just a C student," she lamented. "That's the best I've ever done. I don't understand math. My teacher is the hardest one around."

Fortunately, Jacqueline learned to stop limiting herself by her words. Now each day on the way to school, she says, "I excel in school. I am a quick learner. I have good study habits. I am a good student; I am full of God's wisdom."

Maybe you tend to be critical and judgmental toward people. Don't sit back and say, "That's the way I am."

Instead, look in that mirror and say, "I am compassionate; I am kind. I am sympathetic and understanding; I believe the best in people." As you consistently make these positive declarations, the new attitudes will get down inside you and your relationships will begin to change.

When God told Abraham and Sarah they were going to have a child, they were both well beyond the childbearing years. No wonder Sarah laughed. She must have said, "Abraham, what are you talking about? Me? Have a child. I'm an old woman. I don't think so."

God had to change the image Abraham and Sarah had of themselves before they could ever have that child. How did God do that? He changed their names; He changed the words they were hearing. He changed Sarai to Sarah, which means "princess." He changed Abram to Abraham, which means "father of many nations." Think about it. Before Abraham had a single child, God called him by faith the father of many nations. Every time somebody said, "Hey, Abraham. How you doing?" they were saying, "Hello, father of many nations." He heard that so often, it began to sink down inside him.

Sarah was an older woman who had never had any children. She probably didn't feel much like a princess, but every time somebody said, "Hello, Sarah," they were saying, "Hello, princess." Over time, that changed her self-image. Now, she no longer saw herself as an older, barren woman; she began to see herself as a princess. Eventually, she gave birth to a child, whom the parents named Isaac, as God had instructed.

Perhaps God has whispered something to your heart that seems totally impossible. It may seem impossible for you to ever be well again, or impossible for you to get out of debt, to get married, to lose weight, to start that new business. In the natural, physical realm, all the odds are against you; you don't see how it could happen. But if you're going to see those dreams come to pass, you have to get your mouth moving in the right direction and use your words to help you develop a new image on the inside. No matter how impossible something looks, no matter how you feel, start boldly declaring, "I am strong in the Lord. I can do all things through Christ. I am well able to fulfill my destiny." Call in what God has promised you. The Scripture says, "Let the weak say I am strong." You may not feel well today, but don't go around saying, "I don't think I'm ever going to get over this sickness."

Instead, start boldly declaring, "God is restoring health unto me. I am getting better every day in every way."

Or maybe your financial situation doesn't look good. Start declaring, "I am blessed. I am prosperous. I'm the head and not the tail. I will lend and not borrow."

Don't merely use your words to describe your situation; use your words to change your situation.

Victoria and I have some friends who were trying to have another child. They had a daughter, and they really wanted to have a son. Unfortunately, every time the wife became pregnant, she had a miscarriage. This happened five times over a nine-year period. As the couple grew older, they also grew discouraged and frustrated.

The husband's name was Joe, and he had gone by that name his whole lifetime. But one day it came to his attention that his full given name, Joseph, meant "God will add." When Joe heard that, something clicked inside of him. He knew that was God speaking to him. Joe decided to start using his full name

He told his friends, family members, and coworkers, "Please don't call me Joe anymore; start calling me Joseph." They didn't know what he was doing, and several wrote off Joe's desire to be called Joseph as some sort of midlife crisis. But Joseph didn't care. He knew that every time somebody said, "Hello, Joseph," they were saying, "God will add." They were speaking faith into his life. Joseph took that to mean that "God is going to add to us a son."

Several months after Joseph began believing his name, his wife became pregnant again. And for the first time in ten years, she carried the child full term, and gave birth to a healthy baby boy.

As a testimony to what God had done for them, they named their baby "Joseph" as well — "God will add."

With our words, we can prophesy our own future. Unfortunately, many people predict defeat, failure, lack, and mediocrity. Avoid those kinds of comments and use your words to declare good things. Declare health, joy, financial blessing, happy and whole relationships. All through the day, you can declare, "I have the favor of God. I can do what I need to do." As you do so, you will be blessing your own life and strengthening your self-image.

If you struggle with depression, use your words to change your situation. You may have been through a lot of disappointments. You may have gone through some setbacks in the past. More than anybody, you need to get up every day and boldly declare, "This is going to be a great day. I may have been defeated in the past, but this is a new day. God is on my side. Things are changing in my favor."

When discouraging thoughts attack, instead of complaining and expecting the worst, say it again and again: "Something good is going to happen to me. I'm a victor and not a victim." It's not enough to merely think positively: You need to speak positively about yourself. You need to hear it over and over again. "Good things are coming my way. God is fighting my battles for me. New doors of opportunity are opening."

As you speak affirmatively, you will develop a new image on the inside, and things will begin to change in your favor.

If you will set aside five minutes a day and simply declare good things over your life, you may be astounded at the results. Before you start your busy day, before you leave the house, drive to work, or take the kids to school, take a few minutes to speak blessings over your life. You may prefer to write the statements, so you can have a record of them. It says in Habakkuk to write down your vision. Make a list of your dreams, goals, and aspirations as well as the areas you want to improve, the things you want to see changed. Always make sure you can back it up with God's Word. Then get alone with God and take a few minutes every day to declare good things over your life. Remember, it's not enough to read it or merely think about it. Something supernatural happens when we speak it out. That's how we give life to our faith.

Maybe you struggle with worry. You're always upset about something and your mind tends to fret over insignificant, minor concerns. Start declaring, "I have the peace of God. My mind is at rest. I have a relaxed and easygoing attitude." Declare it by faith and use your words to change that situation.

Betty had tried to quit smoking for years

and years. She had good intentions, and she did her best, but she just couldn't seem to break the habit. She was always saying, "I just don't have what it takes. This is too hard for me; I'll never break this addiction." She even told her friends, "If I ever do quit smoking, I know I will gain so much weight." She was constantly speaking negative words over her life, and this went on for years.

One day somebody encouraged Betty to change what she was saying, to call the things that are not as if they already were. She didn't know any better, so she just started saying, "I don't like to smoke. I can't stand the taste of nicotine. And when I do quit smoking, I'm not going to gain one bit of weight." She said that day after day, month after month.

She later told me, "Joel, I'd be sitting there smoking a cigarette and enjoying it, yet I'd say out of my mouth, 'I can't stand to smoke. I can't stand this nicotine.'" She wasn't talking about the way she was; she was talking about the way she wanted to be. She did that month after month, and then one day, she woke up and lit up a cigarette and it tasted differently — slightly bitter. Before long, the taste grew worse and worse. Eventually, the cigarettes tasted so bad to Betty, she couldn't stand the taste anymore, and she was able to lay them down and not pick them up again.

Amazingly, Betty did not gain one bit of weight because of kicking the smoking habit. Today, she's totally free from nicotine. Betty broke that addiction in part by the power of her words. She prophesied her own future.

Like Betty, maybe you have spent years saying negative things about yourself. "I can't break this addiction. I can't lose weight. I'll never get out of debt. I'll never get married."

Understand, those words have created a stronghold in your heart and mind. You have developed the wrong picture of yourself on the inside. You must begin to change that image and start seeing yourself with the victory or else you will remain in bondage, right where you are.

Decide today that you will speak only positive affirmations about yourself. You may have a thousand bad habits, but don't let another critical word come out of your mouth toward yourself. Use your words to bless your life. Look in that mirror and call in what you need. The image of your life must change on the inside before it can change on the outside.

Start saying every day, "I am excelling in my career. I have the favor of God. I make good decisions. I'm a hard worker and I'm going to rise to new heights." If you hear that long enough, it will create a new image within, an image of victory, an image of success.

Every day, whether I feel like it or not, I declare, "I am anointed. My gifts and talents are coming out to the full. Every message gets better and better. People are drawn to me. People want to listen to me."

Occasionally, I receive letters from people who say, "Joel, I never watch TV ministers. I don't even like them. But for some reason, when I turn you on, I just can't turn you off."

A man wrote, telling me that his wife had been trying to get him to watch me on television for years, but he wouldn't do it. He was quite cynical and sarcastic toward the things of God. One day, however, he was flipping through the channels and came across our program. As usual, he immediately pressed the remote control to change the channel, but for some reason his remote control quit working and he was stuck watching the program. Frustrated and aggravated, he manipulated that remote control, but nothing helped. He changed the batteries and it still didn't work.

In his letter, he admitted, "Joel, even

though I acted like I wasn't listening, what you were saying was applying directly to me." He continued, "Funny thing, the minute the program was over, my remote control started working again." As I read his letter, I thought, *God works in mysterious ways.* Now, that man never misses church on Sunday.

Learn to declare good things over your life. If you are negative and critical toward yourself, your own words can stop God's best plan from coming to pass in your life. That is what almost happened to the Old Testament prophet Jeremiah. God said, "Jeremiah, I saw you before you were ever formed in your mother's womb and I have chosen you to be a prophet to the nations."

Jeremiah was young, and he didn't have a great deal of self-confidence. When he heard God's promise, rather than feeling blessed, Jeremiah was afraid. He said, "God I can't do that. I can't speak to the nations. I'm too young. I wouldn't even know what to say."

God answered, "Jeremiah, say not that you are too young."[27] Notice, God immediately stopped Jeremiah's negative words. Why? God knew that if Jeremiah went around saying, "I can't do this. I don't have what it takes. I'm too young," those negative words would thwart the plan and prevent the promise from coming to pass. God simply said, "Jeremiah, do not say that anymore. Don't use those words to curse your future." Jeremiah changed his words about himself and became a courageous spokesman to a generation that had settled for less than God's best.

God has called you to do great things, as well. He's put dreams and desires in your heart. Sure, there are areas where you want to improve, things that you want to accomplish. Be careful that you don't make excuses: "God, I can't do it. I've made too many mistakes. I'm too young. I'm too old. God, I come from the wrong side of the tracks."

No, God is saying to us the same thing He said to Jeremiah: Stop it. Those negative words can keep you from experiencing My best plan.

Decide right now that today will be a turning point in your life. Prior to now, you rarely have said anything good about yourself. But starting today, get on the offensive and start making positive declarations over your own life. Every day, say things like "I am blessed. I am healthy and prosperous. I am competent; I am called. I'm anointed. I'm creative. I'm talented. I am well able to fulfill my destiny."

If you want to know where you are going to be five years from now, listen to your words. You are prophesying your future. If you want to be stronger, healthier, happier, if you want to break addictions, then start declaring it right now. Remember, you will eat the fruit of your own words, so bless your future. Get in agreement with God, and learn to speak words of faith and victory over your own life. Not only will you develop a better self-image, you will become a better you!

CHAPTER 10
HAVE CONFIDENCE
IN YOURSELF

Each of us has an internal dialogue, an inner conversation going on with ourselves throughout the day. In fact, we talk more to ourselves than we do to anybody else. The question is, What are you saying to yourself? What do you meditate on? Positive thoughts? Empowering thoughts? Affirming thoughts? Or do you go around thinking negative, defeated thoughts, telling yourself things like "I'm unattractive. I'm not talented. I've made many mistakes. I'm sure God is displeased with me." That kind of negative self-talk keeps millions of people from rising higher.

We usually talk to ourselves subconsciously, without even thinking about it. But in the back of your mind, you have these reoccurring thoughts. And for most people those thoughts are negative: I'm clumsy. I'll never overcome my past. I don't have what it takes.

All through the day they allow defeated messages to permeate their mind and self-talk. They see somebody that's successful, somebody that's achieving, and that inner voice tells them, "That will never happen for me. I'm not as smart as that person; I'm not that talented." Or they see somebody that is in good physical shape, somebody that looks healthy, fit, and attractive. That voice tells them, "I'm just not that disciplined. I'll never get back in shape." There's a negative voice on the inside that's constantly telling the person that something is wrong with them.

"You're not a good mother." "You didn't work hard enough last week." "You are a weak person." If we make the mistake of allowing this negative self-talk to take root, it not only saddens our spirit, but it also limits how high we can go in life. Many people are living in mediocrity because they are playing that negative recording day after day, over and over again.

I've discovered that often these wrong-thinking patterns stem from childhood. The people who should have been nurturing us and telling us what we could become, building our confidence, did just the opposite. I know people who are stuck in a rut because as they were growing up, somebody mistreated them, or somebody rejected them. A parent, a coach, or even a peer spoke negative words over the person. They didn't know any better. They just let it take root. Now those wrong-thinking patterns are keeping that person from becoming all God intends him or her to be.

We have to reprogram our minds. Please don't lay in bed every morning thinking about everything that's wrong with you. Don't lie there and rehearse all your mistakes — thinking about what you can't do or how you don't have what it takes. It doesn't matter how many times you've tried and failed. You have to shake off those negative messages and experiences, and put on a new recording. Remind yourself often: "I am a child of the Most High God. I have a bright future. God is pleased with me. I am talented; I am creative; I have what it takes. I will fulfill my destiny." We should be talking to ourselves that way, not in arrogance but in a quiet confidence. Deep down on the inside, all through the day, we should hear things like "I am anointed. I am called. I am chosen. I am equipped. This is my season."

Our internal dialogue should always be positive and hopeful. We should always talk to ourselves with empowering, affirming thoughts. We have to get out of the habit of thinking negative thoughts about ourselves. Don't ever say, "I'm so slow. I'm unattractive. I'll never overcome my past."

No, get those phrases out of your vocabulary. If you make the mistake of dwelling on that junk, it will set the limits for your life. You may have suffered horrible pain in the past. You may have had some unfair things happen to you, but don't allow that to pull you down by constantly playing the negative recording about yourself. You believe what you say about yourself more than you believe what anybody else says. Others can tell you repeatedly that God has a great plan for your life. He has a bright future in store for you. But until you get it down on the inside and start replaying it throughout the day, it's not going to do you any good.

Pay attention to how you talk to yourself. Please don't misunderstand, but in my mind all day long I replay the message, "Joel, you have what it takes. You can do what God's called you to do. You're talented. You're creative. You're strong in the Lord. You're well able to fulfill your destiny."

If you too will talk to yourself in the right way, you'll not only enjoy your life more, but you'll rise higher to a new level of confidence, a new level of boldness. I read a study where researchers gave a test group of college students some special eyeglasses that turned everything upside down, totally opposite of what it should be. For the first few days of the experiment, confusion reigned. The students stumbled over the furniture, they couldn't read or write, they had to be led to class, and they could barely function. But slowly, they started adjusting. By the end of the first week, they were able to go to class on their own. They didn't need any help to get around. The researchers were intrigued so they decided to continue the experiment. After one month, the students had totally adapted. Their minds had compensated for their upside-down world, and they could read without any problem. They could write, do their homework, type on the computer — all upside down.

Something similar can happen to us. If we go around with wrong mind-sets long enough, telling ourselves, "Well, I'm not a good parent. I've made too many mistakes. Nothing good ever happens to me," just like those college students, even though it's totally backwards, and not the way God created us, our minds will eventually adapt and adjust, and we will end up living at that level.

Your world may be upside-down already. Maybe you are living far below your potential, feeling bad about yourself, lacking confidence, and wallowing in low self-esteem. Have you considered that it could be a result of what you are constantly speaking to yourself? Your internal dialogue is negative. You have to change that before anything else will change.

I saw a lady on television who had lost 175 pounds. She had surgery to remove the excess skin and everything went great. They showed the before and after pictures, and she looked fantastic. But several months later they went back to interview her and she was so depressed. She would hardly eat anything. They said, "Hey, what's wrong? You look great. You look fantastic."

She said, "Yes, that's what everybody is telling me. But I guess in my mind, I'll always be a fat, unattractive lady."

As I watched, I thought, *You hit the nail on the head. It's in your mind.* She had changed on the outside, but she had not changed on the inside. She was still playing that old negative recording. "I'm fat. I'm unattractive. I'll never be happy." She could have gotten down to ninety pounds, and she still wouldn't have been happy.

Don't listen to voices that are pulling you down. You may not look like you stepped out of a fashion magazine, but I can tell you this: You were made in the image of Almighty

God. You will be amazed at how much more you enjoy your life and how much better you feel about you, if you'll learn to talk to yourself in a positive manner. And even when you make mistakes, even when you do wrong, don't go around saying, "Well, I can't do anything right. I'm so clumsy. I'm so slow."

I played sports with people who make the mistake of beating themselves up, calling themselves derogatory names. "You idiot!" "Bill, you sorry thing. You can't make a shot." "What kind of jerk are you?"

I know other people who have gone through setbacks in life — disappointments, failures, bankruptcy, or divorce. They go around so defeated, focused on what went wrong. They allow that negative record to play continually. "You blew it. You had your chance. You messed up your life."

Learn to put on that new recording, tell yourself "I am forgiven. I am restored. God has a new plan. Good things are in store."

I'm not saying simply to take the easy way out. I am saying that it does you no good to go around feeling condemned, disgraced, or disqualified over something that is in the past. I know people who live with a black cloud following them around. It's a vague feeling; they can't even put their finger on it, but something is always telling them,

"You're never going to be happy. You might as well forget it."

You cannot sit back and accept those kinds of statements to yourself. You must rise up and start talking to yourself in a new way. All through the day, you should be telling yourself things like, "Something good is going to happen to me. God is pleased with me. I have a bright future. The best is yet to come." You have to change on the inside before it's ever going to happen on the outside.

It would do us all good to lie in bed in the morning and before we get up, think good thoughts about ourselves. *I'm a good parent. I'm a good leader. I'm a good husband. I have a bright future. God is pleased with me.* Learn to think these thoughts on purpose.

I was blessed to be raised by parents who instilled in me this kind of confidence and self-esteem. As I was growing up, my parents always told me that I could accomplish great things; they constantly reminded me that they were proud of me. Having people in our lives who will nurture and encourage us, especially at a young age, when we're forming so many of our thought patterns, is extremely important.

Parents, I would encourage you to instill these qualities in your children. They need your love, your encouragement, your approval, and your affirmation. Don't ever put your children down. Don't say things like "Why can't you make good grades like your brother?" Or "You are just not smart enough to attend college." "If you keep that up, you're not going to amount to anything."

Words are like seeds. They can take root and grow in a person's mind for years. Certainly, when our children are small, we have to correct them, but don't make the mistake of saying things such as, "You are such a bad boy," "You're a bad girl." No, he or she is not a bad person. They may have done something wrong, but they are good children. They're made in the image of Almighty God. God didn't make any junk. Parents, we have a responsibility to instill confidence, self-esteem, and security into our children.

I wonder how many adults struggle today because they didn't get the positive encouragement they needed from their parents or from the people who raised them. Or maybe the parents only corrected the child without showing her the approval side. If you are a parent, please avoid that sad mistake.

My brother Paul and his wife, Jennifer, have the cutest little boy named Jackson. He's always happy and so much fun to be around. Every night when Jennifer takes Jackson to bed, she tells him a story and prays with him. Just before she says good night, she says, "Now, Jackson, let me remind you who you are," then she'll go through this long list of superheroes. "Jackson, you're my Superman. You're my Power Ranger. You're my Buzz Lightyear. You're my Rescue Hero. You're my Lightning McQueen. You're my cowboy. You're my baseball player." Little Jackson just lies there with a big smile on his face, taking it all in.

What is Jennifer doing? She's giving Jackson fuel for his internal dialogue. Even though he's only three years old, Jennifer is saying to him, "Jackson, you are special; you are valuable; you're going to do great things in life." Then she goes through this same routine when she puts my brother Paul to bed! But instead of using Buzz Lightyear, she uses Elvis.

Something funny happened the other day. Paul and Jennifer got home late, so Jennifer put Jackson to bed in a hurry. She didn't take time to go through the long list of superheroes. A few minutes later, she heard this little voice calling out from upstairs. "Mamma, mamma." Jennifer ran to the staircase and called, "Yes, Jackson, what's wrong?" He said, "Mamma, you forgot to tell me who I am."

There's a deeper truth to that simple statement. I have found that if we don't tell our children who they are, somebody else will. I want to tell my children: "You've got what it takes. There's nothing you can't do. Mother and Daddy are behind you. We're proud of you. We believe in you. You are destined to do great things."

Speak words of blessing over your children. Speak victory over their lives. They need your encouragement. They need your approval. Help them to have a big vision for their lives.

When Moses was born, the Egyptian Pharaoh decreed that all the children two years of age and under would be killed. Instead of acquiescing to the absurd, diabolical command, Moses's mother hid him away. Eventually, she put him in a basket and sent him down the Nile River. One of Pharaoh's daughters found him and raised him. Because Moses didn't grow up around a godly father, he didn't have that person speaking blessings into his life.

Many years later, God came to Moses and said, "Moses, I'm choosing you to deliver the people of Israel." Not surprisingly, the first words out of Moses's mouth were, "God, who am I?"

When we don't tell our children who they are and instill confidence and build self-esteem in them, it causes them to struggle with their identity, with who they are, with what they can do. God said, "Moses, don't say, 'Who am I?' You're the one that I've chosen."

Then Moses asked another question. He said, "But, God, who will listen to me? You know I'm not a good speaker. You know I stutter." Notice his lack of confidence. He too was playing the wrong recording in his mind. Possibly his confidence had been undermined by having an absentee father, missing a parent who spoke good things into his life on a regular basis. With God's help, however, Moses overcame that deficit in his upbringing.

Maybe you didn't have a great deal of positive encouragement as a child either. That does not have to hold you back in life. Your earthly father may not have told you who you are, but allow me to help you out. You are a child of the Most High God. You have been crowned with God's glory and honor. You can do all things through Christ. You are full of potential. You are overflowing with creativity. There's nothing in your heart that you cannot accomplish. You have courage, strength, and ability. The favor of God surrounds you wherever you go. Whatever you touch is going to prosper and succeed. You are blessed and you cannot be cursed. That's who you really are. So throw back your shoulders, hold your head up high, and start telling yourself: "I am victorious. I am well able. I am endowed with greatness by God Himself."

You must get your thoughts about yourself moving in the right direction if you truly want to become a better you. All through the day, you should be thinking good things about you. And when the old, negative recordings come to mind, let them remind you that it is time to put on the new recording. Immediately begin quoting some positive affirmations about yourself and about your God. "I am anointed. I am well able. God has good things in store for me!" Keep the right thoughts playing in your mind.

The other day I talked to a young woman in the lobby of Lakewood Church. She was beautiful, and by all outward appearances, she seemed to be happy and on top of the world. On the inside, however, she had a war going on. She didn't like herself. She thought she was unattractive. She thought she was overweight. She had a long list of things she felt were wrong with her.

As I talked with her, I discovered that her father had always put her down. He constantly told her what was wrong with her, what she couldn't do, what she was never going to be. The sad thing is, this young lady in her late twenties had gone through one marriage, gone through a second marriage, and now she was about to end her third marriage.

I told her, "You've got the wrong recording playing on your internal CD player. You're constantly telling yourself, 'I'm fat. I'm unattractive. I have nothing to offer. I'm unlovable.' As long as you're dwelling on those lies, there's going to be a war on the inside. You were not created to live that way. God created you to feel good about yourself. He created you to feel complete, to feel whole, to be confident and secure — not to constantly be against yourself. If you cannot get along with yourself, you'll never be able to get along with other people. It'll spread over into every other relationship."

Maybe there's no peace in your home and the problem is not the other person. You need to get at peace with who you are. Quit allowing the negative voice to play in your mind. Perhaps, like the young woman I mentioned, the root cause was something that happened way back in your life.

Maybe, like many people, you don't know how to turn it off. You think it is normal to go around feeling bad about yourself. You may not have gotten everything that you should have from your parents or the people who raised you, but always remember this: It's not how we start that counts; it's how we finish. Tell yourself every day, "I am the apple of God's eye. I'm His most prized possession. I am crowned with glory and honor. I'm valuable. I'm attractive. I have a bright future in front of me."

Understand that the negative voices always seem to cry out the loudest. You can have twenty people encouraging you and one person will come up and say something negative, and that's what you'll tend to remember. That's what your mind will want to replay again and again. You can do a hundred things right and if you make one mistake, you'll have to fight being guilty and condemned. The negative voices will come at you the strongest, but you must learn to let those go. As long as you stay focused on the negative, you will have a war on the inside. You're not going to feel good about yourself. The only way to change this is to get your internal dialogue going in the right direction. Replace the negative recordings with new, positive, uplifting messages. Start thinking the right thoughts about yourself.

God told the children of Israel in Joshua 5,

verse 9, "This day have I rolled away the reproach of Egypt from you." In other words, they didn't feel good about themselves. They had been hurt and mistreated; they were discouraged, even after being delivered from slavery. God came to them and said, "Stop doing that. I am rolling away the reproach from you." I believe the reproach had to be rolled away before they could go into the Promised Land.

It's the same with us. You may be trying to live in victory, trying to be successful, trying to have a good marriage. But you are negative toward yourself. You don't feel good about who you are. You're constantly dwelling on your past hurts and pains. Until you are willing to let go of those offenses and start focusing on your new possibilities, they will tie you down right where you are. You cannot have a bad attitude toward yourself and expect to have God's best. Quit focusing on what you've done wrong. God has already rolled away your reproach — your shame, embarrassment, failures, and setbacks. God has done His part. Now you must do your part. Let it go so you can go into your Promised Land. Start thinking, feeling, and speaking positively about yourself.

The Scripture says, "Our faith is made effectual when we acknowledge everything good in us." [28] Think about this: Our faith is not effective when we acknowledge all our hurts and pains. It's not effective when we stay focused on our shortcomings or our weaknesses. Our faith is most effective when we acknowledge the good things that are in us. Declare affirmations such as "I have a bright future. I am gifted. I am talented. People like me. I have the favor of God."

When we believe in God's Son, Jesus Christ, and believe in ourselves, that's when our faith comes alive. When we believe we have what it takes, we focus on our possibilities.

Unfortunately, most people do just the opposite. They acknowledge everything wrong with them. Even subconsciously, they are constantly playing that negative recording, causing them to have a low opinion of themselves. If you are in that group, you must change that recording.

I may be naïve, but I *expect* people to like me. I expect people to be friendly to me. I expect people to want to help me. I have a positive opinion about who I am because I know whose I am — I belong to Almighty God.

Don't walk into a room timid and insecure, thinking, *Nobody's going to like me in here. Look at them; they're probably talking about me already. I knew I shouldn't have worn this suit. I knew I should have stayed at home.*

No, get your inner dialogue going in a different direction. Develop a habit of being positive toward yourself; have a good opinion about who you are. "Well, Joel, I'm just a housewife. I'm just a businessperson. I'm just a schoolteacher."

No, you are not "just" anything. You are a child of the Most High God. You are fulfilling your purpose. The Lord orders your steps. Goodness and mercy are following you. You are a person of destiny. Knowing and acknowledging these things can boost your confidence sky high.

Get up every morning and say to yourself, "I am blessed. I am equipped. I have the favor of God. This is going to be a great day." All through the day, play that over and over in your mind. Keep the right recording on. Dwell only on positive, empowering thoughts toward yourself. That's when your faith will be energized. Do not make the mistake of merely acknowledging what's wrong with you. Acknowledge what's right with you. Have a good opinion of who you are. If you'll get in this habit of talking to yourself the right way with these positive empowering affirming thoughts, you'll not only have more confidence, you will rise higher and see God's blessings and favor in a greater way.

1. I refuse to live guilty or condemned because of past mistakes. Instead, I will step into new situations confidently, knowing that I am forgiven by God. I will make this day a fresh beginning.

2. Today, I am choosing to refresh my self-image by speaking positive affirmations and faith-filled words over my life such as:

    "I am blessed; I am prosperous; I am healthy; I am continually growing wiser."

    "I am excelling in my career; God is helping me to succeed."

    "I have a positive opinion about myself because I not only know who I am, but I know *whose* I am — I belong to Almighty God."

3. I am determined to keep my inner dialogue positive about myself. I will reject any negative thoughts toward myself and others, and I will meditate on thoughts such as, "I am valuable. I am well able to do what God has called me to do."

PART THREE:
DEVELOP BETTER
RELATIONSHIPS

■■■■

CHAPTER 11
BRINGING THE BEST
OUT OF PEOPLE

When I was in middle school, I was one of the smaller players on the basketball team. In our first game of the season, we were scheduled to face a real good team, boasting a bunch of big guys. Naturally, at my size, it would have been easy to be intimidated by our opponents.

On game day, I was walking through the school hallways in between classes, when my basketball coach called me over to where he was standing in front of several of my friends. He was a big, strong, tough coach, and in his usual gruff manner, he said, "Joel, you're not that tall, but let me tell you, size doesn't matter. What counts is right down in here." He pointed his finger at his chest as he continued. "Joel, you've got a big heart, and you're going to do great this year."

When I heard the coach's words — spoken right in front of my friends — I stood up taller, threw my shoulders back, and smiled even more than usual! You would have thought I was Michael Jordan. I thought to myself, *The coach believes in me!* My confidence shot up to a completely new level, and I played better that year than I'd ever done before. It's amazing what we can accomplish when we know somebody really believes in us.

That coach took a little time to make a big difference. He took time to instill confidence in me. If we're going to bring out the best in people, we too need to sow seeds of encouragement.

"Well, Joel, nobody's encouraging me," someone might say. "Why should I encourage anyone else?"

If you want your life to increase, if you want your life to get better, then you need to help improve somebody else's life. If you will help somebody else become successful, God will make sure that you are successful.

God puts people in our lives on purpose so we can help them succeed and help them become all He created them to be. Most people will not reach their full potential without somebody else believing in them. That means you and I have an assignment. Everywhere we go we should be encouraging people, building them up, challenging them to reach for new heights. When people are around us, they should leave better off than they were previously. Rather than feeling discouraged or defeated, people should feel challenged and inspired after spending any time with you and me.

The Bible says that love is kind.[29] One translation says, "Love looks for a way of being constructive." In other words, love looks for ways to help improve somebody else's life.

Take time to make a difference. Don't just obsess about how you can make your own life better. Think about how you can make somebody else's life better as well. Our attitude should be: Who can I encourage today? Who can I build up? How can I improve somebody else's life?

You have something to offer that nobody else can give. Somebody needs your encouragement. Somebody needs to know that you believe in him, that you're for him, that you think he has what it takes to succeed. If you look back over your own life, most likely you'll find someone who played a pivotal role in helping you get to where you are today. Maybe your parents or a teacher had confidence in you and helped you believe in yourself. Perhaps it was a boss who placed you in a higher position even though you didn't feel qualified at the time. Or a school counselor who said, "You've got what it takes. You can go to this college. You can be successful in that career."

Maybe they saw something in you that you may not have seen in yourself, and they helped you get to that next level. Now, it's your turn to do something similar for somebody else. Who are you believing in? Who are you cheering on? Who are you helping to become successful? Friend, there's no greater investment in life than in being a people builder. Relationships are more important than our accomplishments.

I believe that God is going to hold us responsible for the people He's put in our lives. He's counting on us to bring out the best in our spouse, in our children, and in our friends and our coworkers. Ask yourself, "Am I improving somebody's life, giving that person confidence, or am I just coasting along, consumed with doing my own thing?"

That's something I've loved about Victoria. She has always believed in me; she's my biggest supporter and my biggest fan. Victoria thinks that I'm the greatest person on the face of this earth. Now, I know that's not true, but I like the fact that she thinks I'm great. Victoria thinks that I can do anything. She's always bringing out the best in me.

One time, a number of years ago, we were

preparing to build a house. We had sold our other home and had bought property on which we planned to build. I picked up the phone to call our builder friend, to get everything lined up to begin construction, but Victoria stopped me. She said, "Joel, what are you doing? We don't need a builder. You can build the house."

I said, "Victoria, I don't know how to build a house. I don't know anything about construction."

"Sure you do, Joel," Victoria replied, her eyes sparkling with excitement. "You were at our other house practically every day when they were building it. You saw how they did it. You can get those subcontractors lined up as well as anybody else."

Sure enough, she talked me into it, and I built our house. It turned out pretty well, considering that I forgot the plumbing!

One thing I know for sure is that Victoria has confidence in me. I don't believe that I would be standing up, speaking to people every week, if Victoria had not told me years ago that one day I was going to be the pastor of Lakewood Church. Keep in mind that when Victoria first began expressing those convictions, I had never preached a sermon in public, much less on television. Furthermore, I had no desire to do so at the time. Yet as Victoria and I sat listening to my father preach, she'd often say, "Joel, one day, that's going to be you up there. You have so much to offer. One day, you're going to be helping a lot of people."

I didn't think I could do it; I didn't like getting up in front of people. I'd never been to seminary. I had no formal training that qualified me to be a pastor. I replied under my breath, "Victoria, I wish you'd quit saying that. That's just not me. I'm not a preacher."

"No, Joel," she answered, "I can see it in you. You have what it takes." Victoria saw things in me that I didn't see in myself, so she kept watering those seeds of encouragement.

When my father went to be with the Lord, and I first started preaching at Lakewood Church, I was extremely nervous, but two factors helped reduce my fears. One, all the seeds of encouragement that Victoria had sown; the other was the congregation's support. Every time I got up to speak, many of the people of Lakewood cheered me on. They applauded even before I began my message. I could have been a terrible speaker, but they kept cheering me on, giving me the confidence that I needed.

After a few months, I realized that they

truly believed in me. I thought, *These people think that I can do it.* It did something on the inside of me as Victoria, my family members, and our congregation at Lakewood Church helped bring out the best in me.

Now, I'm committed to bringing out the best in them and in you. You have things on the inside of you — gifts and talents — that you've not yet dreamed of using. You can go further and accomplish more. Don't settle for the status quo. You can overcome any challenge that's before you. You can break any addiction. You have the power of the Most High God on the inside of you. Start believing in yourself and acting like it's true.

The Bible says in First Corinthians 8, verse 1, that love encourages people to grow to their full stature. When you believe the best in people, you help to bring the best out of them.

Susan Lowell had carved out a successful career, and everything was going great in her life, but she just wasn't satisfied. She had a desire deep down inside to help troubled teenagers. One day, she quit her high-paying job and went to work as a schoolteacher in one of the roughest schools in California, a high school known for drugs, gangs, and other serious problems. Not surprisingly, the school had one of the highest dropout rates in the state. The school board could hardly keep teachers, because the students were so unruly and rebellious. Nobody thought the new lady would last.

But Ms. Lowell took a different approach. On the first day of school, she asked her students to write down their names and addresses and something interesting about themselves. While they were writing, she walked up and down the rows and secretly memorized each student's name. When they finished, she announced to the class they were about to have their first test. The students moaned and groaned. She said, "No, the test isn't for you; this test is for me." She explained, "If I can call each one of you by your correct name, then I pass the test. But if I miss even one of your names, then every one of you will get an automatic 'A' on our first real test."

The students were excited as Ms. Lowell slowly walked up and down the rows, and, one by one, she correctly called out each student's name. The class was duly impressed, and she had their attention. Ms. Lowell spoke softly as she said, "Class, the reason I did this is to show you that you are important to me. When I look at you, I not only like you, but I care about you. That's the reason I'm here."

The students realized that this teacher was different. She was not there simply to get a paycheck; she wasn't trying to get the most compensation for the least amount of work. *This lady believes in us. This lady thinks that we can become something.*

One day Ms. Lowell got word that Armando, one of the roughest students in her class, owed one of the street gangs a hundred dollars. It was an extremely dangerous situation, especially since Armando didn't have the money to pay. Ms. Lowell asked her student to stay after class. When they sat down to talk, she said, "Armando, I've heard about your dilemma and I want to loan you the money to pay your debt, but I'll do it only under one condition."

"What's that?" Armando asked.

She said, "I'll give you this money if you promise to pay me back on the day that you graduate." At the time, Armando was a sophomore, and of all Ms. Lowell's students, he was one of the least likely to graduate. His older brothers and sisters who had attended the same school before him had not graduated. His parents had only a second-grade education.

Ms. Lowell's act of kindness touched his heart. Nobody had ever shown him that kind of love. Nobody had ever believed in him enough to think that he could actually graduate.

Ms. Lowell had the students keep a journal. The week before, she'd asked them to write down the nicest thing anyone had ever done for them. Armando said, "Ms. Lowell, last week I had to make up something, because I can't ever remember anybody doing anything nice for me. But what you did for me today, I will never forget." He went on to say, "Ms. Lowell, I will not let you down. I will graduate, because if you think I can do it, then I know I can do it."

This teacher believed in her students so much, they began to believe in themselves. Indeed, Armando became the first person in his family ever to earn a high school diploma.

Many people simply need somebody to spark a bit of hope, somebody to say, "Yes, you can do it. You've got what it takes."

Are you believing the best in your own children? Are you instilling the confidence in them that they need, telling them that they're going to do great things in life? Are you believing the best in your loved ones? Maybe some of them have gotten off course. Don't give up on them; don't write them off. Make sure they know that you're concerned. Make sure they know that you really believe in them.

Here's the key: Don't focus on what they are right now. Focus on what they can become. See the potential on the inside. They may have some bad habits, or they may be doing some things that you don't like, but don't judge them for it. Don't look down on them critically. Find some way to challenge them to rise higher. Tell them, "I'm praying for you. I believe you're going to break that addiction. I'm believing for great things in your life."

You'll be pleasantly surprised at how people respond when they know you really care. Everywhere Jesus went, He saw potential in people that they didn't see in themselves. He didn't focus on their weaknesses or their faults. He saw them the way they could become.

For example, the disciple Peter had many rough edges. He was hot tempered, loud, bombastic, and impetuous, but that didn't deter Jesus. Jesus didn't say, "Forget it, Peter. I'm going to find somebody a little more refined than you." Instead, Jesus worked with Peter to bring the best out of him. It was in there. He just had to get it out.

Interestingly, Peter's name literally meant "pebble" or "small stone." However, Jesus saw so much more in Peter. He said, "I'm going to give you a new name. Your new name is going to be Cephas, which means 'a rock.' " In other words, God said, "You are a pebble right now, but when I get finished with you, you're going to be a rock. You're going to be strong, solid, and secure."

As a rule, you never bring out the best in someone by condemning and criticizing, or verbally beating a person down. You bring out the best by love. You bring it out by showing people that you care. Your friends, family members, or coworkers may do some things you don't like or that you find offensive; they may have some bad habits, but don't focus on their weaknesses. Find something they're doing right and encourage them for that.

I'm not saying that you just sweep things under the rug, but wait for the right time and opportunity to deal with those negative actions or attitudes. First, you must build your relationship, gain the person's respect and trust, and you can do that by encouraging and challenging him or her to rise higher.

I've found that if I treat people the way I want them to be, they are much more likely to become that sort of person. They're much more likely to change.

For instance, if your husband is not treating you with as much respect as you know he should, don't sink down to his level and act disrespectful as well. No, sow a seed. Treat him respectfully anyway and watch that man begin to change. If he's lazy, treat him as if he were a hard worker. He may do a thousand things you don't like, but find the one thing on which you can compliment him and encourage him for that.

It is easy to nitpick and find fault, but our goal is to bring out the best in people. Our job is to encourage, build up, to challenge people to rise higher.

I heard about a man who went out to get his newspaper one morning, and when he opened up the front door, a little dog owned by the folks living across the street was bringing his paper to him. The man chuckled, hurried back inside, and got the dog a treat. That little dog left there just as happy as can be.

The next morning, when the man went to pick up his newspaper, he opened the door and found that same little dog sitting there. Next to the dog were eight of the neighbors' newspapers!

Human beings respond similarly to treats — especially when we are treated to praise, admiration, and appreciation. Husbands and wives should be each other's greatest cheerleaders. Take time to praise your wife. Take time to compliment your husband. Don't get lazy in this area. Learn not to take each other for granted.

The other day, Victoria walked by me and I noticed that she looked especially beautiful. She was dressed up, and had her hair all fixed. I thought to myself, *Wow, she looks great today.*

But I was busy working at my desk and didn't want to be interrupted, so I didn't say anything. *Besides,* I thought, *she knows I think she's beautiful. I've told her thousands of times.*

I missed the opportunity to sow a compliment. Later, I realized that I was just being lazy. Sure, Victoria may know that I love and appreciate her; she may know that she is physically attractive to me. But as her husband, I have the responsibility to build her up every chance I get.

I heard somebody say, "Complimenting each other is the glue that holds relationships together." With so many things working against good relationships nowadays it's amazing what a kind word here and there will do.

"Honey, you look beautiful today. Thanks for preparing such a delicious dinner," or, "You did great on your project last week." Short, sincere, natural compliments can help keep our relationships strong.

Nearly every time I finish speaking and walk off the platform, Victoria tells me, "Joel, that was great today."

In truth, it may have been the worst message I have ever presented, but that doesn't matter to Victoria. She still encourages me.

We walked off the platform the other day and Victoria said, "Joel, that was spectacular today."

I felt so good. The next Sunday, however, she went back to saying "Joel, that was great today."

"What do you mean, great?" I asked, feigning incredulity. "How about spectacular?"

Victoria just laughed and rolled her eyes. She knows that she's spoiled me!

Be free with your compliments and be quick to vocalize them. Remember, your *thoughts* don't bless anybody but you. You can think good thoughts about somebody all day long, but it's not going to do them one bit of good. You must verbalize those thoughts; speak them out. Every day, try to find somebody you can compliment, someone you can build up. If a waiter at the restaurant gives you good service, don't just think about it. Tell him. "Thanks for being such a fine waiter and taking good care of us today." Those positive words might make his day.

Brent, a man who attends Lakewood Church, was standing in line at the grocery store checkout counter waiting to pay for his selections. The young woman running the register was having a tough time. People in line started getting aggravated and being a bit short with her.

When it was Brent's turn to check out, he decided he wasn't going to add to the problem by responding the way others had done. He smiled and said, "Ma'am, I just want to tell you that I think you're doing a great job. I appreciate you working so hard."

That young woman's countenance brightened instantly. It was as though Brent had lifted a load of heavy bricks off her shoulders. "Sir, I've been working here for three months," the checkout girl said, "and you are the first person to tell me anything like that. Thank you so much."

Our society overflows with critics, cynics, and faultfinders. Many people quickly point out what you are doing wrong, but relatively few take the time to point out anything you are doing right. I don't want to live my life like that. I'm going to be a giver and not a taker. I want to build people up and not tear them down. I'm going to do my best to leave places better off than they were before I passed by.

Recently, I was thinking about the many things in life for which people become known. As I pondered the legacy I would leave, I decided that a hundred years from now, I want to be known as somebody who brought out the best in people, somebody who left the world a better place. Material accomplishments will soon be forgotten. The only thing that lasts is the investment we make in other people's lives.

I want to bring the best out of my wife and children. I want to inspire the best in my friends. I want people to say, "I like being around that Joel Osteen. He encourages me to go higher, to expect more, and to expand my horizons. His actions, attitudes, and the way he treats other people inspire me to be a better individual."

Moreover, I want to spend most of my "discretionary" time with people who will strive to bring the best out of me. The Scripture says, "iron sharpens iron." The way we live our lives with one another should encourage one another to do better.

Ask yourself, Are the people in my life better off or worse off because I passed their way? Am I building them up in our conversations, and bringing out their best, or am I dragging them down? Do I believe in somebody? Do I give them confidence to improve their lives? Or am I focused on myself?

Over the past few years, I've received a number of complimentary letters from famous people — movie stars, government leaders, pro athletes, and the like. I'm flattered and honored by the comments in those letters. But the greatest compliment I ever received came when Victoria stood up in front of our home congregation and said, "After living with Joel all these years, I can tell you that I'm a better person. I've got more confidence. I'm kinder. I have a better attitude. I've grown. And I've been challenged."

Of course, I can say the same thing about the impact she has had on me. She's a "people builder," and we are committed to leaving people better off than they were before they encountered us.

You can be a people builder everywhere you go. That man at the gas station — don't simply pump your gasoline; pump something good into his life. The woman at the office who always seems grumpy — rather than complaining about her, take time to give her a compliment. Build up your friends and coworkers and your boss. Everywhere you go, make positive deposits, instead of negative withdrawals.

When you get up in the morning, instead

of applying your energies to how you can be blessed, find some way to be a blessing to someone else. If you will make somebody else's day, God will make yours.

In my life, I've been blessed to have people who believed in me — my parents, my wife, my family. Now, it's my turn. Who am I believing in? Who am I cheering on? Who am I helping to succeed?

Friend, choose to bring out the best in the people that God has put in your life. You're never more like God than when you give, and the closest thing to His heart is helping others. If you will be a people builder, focused on bringing out the best in others, I can promise you this: God will bring out the best in you.

Chapter 12
Keep the Strife out of Your Life

Relationships are what really matter in life — our relationship to God, with our spouse, children, extended family members, friends, and others within our communities — yet all too often, we allow these relationships to occupy much lower positions than they deserve on our priority lists. If we are not careful, we can allow something or somebody to drive a wedge between ourselves and the people who are most precious to us.

To maintain healthy relationships, we need to learn how to keep the strife out of our lives. God made each of us as unique individuals. We have different personalities and temperaments; we approach issues in different ways, so we really shouldn't be surprised when we grate against one another occasionally. Too often, though, if someone doesn't agree with our opinion, or see eye to eye with us on some matter, we get bent out of shape and allow strife to foment. I've discovered that just because somebody is not exactly like me, or doesn't do things the way I do them, that doesn't necessarily mean that I am right and they are wrong. We're just different, and our differences can cause friction.

It takes maturity to get along with somebody who is different than you are. It takes patience not to start a dispute over minor issues or become easily offended. If we're going to keep the strife out of our lives, then we must learn how to give people the benefit of the doubt.

We will also need to overlook some things. Every person has faults; we all have weaknesses. We should not expect the people with whom we are in a relationship to be perfect. No matter how great a person he or she may be, no matter how much you love him or her, if you are around that person long enough, you will have an opportunity to be offended. There is no such thing as a perfect spouse, a perfect boss, or even a perfect pastor (although I'm very close!).

If we're putting unrealistic expectations on people, expecting them to be perfect, that is not fair to them, and it will be a source of frustration for us. We're always going to be disappointed.

Some people live with the attitude of, "I'll

love you as long as you never hurt me or as long as you never make a mistake." "I'll be your friend as long as you treat me just right." "As long as you do things my way, then I'll accept you, and I'll be happy."

But that is extremely unfair and places too much pressure on that other person. The Scripture teaches that love makes allowances for people's weaknesses. Love covers a person's faults. In other words, you have to overlook some things. Quit demanding perfection out of your spouse, your children, or other people with whom you are in a relationship, and learn to show a little mercy.

I couldn't find a better wife than Victoria. She is an extremely loving, caring, generous person, and yet there are some things I have to overlook, some things for which I have to make allowances. That doesn't mean something is wrong with her; she's just human. If I were a critical faultfinder, keeping an account of everything she did wrong, then our relationship would suffer. Before long, we'd be at odds with each other, arguing, and fighting.

Instead, we make allowances for each other's weaknesses. We've learned not to wear our feelings on our sleeves and not to be easily offended.

Few things are worse than living with a

touchy, overly sensitive person. If somebody offends you or does you wrong, learn to shake it off and move on. The Scripture teaches that love believes the best in people.

"Well, my husband hardly spoke to me this morning. He didn't even thank me for cooking dinner the other night," a wife might say.

Remember, love covers a fault. Instead of going through the day offended and upset, consider the fact that he may not have been feeling up to par. Maybe he's under a lot of pressure at work or stressed out over some other matter. Rather than criticizing and condemning, give him the benefit of the doubt and believe the best in him.

My father used to say, "Everybody has the right to have a bad day every once in a while." If somebody does something you don't like, if they insult or offend you unwittingly, simply swallow your pride and say, "I choose to overlook that offense," and move on.

Instead of immediately drifting to the negative and seeing the worst, it could change your life greatly if you would get in a habit of viewing events from a positive perspective and believing the best in people.

The Scripture says that love keeps no record of wrongs done to it.[30] You might see your relationship with someone go to a whole new level if you'd just get rid of the record book. I know people who have a mental list of everything anybody has done wrong to them for the last twenty years. They have a detailed scorecard, listing every time their spouse hurt them, every time their boss was thoughtless or rude, every time their parents missed the grandkids' ball game. Instead of keeping a list of slights or offenses, throw out your negative record book and look for the good.

Steve told me, "Joel, any time my wife and I have a little disagreement, she brings up every mistake I've made for the last ten years. 'Well, you did this last year. Don't you remember that you did that in 2005? Last month you hurt me.' She keeps stirring up dirt from the past."

As long as you are bringing up pain from the past, you are going to have strife in your present.

"But I'm the one that's right!" I hear you lamenting.

Maybe so, but do you want to be right, or do you want to have peace in your home? Do you want to have your way, or do you want to have healthy relationships? Many times, we can't have both. In all of our relationships, especially in marriage, it is vital that we not keep score of offenses.

Christine was driving through an intersection when she accidentally turned too sharply and sideswiped another car. Worse yet, she was driving her brand-new car, a wedding gift from her husband Eric. Christine pulled over to the side of the road and the driver of the other car, an older gentleman, got out of his car and began to examine his severely damaged front bumper. He then stepped over to where Christine was sitting in her car, crying.

"Are you okay, young lady?" he asked kindly.

"I'm fine," Christine sobbed, "but I just got married and my husband gave me this car as a wedding gift; he is going to be so upset. I don't know what I'm going to do."

"Oh, I'm sure it will be okay." The older gentleman tried to console her. "Your husband will understand." They talked for a few minutes before he said, "If I could just get your insurance information, we'll exchange that, and be on our way."

"I don't even know if I have an insurance card," Christine said through her tears.

"Well, it is usually in the glove compartment," the man suggested. "Why don't you check there?"

Christine opened the glove compartment and found the owner's registration and the insurance information. Attached to the envelope containing the insurance card was a note that read, "Honey, just in case you ever have an accident, please remember I love you and not the car."

That's the kind of person I want to be — a person who shows mercy, even in advance of a mistake or a wrong action. Rather than flaunting somebody's failure, learn to cover some of those weaknesses in the people who are close to you.

CHOOSE TO BE A PEACEMAKER

"But Joel, my spouse and I are simply not that compatible. We just can't get along. We are so different."

No, God may have put you with somebody different from you on purpose. That's not a mistake. Your strengths and weaknesses and that other person's strengths and weaknesses may be quite different, but ideally, your strengths can make up for your partner's weaknesses, and his or her strengths make up for your weaknesses. You complement each other. You should *complete* each other, rather than *compete* with each other. The two of you are much more powerful together than you are apart.

But you must study that other person, find out what he likes and dislikes; find out what her pressure points are, and then don't allow the weaknesses to bring conflict into your relationship.

Maybe you're a neat and tidy person. You like everything put perfectly into place, but your husband is sloppy; he tends to leave things lying around the house. You've told him a thousand times not to leave his shoes in front of the TV. Yet you walk in there one evening, and sure enough, his shoes are there. You go find him and say, "When are you ever going to put your shoes away? I'm so tired of cleaning up after you. That's all I ever do!"

No, why don't you be the peacemaker in your family? Quietly put away his shoes and go on your way so you can enjoy the rest of the evening. In other words, quit making a big deal out of something that is relatively minor. That issue is not worth allowing strife in your home.

"I've asked my wife over and over to turn the lights off when she leaves the room," David huffed. "But she always forgets and I have to go back in there and do it."

"No, instead of harping on your wife, why don't you make allowances for her weaknesses just as she does yours?" I said. "After all, it's not going to hurt you to go back in there and turn the lights off. Maybe you could even get a bit of exercise."

"But when is she ever going to change?" David protested.

You could probably answer David's question for him. When he quits nagging her, stops complaining, and develops a better attitude. That's when she's going to change.

Obviously, these are relatively minor issues, but the same principle applies to matters of more significance. When you cover a person's weaknesses and go the extra mile to keep strife out of your home, you are sowing a seed for God to do a work in that other person. Remember: You cannot change people, only God can. You can harp on that person all day long, but your comments will only serve to make matters worse. The result will bring more strife and more division. Nothing will drive the peace out of your home any quicker than constant criticism. Similarly, you can disrupt the atmosphere in your workplace by incessant griping, snipping, and having a critical attitude.

The Bible teaches, "We need to adapt and adjust in order to keep the peace."[31] It doesn't say that other people should adapt and adjust to us. No, if we are going to have peace, *we* have to be willing to change.

You can't have the attitude, "Well, if my wife would start doing what I ask her, then we'd have peace." "If my husband will start picking up his stuff, then we'll get along fine." "If my boss would start treating me right, then I'd quit being so rude to him."

No, we have to make adjustments in order to keep the peace. In other words, you have to swallow your pride sometimes. Maybe you simply put his shoes away. And then don't go announce to him that you did. "Well, I just want you to know I picked up your shoes . . . again . . . today . . . like I do every day."

No, just put them away and keep your mouth closed. You may not realize it, but when you do your part to keep strife out of your relationships, you are honoring God. When you honor God, He will always honor you. When you sow seeds of mercy and kindness, you'll begin to see your relationships improve.

The key is learning to adapt. We have to be willing to make adjustments. Stop waiting for somebody else to do it; instead, you be the peacemaker in your family or in your workplace.

Sometimes we allow strife to smolder because of the smallest, most insignificant things. We argue over things that don't even matter. One time Victoria and I were driving out of our neighborhood, and we stopped to look at a new house that was being built. I simply made the comment, "I wonder why the builder put the garage over there, on that side of the house. That's not the way I would have done it."

Victoria looked at the house and said, "Well, I think he did that so it would give him more room on his lot."

I studied the landscape and considered how the house was situated, and then replied, "No, that wouldn't give him any more room."

"Sure it would, Joel," Victoria answered. "It would give him a lot more space."

Fifteen minutes later, we were still debating why the builder had put the garage where he did. Our voice tones were getting louder, and our words were getting sharper. Finally, it dawned on me, *Why are we arguing over where this guy put his garage? We don't even know the man!* It wasn't worth losing our joy and peace, so Victoria and I simply agreed to disagree.

Pick your battles wisely. Don't quibble over things that don't really matter. We have enough big issues in life with which to deal.

One day Victoria and I were leaving a Houston Astros baseball game at Minute Maid Park downtown. At that time, the ballpark was relatively new and I didn't really know the best way to exit. When I pulled out of the stadium I asked, "Victoria, should I turn right or should I turn left?"

"I think we need to turn right," Victoria answered.

I looked up and down the street, and didn't recognize anything to the right. "No," I said, "I think we need to go left."

She looked around in every direction, and said, "No, Joel. I know we need to go right."

"Victoria, our house is that way," I said, pointing to the left. "I know we need to go in that direction." I pulled out and turned to the left.

She said, "Well, that's fine, but you're going the wrong way."

We had just enjoyed a relaxing time at the ball game and had such a great time together. Now the whole atmosphere in our car changed. We were uptight, tense, and on edge. We were hardly even talking to each other over something so insignificant. If I would have just swallowed my pride and gone her way, it wouldn't have hurt anything. Even if it had been the wrong way, what's ten minutes going to matter? But no, I had to show her that I was right. I had to prove my point.

I started driving . . . and driving . . . and driving all over downtown Houston. I was trying my best to act as if I knew where I was going, but I might as well have been in Japan! I had no idea where we were. I could see the freeway, but I couldn't figure out how to get on it. (Anyone who has ever driven in downtown Houston can probably relate!)

Every time I looked at Victoria, she'd just smile and say, "Well, you should have listened to me. Maybe we'll get home by this time tomorrow." The more she rubbed it in, the more aggravated I became.

Finally, after wandering around downtown for thirty minutes, I said, "All right, fine. We're going back to the ballpark and we're going to see if you can get us home."

She said, "It's about time."

We drove back to the baseball park and she said, "All right, you need to go right, then you go left." As we drove through a part of Houston that I had never seen before, I was hoping so bad that we were lost. I didn't care if we ever got home. I just did not want Victoria to show me up. We went through several side streets, and she finally said, "Okay, take a right."

Sure enough, that put us on the main freeway headed home. I was so shocked. I refused to believe she could do that. I said, "Victoria, how did you know those directions?"

"Oh, there's a little fabric store down here," she said, "that I used to come to all the time."

Don't make the same mistake that I did. Don't be so proud that you always have to prove your point. Swallow your pride and consider somebody else's opinion. You may think you're right, but there's a chance you could be wrong.

I know people who have gotten a divorce all because they stayed stirred up over something equally as silly or ultimately insignificant. They allowed the sore to fester, and before long they were living at each other's throats. Deep down inside, they may really love each other, but through the years, they've allowed strife to drive a wedge into their relationship.

Jesus said, "A house divided is continually being brought to destruction and it will not stand." Notice, if you allow strife into your relationship, it will be brought to destruction. It may not happen overnight; it might not happen in a couple of months or even a few years. If you allow strife to grow by holding grudges, making sarcastic remarks, or otherwise, you may not realize it, but that relationship is in the process of being destroyed. Strife is chipping away at your foundation, and unless you decide to do something about it soon, your life could crumble into a mess. You could very well look up one day and think, *What have I done? I've destroyed this relationship. How could I have been so foolish?*

Don't be hardheaded and stubborn. Maybe you have been at odds with somebody for months, not speaking to them, giving them the cold shoulder. Life is too short to live it that way. If possible, go to that person and make things right — while you still have the opportunity.

I recently spoke with a man who was broken and defeated. When I asked him what was troubling him, he explained how he and his father got at odds with each other over a business decision. They hadn't spoken in over two years. He said, "Joel, I knew deep down inside that I needed to make it right, but I kept putting it off. Then earlier this week, I received a call informing me that my father had suffered a heart attack and died." Imagine what emotional pain that man is living with.

Don't wait until you cannot make amends with someone from whom you are estranged. Do it today; swallow your pride and apologize even if it wasn't your fault. Keep the peace. Understand, it's not always about being right. It's about keeping strife out of your life. You can win every argument, but if it opens the door to turmoil, brings division, and tears you apart, in the end you didn't win at all — and you may have lost a lot.

I believe that God always gives us a warning, a wake-up call of sorts. He may say simply, "Stop being so argumentative. Quit being a faultfinder. Quit keeping your record books. Start being a peacemaker." When we recognize His voice, we need to respond.

"Well, I'll start being a peacemaker as soon as my husband changes," I hear somebody saying. "I'll do it as soon as my boss starts treating me better."

No, if you wait for somebody else to be the peacemaker in your life, you may wait around your whole lifetime, living your life on hold. Peace starts with you; you make the first move.

"But I apologized first last time. That's not fair. It's his turn to apologize."

It may not be fair, but it can keep you together. Swallow your pride. Be the bigger person. When you do that, you are sowing a seed, and God will always make it up to you.

Abraham, the Old Testament patriarch, moved to a new land with his nephew Lot. The land wasn't big enough to support both of them, so the Bible says in Genesis 13, verse 7, that Lot's herdsmen began to get into strife with Abraham's herdsmen.

Abraham dealt with the situation immediately. He knew if he allowed that friction to continue, it would not only affect the herdsmen, it would affect his relationship with Lot, as well. That strife would eventually bring turmoil to the whole family. So Abraham took the high road and let Lot choose the best piece of land. Interesting, isn't it? To avoid strife, Abraham willingly allowed Lot to take advantage of him. He allowed Lot to have it his way even though Abraham was the elder gentleman and should have been able to choose the best piece of land. Sometimes, no matter how much it hurts, you may have to let the other person do it his or her way just so you can avoid unnecessary conflict. It may not be fair. You may know beyond a doubt that you are right and they're wrong, but that doesn't matter. Let it go and trust God to make it up to you.

The Bible reveals that because Abraham kept the peace and refused to get into strife, God honored him by giving him the whole country. If you will choose to keep the peace, even though somebody is doing you wrong, God will bless you with abundance. He will bring you out better off than you were previously.

The Bible doesn't say it is permissible to live in strife as long as it is not your fault. No, when we're in strife, no matter whose fault it is, destruction and turmoil are sure to follow. Moreover, God may ask *you* to make adjustments to keep the peace.

Bill and Mary had major problems in their marriage. They didn't really have a relationship; they merely existed together. Bill was extremely selfish and argumentative. He was just a hard-to-get-along-with, critical, negative person.

Mary, however, genuinely loved God. She went to church every week and did her best to live with integrity. Bill prided himself on being just the opposite. He wouldn't have anything to do with the things of God and often spoke sarcastically about spiritual matters. Mary prayed nearly every day for God to change her husband. Years dragged by, with little improvement.

One day as Mary was praying, she asked God, "Why do I have to live in such a terrible environment? When are You ever going to change my husband?"

God spoke to her deep in her heart and mind, and said, "Mary, I will change your husband as soon as you change."

"God, what do You mean?" Mary cried. "*He's* the problem. Bill is the one who is mean and argumentative. I go to church every Sunday."

God said, "No, you're not doing all that you can to keep the peace. You've become indifferent to this situation." Then God said, "I'm going to hold you responsible because you know the truth. You know the right thing to do, and when you start doing it, I will change Bill."

Mary took God at His word and started making special efforts to keep the peace in her home. In less than a year, Bill began to change, slowly at first, then more dramatically. Today, they are both serving God and loving each other like newlyweds.

The Bible says, "To him that knows what's right and doesn't do it, then it's sin." [32] So often, we wait for the other person to change. We know he is wrong; she is at fault. We have to realize that God holds us responsible to do what we know to do. When we allow strife in our relationships, we open up the door to all sorts of trouble.

A few years ago, Victoria, I, and our two children went for a bike ride together at a park. The day had not gone real well for me, and I was aggravated over something that Victoria had done. I didn't think it was right, and it irritated me. Instead of letting it go, I chose to hold on to it. I could have overlooked it; it wasn't any big deal. I could have shaken it off and enjoyed the day with my family, but I chose to stay sour.

I placed our daughter Alexandra on my bike seat behind me and pulled away from Victoria and Jonathan. The bike trail was rather narrow, approximately four feet wide, and Jonathan had just learned how to ride his bike a few months earlier. He wasn't yet sure of himself, so he had to go slowly.

I was about a hundred yards ahead of Jonathan and Victoria when another biker approached in the opposite direction, racing past me at a high speed. My first thought was, *I hope Jonathan is careful. That guy is flying!*

Sure enough, as the racer approached Jonathan on the narrow path, Jonathan got rattled and turned his bike right into the path of the oncoming cyclist. They collided head-on, with an awful sound of crunching metal. I thought for sure Jonathan had broken an arm or a leg.

I slammed on the brakes, set my bike down, and ran back to Jonathan as fast as I could. I picked him up and was amazed that he wasn't hurt badly. He was skinned up on his legs and his arms, but he didn't have any broken bones. His bike, however, was such a tangled mess he could no longer ride it.

Fortunately, the other rider was okay as well. When everything calmed down, something on the inside of me said, "Joel, you brought all this on yourself. You had the choice to make things right. You had the choice to diffuse strife, but you chose not to."

I knew better, yet I continued to hold on to the offense. I wasn't treating Victoria right, and the accident happened, at least partly as a result. The Scripture says don't give any foothold to the enemy, a foothold of strife, a foothold of arguing, a foothold of unforgiveness. Of course, not every accident is because of strife, but I knew I had brought this one on us, so I apologized to my family members.

When we hardheadedly choose to hold on to strife, we are choosing to step out of God's protection. We step out of God's blessings and favor. Certainly, there are times when we must confront issues head-on, but there are also times that we can choose to avoid strife in a relationship by giving up our right to be right. Take the initiative to keep strife out of your life. Get rid of pettiness that produces division and discord. Make a decision that you're going to make the necessary adjustments so you can live a more peaceful life.

Friend, if you will swallow your pride and do whatever it takes to keep strife out of your life, you will sow seeds for God's blessings and promotion. When you do that, you'll see your relationships begin to flourish. God said, "Blessed are the peacemakers." If you'll have that kind of attitude, your relationships will continually get better and better.

CHAPTER 13
TAKING A STAND FOR YOUR FAMILY

One of the greatest threats we face in the twenty-first century is not a terrorist attack or an ecological catastrophe, but an attack on our homes. The enemy would love nothing more than to ruin your relationship with your husband or your wife, your parents, or your children. Too many homes are being destroyed through strife, lack of commitment, wrong priorities, and bad attitudes. If we're going to have strong, healthy relationships, we must dig our heels in and fight for our families.

The Old Testament records a time when Nehemiah was rebuilding the walls of Jerusalem. The walls had been torn down years previously, and the enemy was coming against God's people, against their homes, their wives and children, while the men worked on the construction crews. The situation got so bad that Nehemiah instructed his men to work with a hammer in one hand

270

and a sword in the other. He encouraged them, "Men, fight for your sons, fight for your daughters, fight for your wives, fight for your families" (Nehemiah 4:14). He went on to say, "If you will fight, then God will fight."

I believe God is saying something similar to us today. If we will do our part and take a strong stand for our families, God will do His part. He'll help us to have great marriages and great relationships with our parents and children.

Certainly, not everyone will get married, but if a man and a woman choose to marry, two issues must be settled first. Number one: As a couple, we are committed to God. We're going to live a life that honors Him. We will be people of excellence and integrity in all that we do.

The second settled issue must be that as a couple, we are committed to each other. Occasionally, we may disagree, say things we shouldn't, we might even pout or get downright angry. But when it's all said and done, we're going to get over it, and we will forgive and move on. Leaving is not an option. We're committed to each other through the good times and the tough times.

If bailing out of the relationship is an option or an alternative, then you will always find some reason to justify it. "Joel, we just can't get along. We're not compatible. We tried, but we just don't love each other anymore."

Truth is, no two people are completely compatible. We have to learn to become one. That means we may have to make sacrifices; we may have to overlook some things. We must be willing to compromise for the good of the relationship.

The perfect spouse does not exist. Victoria sometimes tells people, "Oh, my husband, Joel, is the perfect husband."

Don't believe that for a minute. She is saying that by faith!

Stick with your spouse and make that relationship work. As one lady quipped, "My husband and I got married for better or for worse. He couldn't do any better and I couldn't do any worse."

When you do have disagreements, learn to disagree from the neck up. Don't let it get down in your heart. Victoria and I don't always see eye to eye, but we've learned how to agree to disagree. When you present your case, don't try to make that other person change his or her mind. Give others the right to have their own opinion. If you're not going to be happy unless they agree with you, then really you're simply trying to manipulate your partner. You're trying to force your opinion on that person. The better approach is to present your case, share your heart, and then step back and allow God to work in that person or situation.

As long as we are argumentative and we're trying to force our opinions, then there's going to be strife in our homes. Wherever there's strife, there's confusion. And there's nothing worse than living in a home that's tense. Everybody's on edge. You feel that at any moment something could explode.

You don't have to live that way. Do your best to create an atmosphere of peace and unity in your home. When you're tempted to pop off and say hurtful, critical, counterproductive things that you know you shouldn't, next time you have that opportunity, do yourself a favor. Take a deep breath, pause about ten seconds, and think about what you're going to say before you speak. Words can cut like a knife. You may say them in a matter of seconds, but three months later the person to whom you spoke them may still be feeling the sting.

Have you ever touched the stove and then pulled your hand off immediately? But weeks later, it still stings. That is what hurtful, critical words can do.

Never threaten your spouse with divorce. I've heard people say, "Well, if you ever do that again, I'm out of here." "If you don't do this, I'm leaving."

No, don't even let those words out into the atmosphere. Your words have creative power, and when you speak like that, you're just giving the enemy a right to bring it to pass. Besides, the Bible tells us "to be angry and sin not." Certainly, at times we're going to get angry. Anger is an emotion God built into us. But we don't have to blow up and say hurtful things that are going to damage our relationships. Learn to take a step back, collect your thoughts, and think about what you want to say.

One time, my mother and father got into a disagreement. My dad was extremely upset, so he decided he was going to give my mother the silent treatment. When Mother spoke to him, Daddy would answer back in the shortest, most unfriendly way he could. This went on for an hour or two, and he was doing his best to ignore my mother.

My mother is rather feisty, so she decided to do something about the situation. She went and hid behind a door, and she stayed there as still and quiet as she could be. Before long, my father realized that she wasn't around and he began searching for her. He looked all over the house, and he couldn't find her anywhere. The more he looked, the more frustrated he became. He said, "It's terrible to try to ignore somebody and you can't even find them." This went on for about fifteen minutes.

Finally, Daddy started getting worried. About that time, he walked past the door where my mother was hiding. Quick as a cat, my mother leaped onto my father's back, wrapped her arms and legs around him, and said, "John, I'm not getting off until you cheer up." They laughed so much that my father forgot what he was mad about.

Try to create a fun-filled atmosphere in your home. Everyone experiences stressful times; we all get uptight. We all have disagreements, but we should not allow that to linger. Too often we get complacent. "Well, I know I shouldn't say this, but I'm mad. I'm going to say it anyway." Or "I know I need to forgive, but I don't feel like it." Little by little, the relationship gets worse. Don't play those petty games. Do whatever it takes to keep the peace.

Victoria and I have been married for more than twenty years, and we don't agree on every single thing, but we are committed to each other. We're committed to our children, and to our extended family. We have committed in advance that we will work through any differences with each other that we may have.

Some people are committed while they're dating, or for the first few years of marriage. They're committed while everything is rosy, but how about when the sizzle subsides? Now, instead of scintillating romance, you are picking up his dirty socks or washing his sweaty workout clothes. That takes commitment. Or when you were dating, she always looked perfect, dressed to the nines. You never saw her without her hair in place and her makeup perfectly done. Now, you wake up in the morning and say, "Who is that woman over there?"

But marriage is a commitment, not a feeling.

I heard a true story about the president of a prestigious university. He was an older gentleman and a well-respected leader. Later in his life, his wife developed Alzheimer's. Month after month, her condition grew progressively worse. Several years down the road, the disease had so impaired her mind that she could not even recognize her husband anymore. They were a relatively affluent couple, so the gentleman hired nurses to help care for his ailing wife.

Then one day, he went in and announced to the university board of directors that he was going to resign so he could spend his full time taking care of his wife. The board members tried to talk him out of it, reminding him how needed he was. One board member spoke up and said, "In all respect, sir, why would you want to do this? Your wife doesn't even know who you are."

The university president looked the board member in the eye and said, "I made a commitment to this woman over fifty years ago. She may not know who I am, but I know who she is."

That's the kind of commitment that we need to have in our relationships as well.

Interestingly, God holds the husband and father responsible to keep the family together. The word *husband* comes from a Latin word that means "house band." Think of a rubber band that wraps around something, holding it together. That's a picture of what a good husband is supposed to do for his wife and family.

Solomon was the wisest man who ever lived. His book of wisdom encourages a husband to look his wife in the eyes and tell her, "There are many beautiful women in the world, but you excel them all." Solomon started his day off by praising and encouraging his wife. Men, you can imagine how our relationships would improve if we'd start complimenting our wives like that. Some women haven't had a compliment in years, not because they are undeserving, but because they are not appreciated. All they hear is what they're doing wrong. How the dinner wasn't any good. The kids are too loud.

Listen carefully to the words and tone of voice you use with your spouse. Are you complaining all the time and telling her what she's not doing right? Or are you doing like Solomon — blessing, encouraging, and uplifting that woman?

A WORD FROM THE WISE

The Song of Solomon is a biblical love story. In eight short chapters, Solomon praised his wife forty times. He wrote of her strength, beauty, and intelligence.

"Well, Joel, you don't know my wife," Chuck said. "She's the problem. She's argumentative. She's hard to get along with."

"Maybe so, Chuck," I replied, "but if you start praising your wife, if you start telling her how beautiful she is, and how glad you are to have her in your life, when you talk about the good, you will draw out the good. If you talk about the negative, you'll draw out the negative. It's up to you."

Men, learn to speak blessings over your wife and you will see that woman rise to a new level. She will respond to your praise and encouragement. Your words don't have to be poetic, fancy, or profound. Tell her simply but sincerely, "You're a great mother to our children. And you are a great wife to me. I'm so glad I can always count on you."

If you'll treat your wife like a queen, she will be much more willing to treat you like a king. As a husband, you must understand that your wife needs your blessing. She needs your approval.

"Well, Joel, I'm just not a real romantic kind of guy," you may be saying. "I don't say all those mushy, gooey things."

Understand, this is not an option; it's a necessity, if you're going to have a healthy marriage. Like Solomon, get in the habit of looking at your wife and saying, "You are beautiful. I'm glad you're in my life. There are a lot of pretty women, but you excel them all."

The Bible says, "The wife is reflection of the man's glory."

If Victoria appeared in public with her countenance downcast, her hair disheveled, and her clothes dirty and wrinkled, her appearance and demeanor would be a be a sad reflection on me. I would need to examine my life and ask myself, "Am I treating her well? Am I making her secure? Does she know I'm proud of her?"

Husband, you need to look at your wife

and see if she is reflecting your glory. Your wife should be strong, confident, secure, beautiful, radiant, and healthy. You should see it in her smile. You should see it in the way she carries herself.

I used to play basketball with a guy who disrespected his wife. After the game, he'd say things such as, "Well, I'm going home to see my old lady."

I often wondered, *If you talk about your wife like that, you must not think too much of yourself, either, because she's reflecting your glory.* I'd smile and say, "Well, I'm going home to see Queen Victoria."

It's true! Victoria is the queen of our house. Since I've made her the queen, that makes me the king, and I rather enjoy that.

Because the writer of Proverbs 31 praised his wife, his children rose up and blessed her as well.[33] Unquestionably, when a husband praises and blesses his wife, their children will follow his example. How a man treats his wife will have a profound impact on how his children will respect and honor their mother. Your children subconsciously take in voice tones, body language, and personal demeanor.

And Dad, your daughter will most likely marry somebody much like you. If you are hard-nosed and disrespectful, speaking rude, hurtful things to your spouse, don't be surprised if your daughter gravitates toward somebody with those same characteristics. I realize I need to treat my wife the way I want somebody to treat my daughter.

And Mom, you need to treat your husband the way you want somebody to treat your sons.

Men, open the car door for your wife. Take her coffee in the morning. Go out of your way to show her love, honor, and respect. I heard somebody say, "If a man ever opens the car door for his wife, he's either got a new car or a new wife." Perhaps we need to return to a society that encourages men to respect and honor women.

"If I do that sort of thing, my friends may think I'm a weakling," a guy might say. "They may give me a hard time."

If that's the case, you probably ought to find some new friends. A real man's masculinity is not diminished because he opens the car door for his wife. Being male doesn't necessarily make you a man. Treating people with dignity and respect makes you a man. Taking care of your wife and family makes you a man. Watching over your children makes you a man. Speaking blessings over your wife and kids — that's being a real man.

Granted, you may not have grown up in

that kind of loving environment, but you can set a new standard. You can raise the bar.

In the reproduction process, the father provides the child's identity. The female contributes two X chromosomes; the male contributes an X and a Y chromosome. If the father gives the female an X, the child will be a baby girl. If he gives a Y, the baby will be a boy. The mother does not determine the sex of the baby. The child's identity comes through the father.

Father, you need to make especially sure that you affirm your children. You have incredible influence over them. Every day, just as you bless your wife, bless your children as well. Look at each child and say, "I'm so proud of you. I think you're great. There's nothing that you can't do." Your children need your approval. You're helping them to form their identity. If we're too busy as fathers, we're never there, or maybe we're just always correcting our children without providing them with affirmation, our children are not going to be as confident and secure as they should be.

Certainly, there are times when the father can't be there for his children because of other responsibilities. Nonetheless, do your best to keep your priorities in order. No amount of success in your career can make up for failure at home. I've seen some men accomplish great things in the corporate world as business leaders but at the expense of their children. Their children grew up without a father figure.

Fathers, take your children to church; don't send them. Be at their ball games as often as possible. Know who their friends are. Listen to their music. Children are looking for direction and guidance. When that young man comes over to take your daughter out on a date, be the first one at the door. Let him know there's a man in the house watching over that young lady. Parents, we have to fight for our children. If we will fight for them, God will fight with us.

A lifelong friend told me that as a teenager he had a drug problem. I thought that was strange, since I knew him well and remembered him as a good kid. He didn't look or act like someone on drugs. He said, "Yeah, Joel, every Sunday my parents drug me to church. They drug me to Sunday school. They drug me to Bible Study!" He laughed as he said, "And those 'drugs' are still in my veins. They affect everything that I say and do."

Years ago, at the largest game reserve in South Africa, they developed an overpopulation of elephants. The curators decided to take three hundred of the youngest male elephants and separate them from their parents and other adult elephants. The "orphans" were transported to another national park, where the white rhinoceros reigned as the dominant "king of the park." The rhinoceros has no natural enemies. Nothing stalks it, not even a lion, a tiger, or a bear. The rhino is simply too powerful. As such, the curators felt there would be no problem mixing the orphan elephants in with the rhinos. Over time, however, they began to find dead rhinos out in the brush. They couldn't understand what was happening, so they set up surveillance cameras to observe the park. Much to their surprise, they found that those young male elephants, the ones that no longer had a father or mother figure, had formed gangs and they had viciously attacked the rhino population. It's not even in the elephant's God-given natural instincts to act that way, but the lack of parental influence spawned the strange, deadly phenomenon.

I believe a similar plight threatens our children. The reason that children get in trouble can often be traced to the fact that they do not have positive role models in their lives. They don't have anybody speaking blessings over them and praying for them; they don't have father figures, and many don't have healthy, positive mother figures. It doesn't mean these children are incorrigible; it is simply a fact that without parental guidance, children sometimes do things they might not otherwise do if Mom or Dad were around.

We have a responsibility to reach out to children who don't have a father figure or a mother figure. Maybe you can mentor a young man or a young woman. If you really want to be blessed, don't just fight for your family, fight for somebody else's family. Stand in the gap for that single mom or single dad. When you take your son out to hit baseballs, swing by and pick up that young man who doesn't have a father figure. Reach out to some other children. Help them discover their identity.

Mandy grew up in a dysfunctional home. Her father was never around and her mother had plenty of problems of her own. As a teenager, Mandy raised her younger brother. To all observers, it appeared that Mandy was handling the situation reasonably well, but on the inside, she was crying out for help.

One day a friend of hers at school mentioned that her father owned a fast-food restaurant. "Come on down, Mandy. Maybe my dad will give you a job," her friend suggested. Mandy visited the restaurant, and that gentleman not only gave her a job, but he also took her under his wing. He began to watch after her, making sure she changed the oil in her car, checking to see that she was doing okay in school, and on and on. He didn't even realize it, but he became the father figure for which Mandy longed. Years later, when Mandy was about to get married, her real father was nowhere to be found. Can you guess who gave Mandy away at her wedding?

That's right; it was the man from the fast-food restaurant. He made time to care. He fought not only for his own family; he fought for somebody else's child, too. Today, Mandy is healthy, whole, and happily married, much to the credit of a man who became a father figure to her. Stand up for your family and then be "family" to someone else who needs a father, mother, sister, or brother. As you take time for others, God will provide for you.

CHAPTER 14
INVEST IN YOUR RELATIONSHIPS

"Just a minute, boys," Terry said as he wheeled his car toward First National Bank's outdoor automated teller machine. "I have to stop and get some money, and then we'll be on our way. I'm glad you guys accepted my invitation to go to the ball game." Terry pulled alongside the money machine and punched in his password. He pressed the keys and entered $200 as the amount of money he wanted to withdraw. The machine buzzed, whirred, and in a few seconds spit out a slip of paper . . . but no money. Terry pulled the paper off the machine, read it, and quickly stuffed it into his pocket. "Silly machine!" he said. "These things never work right. Does anyone have any cash?"

"Yeah, sure. No problem," one of the guys said from the backseat. "I have plenty of cash. You can borrow some from me till Monday." Terry's friends looked at each other knowingly. Whether Terry was willing to admit it or not, they all knew that the reason Terry was unable to make a withdrawal from his account was simple: He hadn't made a deposit into his account. Terry was pretending to be a generous giver, when in fact he was a selfish "taker."

If you want your relationships to thrive, you must invest in them by being a giver rather than a taker. Everywhere you go, strive to make relational deposits into people's lives, encouraging them, building them up, and helping them to feel better about themselves.

Granted, it's not always easy. Some people are difficult to be around, because they tend to draw the life and energy out of you. They're not bad people; they just drain you. They always have a problem, or some major crisis that they are convinced requires your help to solve. They talk all the time, so much so that you can't get a word in edgewise. By the time the conversation is done, you feel as though your emotional energy is gone. Difficult people don't make positive deposits; they are too busy making withdrawals.

Please don't misunderstand. It's okay to be down and discouraged occasionally. Everybody has a right to have a bad day. But if you do that all the time, that's a problem. You're not going to have good friendships if you're always draining the emotional reserves of the people around you.

Let me tell you something that your friends may not tell you: Your family members, friends, and coworkers don't want to hear about your problems all the time. They have enough problems of their own. They're already carrying a heavy load without you dumping your heavy burdens on them, too.

If you're always talking about what's wrong in your life, or how badly people or circumstances are treating you, that's an extremely selfish way to live. Try to get your mind off yourself and quit living with that "What can you do for me?" attitude. Replace it with questions such as, "What can I do to help someone else? How can I make your life better? How can I encourage you?" Make sure you are investing in people, rather than constantly making withdrawals from their emotional reserves.

I like to think of my relationships as "emotional bank accounts." I have an account with every person with whom I have a relationship — whether a family member, a business associate, friends, even some of the people I meet in passing; I have an emotional account with the security guard at work, the man at the gas station, and the waiter at the restaurant. Every time I interact with them, I'm either making a deposit or making a withdrawal from that account.

How do you make a deposit? It can be something as simple as taking the time to walk over and shake that man's hand. "How are you doing today? Good morning. Good to see you."

Just the simple fact that you went out of your way to make him feel important made a deposit into that account. Your act of kindness built trust and respect. You can make a deposit simply by smiling at somebody, acknowledging them, being friendly, being pleasant to them in ordinary circumstances.

When you compliment people, you're making a deposit. Tell that coworker, "That was an outstanding presentation. You did a great job." Tell your husband, "I appreciate what you do for this family." Tell your wife, "You make it so much fun to live around here." When you do such things, you are not merely giving a compliment, you are making a deposit into the account you share with that person.

At home, you can make deposits in your emotional bank accounts by giving your wife a hug and a kiss, telling her that you love her. You make deposits into your accounts with your children by spending time with them, by listening to your daughter when she's playing the piano, by going down to the park and watching your son skateboard.

A subtle yet amazingly effective means of making a deposit is by overlooking a fault. Maybe a coworker is rude to you and he jumps down your throat about some meaningless matter. Instead of retaliating, you let it go. The next day when he apologizes, you say, "Don't even worry. I've already forgiven you. I didn't think twice about it. I knew that wasn't your normal self."

When you do such things, you make huge deposits into your account with that person. Your stock goes up significantly on his scale. Perhaps one day when you're a bit stressed and on edge, and maybe you don't treat him as well as you normally would, you'll have plenty in your account to cover it.

How do we make withdrawals from our relationship accounts? The most common way of making withdrawals is through selfish behavior. When we're thinking only about what we want and what we need, we will inevitably withdraw resources from our relationship accounts. We make withdrawals when we don't take time for people. You go into the office and you just blow past the receptionist. You don't smile or even notice her. Whether your mind was somewhere else or you were simply being rude is irrelevant.

You just made a withdrawal from your account with that person; you lowered her opinion of you.

Other ways of making withdrawals include those incidents in which we don't forgive, when we don't keep our commitments, when we don't express appreciation to someone to whom it is due. Maybe somebody does something nice for you by going out of her way, but you take it for granted. You don't say thank you; you're too busy or, worse yet, maybe you feel that you're too important to say something such as, "I appreciate your effort." Failure to appreciate the kindnesses of others will always result in a withdrawal from your account with those people.

The problem in many of our relationships is that our accounts are overdrawn. When we make a mistake and we need a little mercy, understanding, or the benefit of the doubt, that person goes to our relationship account and discovers it is already empty. Now we must live constantly on edge. Minor issues become magnified. We have to guard every little word that we say, because there's no reservoir of grace from which to draw in that relationship. We've exhausted the resources. And that's when little things suddenly turn into big things.

For instance, you correct your teenage son, and seemingly out of the blue, he blows up on you. "Who are you to tell me that?" he rails. "I don't have to listen to you."

Through such statements he is revealing that your relationship account with him is depleted. "You haven't built in trust recently. You haven't taken an interest in me; you haven't let me know that I am important to you."

He's saying, "You're trying to make a withdrawal, but there's nothing in the account, because you haven't made any recent deposits."

That situation doesn't come about overnight. The teenager doesn't wake up one morning and decide he doesn't have any respect for his parents. Rather, through the years he's not been getting what he needs. The deposits in the account between the teenager and his parents have been drained.

If you're going to correct someone, or maybe you're going to offer some constructive criticism, you need to make sure that you've made plenty of deposits into your account with that person. Make sure you've earned that person's respect.

In disciplining your children, ask yourself, "Have I encouraged him? Have I complimented her? Have I been interested in what he's interested in, or have I simply been making withdrawals?" If all your child has heard for the last couple of months is "Clean your room, do your homework, take out the trash, tuck your shirt in, be home by ten . . ." you are merely making withdrawals. And let's face it: Parents must make many withdrawals during their children's teenage years, but you cannot expect to speak effectively into your child's life unless you have first made plenty of deposits. You must invest in that relationship, nurture it, and build trust.

A dad was having a terrible time with his teenage son. They just couldn't seem to get along. They couldn't connect with each other and had little in common. The son was a star athlete, but the dad was more interested in his own career. He was working all the time, and hardly saw any of his son's ball games. Over time, their relationship deteriorated.

One day, the dad recognized that he had to make some changes. He realized if he was ever going to earn his son's respect, and be able to speak into his life, he needed to start making some deposits. He knew that his son was a huge baseball fan, so even though the dad didn't care for baseball, he decided to take a whole month off work and take his son to see every Major League Baseball team play. It was expensive and time-consuming as they traveled to numerous cities all across America. But it was a priceless time of healing, a time when their emotional accounts were replenished. That month-long trip was the catalyst that began a turnaround in that father-son relationship.

When the dad got back home, one of his business partners found out what he had done. He was shocked that this father had put forth such an enormous effort and expense to attend the baseball games with his son. He asked his partner, "Do you really love baseball that much?"

The dad said, "Not at all, but I really love my son that much."

Start investing in your children. You may not be able to do what this man did, but you can take time for your son, let your daughter know that you care. Keep those emotional accounts maxed out.

DEPOSIT BEFORE WITHDRAWING

It's amazing how people will respond when they know that you're rooting for them, that you are in their corner, wanting them to do well. Oftentimes, they will be willing to change when they know you're not trying to condemn them, that you are not trying to put them down or make them feel bad about themselves. True correction always inspires people to want to do better.

Often after one of our services at Lakewood Church, or at one of our special events around the country, Victoria and I will talk candidly about how things went and what we could have done better. When I have what I think is a good suggestion or some constructive criticism, I don't just get in the car and blurt it out. "Well, Victoria, if you'd have said this or that, things would have been better; if you'd have just done it my way." No, when I have a suggestion that I feel would help her, I always start off with something positive. I'll tell her, "Victoria, you did great up there. You spoke into the people's lives. This point was so good. That was clear and helpful, but maybe next time you could add this, and it would be more effective. You would do even better." When I begin with something positive, the defenses come down, and she's willing to consider my suggestion. She does something similar with me when she notices some area in which I can improve. Rather than condemning each other, we've chosen to encourage each other.

If you'll make it a priority to keep your emotional accounts full in your relationships, you will have far fewer problems with people receiving suggestions and receiving correction from you. In fact, one expert says the first thirty seconds of a conversation will determine the next hour. So when you have something sensitive to talk about, when you have something that has potential to cause conflict or problems, always start positively. Make sure it is the right time to broach that matter. Make sure that you've thought about how you're going to start the conversation and be aware of your voice tones. Watch your body language. Keep a pleasant expression, and choose to discuss the matter in love.

When you are trying to improve a relationship, if your words or actions cause the other person to become defensive, you've defeated your purpose. They are not going to receive what you have to say. They may get their feelings hurt, or they'll start pointing out your faults. "Well, who are you to tell me that?" he or she may retort. "You're no better than I am! Do you think you're perfect?" If you approach matters in a better way, all that turmoil can be avoided.

Studies show that it takes five positive charges to override one negative charge. In other words, before you correct someone, make sure that you have already given that person five compliments. Sadly, the correction-to-compliment ratio is nearly opposite that in our society today. We hear five things we're doing wrong to every one thing that we're doing right. No wonder our relationships are not what they should be! Our accounts are overdrawn.

When we correct people, we should never belittle them or make them feel insignificant. At the office, don't have the attitude, "How could you come up with that? Whose lousy idea was this?" Instead, do your best to find the good in every suggestion, even if you can't use it.

Sometimes, in our organization, somebody may start a new project and it simply doesn't work; it doesn't catch on. We know that we are going to have to discontinue it. However, when that happens, I always go overboard to let the people involved know that I have initiated plenty of projects that haven't worked. For one reason or another, some program that I really thought would fly never made it off the ground. I want my coworkers to know that I'm right there with them. We should never make people feel small for having attempted something great and failing. We should never talk down to someone, whether it is a spouse, a coworker, or a child. Treat people with respect.

Remember, genuine love overlooks a fault. Love makes allowances for mistakes. True love sees the best in every person. If you want to make a huge deposit into somebody's life, when he makes a mistake and he knows he is wrong, don't make a big deal about it. Don't embarrass a child in front of other family members or friends. Don't embarrass an employee in front of his or her coworkers. If you must confront them about a matter, deal with them in private if at all possible, and always do your best to protect their dignity. It does not do anything positive to show somebody up or to humiliate someone in front of others.

Occasionally, you may be tempted to pay back a person for something painful that he or she did to you, but if you succumb to that temptation, in the long run, you will lose out in that relationship. When you embarrass somebody that you could have easily covered for, it will drain your account with that person and destroy any sense of trust and loyalty that existed between the two of you.

Years ago when Colin Powell worked for President Ronald Reagan, he and several other cabinet members came up with a new policy. They were excited about it and went to a meeting with President Reagan to explain the details.

General Powell felt strongly about it because it was his idea, so he was selling the program to the best of his ability. He told President Reagan how helpful the new system could be, but President Reagan wasn't convinced. He saw what he thought were some major flaws in the policy, and he debated Colin Powell back and forth for some time. Finally, even though President Reagan disagreed, he decided to trust General Powell and he accepted the new policy.

Unfortunately, it was a big mistake. The policy totally failed and created a huge mess. At a press conference, President Reagan was questioned about what went wrong. After intense grilling of the president, a reporter finally asked the question that General Powell was hoping wouldn't be asked: "President Reagan, tell us, was this new policy your idea?"

Without hesitation President Reagan said, "I take full responsibility for it." General Powell stood on the side of the room, and when President Reagan looked over at him, the general had tears in his eyes. President Reagan had just made a huge deposit into his account with Colin Powell. The president had protected Powell's reputation and covered a mistake. As General Powell was leaving the room, he told one of the other cabinet members, "I'll do anything for that man."

If you want to build lifelong, loyal friendships, if you want to build trust, learn to protect your family members and friends even when they make mistakes. Learn to show mercy. Take the heat even though it wasn't your fault. Do your best to protect a reputation. Don't embarrass somebody when you have the opportunity or wherewithal to build up that person.

Certainly, we are not to condone evil or to cover intentional wrongdoing. But whenever it is simply a mistake or a failure on the part of somebody with whom we share an account, do your best to guard that relationship carefully and with integrity.

Everywhere we go we should be making deposits — whether at the grocery store, ballpark, school, or office. Develop a habit of sowing good things into people's lives. Make it your business to help somebody else feel better about himself or herself. Be interested in people. Take time to let someone know that you care. Go out of your way to show somebody that he or she is special. When you leave the office, instead of rushing out of the parking garage, take a few moments to ask the attendant, "How are you doing today? How are you feeling? I'm so glad you are part of this company." Encourage him in some way; make him feel important; help him to know that somebody cares.

Learn to appreciate people. Learn to say thank you. Just because somebody works for you doesn't mean you are exempt from expressing appreciation to that person. "Well, Joel, I pay him good money. I pay her good money. I shouldn't have to coddle him or her." Or "I pay high enough taxes. I shouldn't have to thank that policeman. I shouldn't have to thank that schoolteacher. They should do their jobs." No, learn to sow positive deposits into people's lives.

A while back, I was working at my house out in the yard. It was a hot, humid morning, so I decided to go inside and get some water. On my way, I noticed the garbagemen working their way down the street collecting trash. I thought, *I'll get a couple of extra bottles of water and give some to them.* When they came by our home, I ran out and gave them that water. The response was surprising. You would have thought I had given each of them a hundred-dollar bill. They were so thankful. I didn't think much about it at the time; it was no big deal. But I had just made a deposit into that account.

A few months passed, and one day, Victoria and I were late in getting our trash out. The sanitation truck came by early in the morning and we missed it. I didn't want the trash in the garbage cans to stay out on the street for three or four days, but there was not much I could do about it.

Later that day, those garbage men made a special trip back by our house to see if we'd put our trash out before they went to the dump. That sort of unanticipated, reciprocal help happens frequently when you make deposits into people's lives.

Don't make the mistake of living your life self-centered, rushing through your day concerned only about yourself. Take time for people; make them feel special; learn to appreciate them. When you see your mailman dropping off the mail, call out to him, "Hey, thank you. I appreciate that." When you go to the grocery store, encourage the cashier. Be friendly. Sow a seed with the bank teller, the woman who cuts your hair, the man at the gas station; make a positive deposit in each of their lives as you pass their way.

"Why bother?" you may ask. "I'm never going to have a long-term relationship with them."

Maybe not, but as part of your relationship with God, you can still extend kindness and appreciation to every person you meet. The Scripture says, "We should encourage one another daily."[34] That means every day you should find somebody you

can help build up. Each day look for somebody for whom you can make a deposit of
encouragement. A simple compliment may
turn somebody's whole day around. "You
look great today. That color really looks
good on you." Or you can tell somebody, "I
appreciate you being my friend. That means
a lot to me."

I remember when I was at my father's
house and he would see the mailman coming, Daddy would get a big smile on his face,
and he'd say, "Well, look-ee here, here comes
the finest mailman in all the world." That
mailman's countenance would light up. My
father's simple compliment brightened the
man's day. It didn't take a lot of effort; it
didn't require much of Daddy's time. He
had developed a habit of investing in people,
in helping other people to feel better about
themselves.

Your words have the power to put a spring
in somebody's step, to lift somebody out of
defeat and discouragement, and to help pro-
pel them to victory. A potentially uplifting
deposit such as Daddy made in the life of
that postman doesn't take much more than
ten or fifteen seconds to make. Yet somebody
in your realm of influence may need just
such a fifteen-second investment in the account they share with you.

Understand that every person needs encouragement, no matter who he or she is or how successful they appear. Frequently, someone will tell me, "Joel, you've really helped me." Or "You've made such a difference in my life." Every time I hear a statement such as that, it encourages me to be better; it does something deep down on the inside of me that lets me know that my life has significance and that I've been able to make a difference in this world. Everyone you know needs that sort of encouragement.

Husband, your wife can never hear you say too many times, "You're beautiful. I think you're great. I'm so glad that you're my wife." Keep those emotional accounts growing.

Learn to give compliments freely. Learn to be friendly and avoid anything that exudes the attitude that you are so important that you can't take time for somebody who's not up to your level. Instead, make everyone you meet feel important; strive to make every person with whom you have contact feel special. After all, every person you meet is made in the image of God.

Victoria and I share a favorite restaurant, a place with great food, wonderful atmosphere, and valet parking. I noticed, however, that many customers drive up and toss their car keys to the parking attendants, treating them as though they were servants. I refuse to do that. Instead, I always make an effort to be friendly to the valet parking attendants. I'll take fifteen seconds or so and say, "How are you doing? How's everything been going?" It is amazing how that little bit of time and interest makes a deposit in the lives of those young men.

I've also noticed that when Victoria and I leave that restaurant, there may be five or ten people waiting for their cars, but somehow our car always seems to get to the doorway ahead of the others. It almost embarrasses me. I never ask the parking guys to do anything special for us, nor do we expect it. Yet they do it.

I'm convinced that people want to be good to you when you have sown good things into their lives. I probably haven't spoken to those young men more than five minutes in my whole lifetime, but they know I've made some deposits into my emotional account with them.

Rather than trying to figure out what everybody can do for you, start looking for things that you can do for somebody else. Make relational deposits wherever you go. Be a giver rather than a taker. As you do so, your relationships will not only get better, but you also will see God's favor in a greater way, and you will experience more of His blessings.

CHAPTER 15
BEING GOOD TO PEOPLE

Do you want to get more out of life? Who doesn't, right? Okay, try this: Get up every day and rather than trying to be blessed, do everything in your power to be a blessing to someone else. If you will do that for six weeks — trying to be a blessing to someone every day — your life will be filled with so many blessings you won't be able to contain them all.

I've discovered that if I meet other people's needs, God will meet mine. If I make somebody else happy, God will make sure that I'm happy. Every day, we should look for opportunities to be good to people. Maybe you can buy somebody's lunch, or give someone a ride, babysit somebody's children, tip a little more than is expected. Get in a habit of doing some good for somebody every day. Don't make the mistake of living selfishly. That's one of the worst prisons you could ever live in. You were not created to be focused only on yourself. Almighty God made you to be a giver. The best way for you to be fulfilled is to get your mind off yourself and reach out to others.

Get up in the morning with the attitude, "Who can I be a blessing to today? Who can I encourage? Where is there a need that I can meet?"

I don't believe that we see enough good works today. We hear a lot about success and about the good things that God wants to do for us, but let's not forget we are blessed, so we can be a blessing. We are blessed so we can share God's goodness wherever we go. If you want to make an impact on somebody's life, you don't necessarily have to preach a sermon to that person; just be good to them. Your actions will speak much louder than your words. You can say, "I love you and I care about you," but we demonstrate true love by what we do.

If I love you, I'll go out of my way to help you. If I love you, I'll give you a ride to work or school, even though I have to get up earlier than usual to do it. If I love you, I'll babysit your children when I know that you're not feeling well. True love turns words and feelings into action.

Learn to be good to people in your everyday life. When you go to the lunchroom, bring your coworker back a cup of coffee. You may be thinking, *I'm not going to do that. He never does anything for me.*

Be bigger than that; do it unto God. Don't miss an opportunity to do something good for someone. On the freeway, when traffic backs up, let that car squeeze in front of you. At the grocery store, when you have a large basket full of groceries and the person behind you is carrying just a few, let him or her go ahead of you. In the parking lot, when you pull up to that last spot at the same time as another car, back up and let the other person have that space. Prefer them over you. Be good to them.

"Well, I thought that was God's favor, helping me beat them to the parking spot," you might say.

No, that's our old selfish nature wanting to be first. If you will be good to people, you will have more of God's favor than you will ever need.

When you are eating at a restaurant, be a good tipper. Please don't leave that young waitress a dollar bill when you just spent thirty dollars to eat. "But Joel, I shared my testimony. I invited her to come to church."

No, you canceled out your testimony with your lousy tip.

Victoria and I went to a restaurant where

we had eaten a number of times before. We practically knew the menu by heart, and we knew exactly what we wanted. When we sat down, we ordered right away. I was hungry, but it seemed to take forever for the cooks to prepare our food. We waited and waited. It didn't make sense. The restaurant wasn't even busy. When the waitress finally brought the food, our order was incorrect. She returned my dinner to the kitchen, and it was another long delay. Finally, I got tired of waiting and began eating off Victoria's plate. It was the worst service that we'd ever had in that restaurant.

When it came time to pay the bill and leave a tip, I thought, *God, now You just saw what happened. And I know that You're a just God. Surely, You don't expect me to leave a good tip.*

Almost immediately, I knew I was wrong. I said, "Okay, God; how about five percent?"

Let me tell you a secret. Don't ever negotiate with God, because you will never win. I said, "Okay, God, how about ten percent, fifteen percent? That's the normal amount. God, You know that's the going rate. I should be able to do that." But I still didn't have any peace. I knew God was saying, "Don't miss this opportunity to do good. Don't miss this opportunity to show My mercy." We can be good to people when they're good to us. That's easy. But God wants us to be good to people even when they're not so good to us.

I eventually changed my attitude and thought, *I'm not just going to give this girl a tip, I'm going to sow a seed in her life. I'm going to go the extra mile and be good to her.* We left a twenty-dollar tip for a thirty-dollar meal. But we did it as sowing a seed.

A few weeks later, I received a letter from that young lady. I had no idea that she had recognized Victoria and me; she hadn't given us any indication that she knew us.

Her letter began by asking, "Do you remember me? I'm the girl who waited on you at what was probably your worst restaurant experience ever?"

I smiled as I read and thought, *I know exactly who you are.*

She went on to tell how she had been raised in a good Christian family. They went to church every Sunday, but in her late teens, her family was hurt by a leader in their congregation. Somebody did them wrong. Consequently, the entire family had given up on God and dropped out of church. Over the last year or two, however, they had been watching me on television. The waitress related in her letter, "I told my parents I know those people are real. Something on the inside tells me they're sincere and we need to get back in church."

She continued, "Joel, when you and your wife came in the restaurant, and we got your order all mixed up, most people would have really gotten aggravated and upset, but you two were so nice and kind. And on top of that, you left us that big tip." She said, "That confirmed what I already knew in my heart. I went home and told my parents what happened, and now we've gotten our lives back on track, and we're worshiping the Lord at Lakewood every Sunday morning."

Learn to be good to people. That's one of the best witnesses we can possibly have. Now, when I tip people, I tell Victoria, "We're going to sow a seed into their life. Here's an opportunity to do good." When I leave that place, I want them to be able to say, "That couple sure is generous; they are good to people."

The world does not need to hear another sermon nearly as much as it needs to see one. Learn to give your time, your money, and an encouraging word; meet a need. When you show love, you are showing God to the world.

Don't worry about it if you don't get any credit. If that young lady hadn't written to Victoria and me, it wouldn't have mattered one bit. I would still feel that we did the right thing. When you let somebody in traffic in front of you, you may never see that person again. When you give somebody twenty dollars simply because you felt compassion in your heart, you may never hear back from them. That's okay; God is keeping the records. He sees every act of kindness you show. He sees every time you are good to somebody. He hears every encouraging word you speak. God has seen all the times you went out of your way to help somebody who never said thank you. Your good deeds do not go unnoticed by Almighty God.

In fact, the Scripture teaches that when you do things in secret, without getting any credit, you will receive a greater reward. It's one thing to make a big splash and let everybody know how generous you are, but if you really want to be blessed, do something good for somebody and don't tell anybody about it. Leave some cash in an unmarked envelope on the desk of that coworker who's struggling. At the restaurant, buy somebody's dinner and remain anonymous. Clean up the kitchen at the office and don't tell anybody that you did it. When you do things in secret, when nobody thanks you and you don't get any credit, you are sowing a seed for God to do great things in your life.

I want to be the kind of person that does good for people whether I get paid back or not, whether they say thank you or they don't. I don't want to do something kind so I can be seen. I don't want to do it so people can say, "Look how great he is." No, I want to do it unto God. I believe when we have that kind of attitude, we will see God's favor in ways we've never seen before.

At a tollbooth on a busy section of the freeway, instead of paying the normal one-dollar toll, a man often gave the clerk five dollars and paid for the next four cars behind him. When that next car pulled up, the clerk told the driver, "Your toll has already been paid by somebody in front of you." It happened so frequently that eventually, a reporter heard about the generosity and wrote about it in the news.

It's amazing how just one little act of kindness can brighten somebody's whole day. Who knows, maybe that person whose toll was paid was down and discouraged, or otherwise stressed out, but then the clerk said, "Your toll has been paid." Maybe the passengers in the four cars following the phantom toll payer were about to go home uptight and irritated, but suddenly, they were going home to be a better father or a better wife all because somebody sowed a seed, somebody didn't miss an opportunity to do good.

I wonder what our world would be like if every person would find some way to do good every single day. What would our cities be like? What would our offices be like? What would our schools be like if we made it a priority to brighten somebody else's day, to do something good for somebody else?

The Bible says, "Every opportunity we have we should do good to people."[35] That means we need to be proactive, on the lookout for opportunities. Who can I bless today? For whom can I do a favor? You can't sit back and wait for the need to come to you; go after it. Be sensitive; pay attention to the people around you. If you see one of your friends wearing the same clothes over and over again, step up and say, "Let me give you a new suit or two." Or "Take this gift certificate and go get yourself some new clothes."

Maybe you overheard one of your coworkers saying, "Next week, I have to take my car in to the shop. I don't know how I'm going to get to work."

Tell your coworker, "Let me swing by in the mornings and pick you up."

"No, that's too far. My home is out of your way."

"It's okay; no big deal. I'll be glad to do it."

Listen to what people are saying around you.

Of course, we can't spend all our time and money like that. Most of us could probably do more than we are currently in this regard, though. The Scripture says people will know us by our fruit.[36] They're not going to know us by how many verses of Scripture we quote. They won't know us by how many bumper stickers we have on our car. People are going to know that we're believers when we meet real needs by doing good works.

You may have plenty of money. If so, when you see that single mom who's really struggling, why don't you pay her rent for a month or two? Tell her, "Let me pick up the car payment for the next several months. Let me lighten the load just a little." Jesus said, "When you do it to the least of one of these, it's like you're doing it unto Me."[37]

Moreover, it says in Proverbs, when you give to the poor, you are lending to God. You may not be able to do that, but you can babysit some children. Why don't you give a young couple or a single mom a break one night? Say, "You go do something special for yourself. Here's a gift certificate. You go up to the mall. You go get your nails done. You go get a massage, or whatever you want, but our family is going to keep your children tonight."

Perhaps you can be a mentor to a young man or young woman who doesn't have a positive role model in his or her life. That doesn't take a lot of money. It just takes time and somebody who cares, somebody who is willing to make a difference.

A young man who sings in our Lakewood children's choir comes from an extremely dysfunctional family. His father is in prison, his mother has a serious drug addiction, and he was not receiving the care and attention that he really needed. Somehow, one of our families at Lakewood came across the boy's path, and they took an interest in him. They had a son the same age as this young man, so they started taking the young man to church and showing him love. He began to see what a family was all about, as he received the love and attention that he needed. He'd never been to church before, but he loved coming to Lakewood. That was the highlight of his week. He couldn't wait till Sundays.

He eventually got involved in our children's choir and discovered that he loved to sing. Now the family that had taken an interest in the boy not only had to bring him to church on Sunday, but they also had to bring him back during the week for choir practice. It was more time, effort, and energy, but they never complained. They gladly did it. They were sowing into his life.

Unfortunately, that young man lost his mother in a tragic accident at home. She died right before his eyes. Of course, he was devastated and heartbroken. A couple of days after the funeral, the family members and relatives gathered in that home to try to figure out what they were going to do. But this young man was nowhere to be found. They finally went to his room and found his door closed. When they opened it, they discovered the young man listening to his choir tapes, practicing for his next song, getting ready for that next special.

When I heard about that incident, I wondered what that young man would have done had somebody not taken an interest in him. How would he have coped in that situation, if that surrogate family had not taken time to care? What if they had been too busy? What if they had the attitude, We'll take you to church, but we're not going to take you to choir practice; that's just asking too much.

No, they were willing to be inconvenienced. They sacrificed their own time and resources to help meet that boy's need. They took time to care, and that's what true living is all about. The closest thing to the heart of God is helping people who are hurting. If we're too busy for our friends and neighbors, and for the less fortunate, then we're too busy. Our priorities are out of line.

The Scripture says that in the last days the love of the great body of people will grow cold.[38] That simply means that people will be so busy, they'll be so focused on their own needs, they'll be so caught up in their drive for success they won't take time to make a difference.

Friend, don't let that description apply to you. All around you people are hurting. They need your love and your encouragement. Don't miss the miracle of the moment. You may have someone in your life right now who needs your time and energy. Are you paying attention?

Maybe one of your coworkers is just about on the brink of giving up. He desperately needs your encouragement. She needs you to take her to lunch and let her know that you care. Don't be too busy. Don't be insensitive to the needs around you. Be willing to be inconvenienced.

When you study the life of Jesus, you'll notice that He always took time for people. He was busy. He had places He wanted to go, but He was always willing to change His plans to do good for somebody else. As He walked through the villages, people called out to Him, "Jesus, please come over here and pray for us." He would stop and go out of His way to bring healing to those people. One time they came up to Him and said, "Jesus, please come to our city, our relative is so sick. You've got to pray for him." Jesus changed His plans and went that way.

When they tried to bring the little children to Jesus, the disciples said, "No, don't bother Him. He's busy. He's too important."

Jesus said, "No, no; let the children come to Me."

It's so easy for us to get caught up in our own little worlds and focus only on ourselves. "I've got my plans. Don't get me off my schedule." Instead, take time for people. Don't miss any opportunities to do good. Make a difference in somebody's life. It doesn't have to be something big. Often, small gestures of love and kindness can make a big difference. A women's group at our church makes blankets, and then the women embroider Scripture verses on them and take them to cancer patients at M. D. Anderson Cancer Center, in Houston. Those handmade blankets remind the men and women struggling with cancer that somebody cares; the expression of love gives them an extra ray of hope. Those ladies are using their talents to do something good for somebody else.

You may not have a lot of extra money, but maybe you can make a blanket or bake a cake. You can mentor a young man. You can visit the nursing home. You can get involved in a prison outreach and encourage the inmates to trust God. Do something good for somebody.

O. A. "Bum" Phillips, the legendary NFL football coach, retired from the game a number of years ago, but Phillips isn't really retired. He's at the prisons every chance he gets, encouraging the prisoners and giving them hope. That's what life's all about — doing something good for somebody else. John Bunyan, the author of the classic *Pilgrim's Progress,* said, "You have not lived today until you have done something for someone who can never repay you."

"But, Joel, I bought this book to find out how I could get blessed," you may be saying. "I wanted how to find out how I could get my needs met."

Friend, this is exactly how it happens. If you will meet somebody else's needs, God will meet yours. What you make happen for others, God will make happen for you. When I start to feel discouraged or down, or feeling as though I have the weight of the world on my shoulders, I go up to the hospital and pray for people. I find when I start giving encouragement, giving people hope, my joy quickly returns. It changes my focus.

A while back, I was at one of the hospitals praying for a family. As I left their room, four or five people came up to me and asked me to go into their loved ones' room and pray for them. I gladly did it. One family member asked, "Would you go in there and pray for our father?"

"Sure I will," I said, "but why don't you come with me?"

They said, "No, we'll wait out here, if you don't mind." I went in and talked with the man and treated him as if he were my best friend. I prayed a strong prayer over him. When I came out of the room, his family was so surprised. One of them said, "Joel, we can't believe that he let you pray for him. He makes fun of us for watching you on television."

I thought, *If I had known that earlier, I might have prayed differently!* Regardless of what he thought of me, I was refreshed by praying for him.

There are two kinds of people in this world: givers and takers. Be a giver and not a taker. Make a difference in somebody's life.

I heard a story about a young boy who lived in the inner city. He was about eight years old, and his family was extremely poor. One cold fall day, he was up at the local store looking in the window admiring a pair of tennis shoes. As he stood there, cold and barefoot, a lady came along and said, "Young man, what are you doing staring so intently in this window?"

Under his breath, and almost shyly, he said, "Well, I was just sort of praying and asking God if He'd give me a new pair of tennis shoes."

Without hesitation, the woman took him into the store and very gently and lovingly washed his cold dirty feet. Then she put a brand-new pair of socks on him and told him to pick out three new pairs of tennis shoes. He couldn't believe it. He was so excited. He had never owned a new pair of shoes. He'd always worn hand-me-downs.

After the woman paid for the purchases, she returned to the little boy. He looked at her in disbelief. Nobody had ever taken that kind of interest in him. With tears running down his cheeks, he said, "Lady, can I ask you a question? Are you God's wife?"

Friend, you are never more like God than when you give, when you take time for people, when you do something good for somebody who can never repay you. Don't get sucked into society's narcissistic way of thinking — it's all about me, me, me! You will never be happy catering to yourself. Real joy comes as you give your life away.

Do you really want to be a better you? Make a decision with me that you're going to start being good to people. Pay attention to those around you — your friends, coworkers, relatives, even strangers. Listen to what they're saying. Be sensitive and don't miss any opportunity to do good. Remember, true love is always backed up with actions.

1. I will help somebody else become successful and trust God to make me successful. This week I will build up, encourage, or otherwise improve the lives of at least three people.

2. I will (on purpose) find somebody that I can be good to today. I will attempt to make somebody's day. I will look for ways to be a blessing, especially to someone who cannot repay me.

3. I will be determined to keep strife out of my home. I will remind myself regularly:
   "I am a peacemaker, not a trouble-maker."
   "I will overlook minor matters and I will forgive quickly."
   "I choose to see the best in other people."
   "I appreciate my spouse, my family members, my friends, and my coworkers."

4. Today I will make relational deposits in the lives of people around me. I will give compliments freely and seek to make every person I meet feel important.

■ ■ ■ ■

PART FOUR:
FORM BETTER HABITS

■ ■ ■ ■

CHAPTER 16
FEED YOUR GOOD HABITS

An old Cherokee tale tells of a grandfather teaching life principles to his grandson. The wise old Cherokee said, "Son, on the inside of every person a battle is raging between two wolves. One wolf is evil. It's angry, jealous, unforgiving, proud, and lazy. The other wolf is good. It's filled with love, kindness, humility, and self-control.

"These two wolves are constantly fighting," the grandfather said.

The little boy thought about it, and said, "Grandfather, which wolf is going to win?"

The grandfather smiled and said, "Whichever one you feed."

Feeding unforgiveness, impatience, low self-esteem, or other negative traits will only make them stronger. For instance, maybe you complain frequently about your job. You're always talking negatively about your boss, how that company doesn't treat you right, and how you can't stand the drive to work. Ironically, when we complain, we feel a sense of release. It feels good to feed those negative thoughts. But the wolf we feed will always want more.

The next time you are tempted to complain, ask yourself, "Do I really want to keep feeding this negative habit?" "Do I really want to stay where I am?" Or, "Do I want to starve this complaining spirit and step up higher?"

If you will start feeding peace, patience, kindness, gentleness, humility, and self-control, you will see those character traits developing in your life. Make the better choice and instead of complaining about going to work, learn to say, "Father, I thank you that at least I have a job. And these people may not be treating me right, but I'm not working for man; I'm working unto You." When you do that, you're feeding the right thing and the new habit develops.

A habit is an acquired, learned behavior that we do without even thinking about it. It's almost involuntary. We've done it so much it becomes practically second nature. If we have good habits, that may be fine. But sometimes our habits are keeping us from God's best, and we may not even realize it.

Many of the habits that we've developed stem from the culture in which we were raised. If you grew up in a home where people were disorganized, sloppy, or perpetually late, you may have formed some of those same negative habits. Or if you were raised around people who tended to be harsh, sarcastic, or rude, you may have picked up some of that same behavior. You may not even realize that such attitudes and behaviors are offensive, since that is all you've ever known.

On the other end of the spectrum, some people grow up around people with positive habits such as neatness, godliness, cleanliness, and order. Many people have established positive habits concerning diet and exercise. Other individuals have a habit of getting up at a particular time and going to bed at a time that will allow his or her body to rest and be refreshed. These are positive learned behavior patterns.

Your habits — whether good or bad — will greatly determine your future. One study says that 90 percent of our everyday behavior is based on our habits. Let that sink in for a moment: From the time we get up in the morning to the time we go to bed at night, 90 percent of what we do is habitual behavior. That means how we treat people, how we spend our money, what we watch, what we listen to — 90 percent of the time, we're on autopilot. We do what we've always done. It is no wonder that if you want to change your life, you must start by consciously changing your everyday habits. You can't keep doing the same things you have been doing and expect to get different results.

To become a better you, take inventory of your habits. Do you have a tendency to be negative in your thoughts and conversations? Are you always late to work? Do you worry all the time? Do you overeat? Do you regularly succumb to addictions?

Understand, your habit may not be legally, ethically, or morally wrong. It can be a seemingly innocuous action or attitude, a little thing, but if you don't do something about it, you can go for years wasting time and energy, being unproductive and unprofitable. That is not God's best.

The good news is you can change. You can develop better habits. Most studies of habitual behavior indicate that a habit can be broken in six weeks; some studies tell us that you can break a habit in as little as twenty-one days. Think about that. If you will discipline yourself for a month or so, and be willing to suffer through the pain of change, you can rid yourself of a negative behavior, form a new healthy habit, and rise to a new level of personal freedom.

The Apostle Paul said, "All things are permissible to me, but not all things are profitable. All things are lawful, but I will not be mastered by anything." Notice, Paul is saying in effect, "I'm going to rid myself of anything that is not profitable or productive in my life." He was saying, "I'm not going to stay under the control of any bad habits."

It's a fact: Successful people develop better habits. That's why even professional golfers practice hitting golf balls nearly every day. Some pros hit as many as five hundred to a thousand balls a day when they are not competing in tournaments. They work for hours to repeat their golf swing so they can do it without even thinking about it. Then, when they get in a tournament under intense pressure, their bodies perform the correct swing almost automatically. No wonder those golfers are successful! They have formed successful habits.

If you have a bad habit of not getting to work on time, change that behavior. People who get ahead in life are usually punctual. Get up fifteen minutes earlier on days you must go to work, attend school, or go to a meeting. Plan your travel so you can arrive with time to spare. Establish a new routine of being on time. Don't allow yourself to be late when punctuality is such an easy habit to develop.

Or if you have a habit of eating a bunch of junk food and drinking several sodas every day, commit yourself to forming better eating habits. Don't go on a crash diet; just change one small thing at a time. Before long, you will notice a marked difference in your energy level as well as your personal appearance.

Our habits become part of our character. If you allow yourself to be disorganized or you are always running late, that becomes a part of who you are. If you've trained yourself to get upset and have a fit whenever you don't get your way, unfortunately those bad habits become a part of you, too. The first step toward changing is to identify what's holding you back. Identify any bad habits and then make a decision to do something about them.

How do we change a habit? Simple: Quit feeding the bad habit. You have to starve your bad habits into submission and start nourishing your good habits.

I heard somebody say, "Bad habits are easy to develop but difficult to live with." In other words, it's easy to pop off and be rude, saying whatever you feel and making snide, cutting, sarcastic remarks. That's easy. But it's difficult to live in a home filled with strife and tension.

It's easy to spend money that we don't have and charge everything on our credit cards. It's hard to live with the pressure of not being able to pay our bills. It's easy to give in to temptation and do whatever we feel. It's difficult to live in bondage, feeling guilty and condemned.

Consider a person with a chemical addiction. It is easy to get hooked. It may seem fun and exciting at first. Before long, however, that addiction controls the person. He becomes a slave to it. Bad habits are easy to acquire but hard to live with.

On the other hand, good habits are difficult to develop. A good habit results from a desire to work and sacrifice, and sometimes a willingness to endure pain and suffering. But good habits are easy to live with. For instance, at first it's hard to hold your tongue and overlook an offense when someone criticizes or insults you. It's hard at first to forgive. But it sure is easy to live in a home filled with peace and harmony.

If you are willing to be uncomfortable for a little while, so you can press past the initial pain of change, in the long run, your life will be much better. Pain doesn't last forever; in fact, once you develop the new habit, the pain often disappears.

Victoria knows that I won't argue with her.

We don't allow strife and conflict in our home. In our marriage, it's not hard for me to overlook things or to forgive an offense, because I've simply trained myself to be a peacemaker. I've trained myself to apologize even when it's not my fault, which of course is every time we have a disagreement!

However, in the early years of our marriage, I didn't respond that way. Instead, I'd put up a good argument, and I'd tell her what I thought and the way I felt it should be. One day I realized, *That's not the way God wants me to live.* That's not His best. I could hear the still, small voice down inside, saying, "Joel, let it go. You're better than this. Don't live on this low level."

I recognized that I had to make a decision: Did I want to prove I was right, or did I want to have peace in our home? I began to change, and relinquishing my right to fight gradually got easier. Today, it's not difficult at all for me to be easygoing; it has become part of my character. It's natural to me. Truth is, I could still be floundering where I was twenty years ago, when Victoria and I first married: arguing, pouting when I didn't get my way, and always wanting to have the last word.

Thankfully, I developed better habits. I pressed past the pain of change and today I can say it has been worth it. Sure, I have other areas in which I need to improve — maybe one or two!

If you, too, will press past the initial pain — whether it takes a week, a month, or a year — eventually the pain will go away, and you will not only enjoy your life a lot more, but you'll be living at a much higher level.

DELAYED REACTIONS

The subtle danger associated with many bad habits is that we may not suffer their consequences until later on in life. If you abuse your body with tobacco or alcohol, it may be years before you develop cancer, emphysema, or cirrhosis of the liver. If you mistreat your body by eating poorly and working long hours all the time, getting insufficient nutrition and rest, you may get away with it for a while, but one day those bad habits will catch up with you. If you're rude and harsh to your family, friends, and coworkers, they may put up with it now, but one day you could be a very lonely person. People may tolerate your insolence for a season, but eventually your relationships will suffer.

Usually, when we consider habits, we tend to think of destructive patterns such as drug addictions, alcoholism, or some other kind of abuse. Yet the habits that are likely to make or break most people are much more mundane. Look at your everyday habits. If you waste four or five minutes each day trying to find things that you have misplaced — your keys, cell phone, glasses, notebook, or something else — at the end of a year, you will have wasted almost a week of your life. The Bible tells us to make the most of our time. Living sloppy and disorganized is not being a good steward of the time that God has given to you.

I heard somebody say, "Habits are like gravity; they will always pull you toward them." If you develop good habits, they'll make your life easier, more successful, and more productive. You won't be struggling constantly to do the right thing. When you practice good habits, your life will produce good fruit. You'll be happy, naturally, and you will experience God's abundant life. But if you establish bad habits, they will inevitably drag you down. You'll gravitate toward them.

Certainly, if you've been set in your ways for twenty or thirty years, you may not overcome that habit you want to change in a mere twenty-one days. But if you will make up your mind, and ask God for His help in breaking that habit, it won't take you years to do it either. Make a decision to change, stick with it, and you will be amazed how soon you begin to form that new habit. It will get easier every day, to the point when, eventually, you'll do the right thing automatically. You won't even have to think about it.

When Victoria and I first got married, we often misplaced our car keys. I'd come home and put them on the table, or maybe take them up to the bedroom with me. Victoria might leave them in her purse or put them in the kitchen. It seemed like every time we got ready to leave, we'd have to search to find the car keys. One day, I realized how much time we were wasting. I found a hammer and two little nails and I pounded those nails right inside a cabinet by our back door so we could hang our keys on them. The next few times I came home, I did the same thing as I'd always done. Without even thinking about it, I took the keys up to our bedroom or left them in my gym bag. I had to remind myself, *Go back downstairs, and put the keys where they now belong, on the tiny nails in the closet.* I did this day after day after day.

Changing a habit is not easy at first, but eventually, once you retrain yourself, the new habit comes naturally. Now, Victoria and I don't even think about where we are supposed to keep our car keys. When we go home, we go right to the cabinet and hang up the keys. A habit works that way whether positively or negatively. Repeated behavior tends to become almost automatic.

Friend, don't stay stuck in a bad habit. Make a decision that you are going to develop better habits. To change, you must be consistent. You have to do it day in and day out. You need to have a "no exceptions" policy. That means no matter how you feel, no matter how much you want to go back to your old ways, you're going to stick with your new plan. No exceptions.

A second key to change is that you must be willing to press past the pain and discomfort at the beginning of your new regimen. After all, if you've trained your body in a certain way year after year, you've developed behavior patterns to which you have grown accustomed. Don't be surprised if your own body revolts against you when you try to establish new patterns. But if you will discipline yourself and stand your ground, in a few months, you can form new habits and your life will be much more rewarding.

For a runner preparing to race in competition, the first few days of conditioning are awful. His stomach wrenches, his legs ache, and at every turn the temptation to quit looms. As he conditions his body day after day, he is able to run farther, faster, with less fatigue and fewer interruptions in his progress.

Understand, once you get past that initial pain, establishing the new and better pattern will be much easier. Think of a rocket being launched into space. Liftoff takes an enormous amount of thrust. The majority of the energy expended in that launch is spent as the spacecraft breaks free of earth's gravitational pull. Once it pushes into outer space, it is much easier to keep moving forward. In the same way, when it comes to breaking habits, if you can just get past the first few weeks, it will get easier, and one day you will be home free.

Think about all the people you know who are trying to lose weight. The diet business is a multibillion-dollar industry nowadays. Although diets can be helpful at times, the long-term solution to keeping your weight under control is not to run from one new "wonder" diet to another. Most of the success achieved by those kinds of diets is temporary. Unfortunately, most dieters end up regaining that weight — and more!

The better way to get your weight under control and maintain it is to establish new habits. Start exercising, start watching what you eat, when you eat, and how much you eat. Granted, it's not always easy; especially at first, you will have to be extremely disciplined. Every time you resist a temptation, every time you make a better choice, it will get easier. One day, you'll notice that you are living a healthier and more productive life.

Remember, in forming a new habit, it is always the most difficult at the beginning. You'll be tempted to turn around or to return to your old routine, but you don't have to give in.

You may say, "But Joel, I just couldn't live without that bowl of ice cream before I go to bed each night."

Yes, you *can* live without it, and you will probably live longer and better without it! If you are going to break that habit, the first step is to quit going into the kitchen late at night. The Bible says to run from temptation, so whether it is sexual temptation or sugar temptation, the key to success is the same: You have to stay far away from it!

When you go to the grocery store, don't even go down the aisle where all that delicious, *fattening* ice cream is hiding, waiting to seduce you. Don't make excuses such as, "Well, I'm just going to pick up this one half gallon of Cookies and Cream in case we have some guests come over."

No, you know you will be the only guest who eats that ice cream. Stay far away from it. Run from that temptation. Don't make eating right harder on yourself than it has to be. I'm teasing (a little), but seriously, you cannot mistreat your body and expect it to function the way God intended.

TIME FOR A CHANGE

Just as some people don't manage their diets well, others don't manage their time well. They're not living a balanced life; consequently they are stressed out, always rundown. They've gotten into a habit of overworking. They rarely relax; they hardly ever exercise. They never take any free time for themselves. Unless they make changes and bring some balance into their lives, one day, that's going to catch up to them. You can live stressed out for a while, especially when you're young. But don't be surprised when your body suffers the consequences.

It's much better to develop good habits right now. Look at the way you live, and ask, "Why am I doing what I'm doing? Is this something that's been passed down to me by my family? Is this a good habit? Is it helping me become a better person?" If, in your analysis, you discover some habits that are not productive or profitable, dare to make the changes that will help you to replace them. Make sure that you're not allowing anything but God to master you.

I'm familiar with a woman who was trying to quit smoking, after having been addicted to cigarettes for many years. She was determined that "this time" she was going to stop. And she did well for several weeks. But one day, she had an argument with her husband. She became aggravated and upset, so she went down to the store and bought a package of cigarettes. She thought, *I'll show him, I'm going to smoke this whole pack!*

But when she started to light up the first cigarette, something down inside her said, "You are about to waste all you've been through. If you smoke that cigarette, you will have to start all over and retrain yourself from the beginning, just because you can't control your emotions."

When she thought about the toil and discipline it had taken to kick the habit, and about all she had been through, and how much she had already endured to get to that point, she made a decision. She put down those cigarettes and determined never to pick them up again.

You will always have plenty of excuses and rationalizations why you should not change. You can usually find a reason to give up, turn around, go back, and keep living the same way you've always lived. Don't be surprised when you are tested. Simply remember that the Scripture says, "There is no temptation that will come to you that you can't overcome. God will always make a way of escape." [39] No matter how intense the pressure, or how difficult it seems, you need to know that you can withstand it. God will help you. He will make a way of escape, but you must take it.

If you see an area where you're not responding in a positive manner, don't make excuses. Take responsibility and say, "I recognize what's happening and I choose to change. I'm going to develop better habits."

In reality, it's not so much that we *break* bad habits; we must *replace* them. In other words, if you have a problem with worry, and your mind is always racing ninety miles per hour — worried about your children, worried about your finances, worried about your health — you need to recognize that worry is a bad habit you've developed. It is hard to worry and trust God at the same time. God wants your mind to be at peace. You can rest assured, knowing that God has you in the palm of His hand. When you've been worrying for a long time, however, it's almost second nature to you; you don't even think about it. You just get up in the morning and start worrying about what the day will bring.

In most cases, you can't simply decide to stop worrying. You have to replace the negative thoughts with positive faith-filled thoughts. Then every time you're tempted to worry, use that temptation as a reminder to dwell on good things. The Scripture tells us to "Dwell on things that are pure, things that are wholesome, things that are of a good report." [40] If you will replace those thoughts of worry with thoughts of hope, faith, and victory, then you will retrain your mind. Do that day in and day out, and before long, you will have formed a habit of dwelling on good things, and you'll have broken that old habit of worry.

The key to success is to find something with which you can replace the negative habit. If you habitually run to the kitchen and eat every time you are stressed out, find someplace else to go, something else to do. When you feel tense, go outside and take a walk. It doesn't have to be a two-mile jog. Simply walk around the block or down the street. When you come back, stay busy and stay out of the kitchen!

"Practice makes perfect," the saying goes. That may be so, but sometimes we practice the wrong things. I've had people tell me, "Joel, I'm just a real negative person. My parents were negative. My grandparents were negative. This is just who I am."

With all due respect, that's *not* who you really are. That's who you are *allowing* yourself to be. That is not the person God made you to be. God made you to be free. He didn't make you to be bound by addictions. He didn't make you to be disorganized, hot-tempered, frustrated, or negative. God made you as a person of excellence. He made you to be happy, healthy, and whole. But too often, we've developed wrong mind-sets. We tell ourselves, "I can't change. I can't break this habit." No, the problem is we're practicing the wrong things.

Interestingly, the Apostle Paul said in Romans, chapter 7, "The things I want to do I don't. And the things I don't want to do, I end up doing." Paul was struggling to do the right thing. In verse 19, he gives us insight into why he was having that struggle. He said, "For I failed to practice the things I desire to do." He was basically saying, I haven't developed good habits in these areas. I'm not practicing what I know I should be doing. Truth is, we are all practicing something, and the way to develop good habits is by practicing the right things. You may be good at losing your temper because you practice it a couple of times a week. Some people are good at being impatient because they practice it every morning on the drive to work. I know people who are good at being negative because they constantly practice negative thinking. Remember, repetition is what forms a habit. That's what puts us on autopilot. So we have to make sure we are practicing the right things.

For instance, every one of us should be practicing forgiveness. The next time somebody offends or hurts you, don't return evil for evil. Immediately forgive the person who hurt you; let it go and start practicing forgiveness.

Let's practice being disciplined in our spending and making good financial choices. Many people are way out of balance in their finances because they've developed bad habits, such as spending money that they don't have and charging purchases on their credit cards. It doesn't take a lot of wisdom to realize that paying twenty-some percent interest on a credit card is not a good thing.

I've heard people say, "Joel, I just can't make it without my credit cards. I can't live without them." You can make it, but you may be a little uncomfortable. You may have to suffer through that period of change. As my father often said, "Learn to sit on an apple box until you can afford a chair." What he was really saying was if you'll use what you have wisely, then God will give you more. Many people today are praying for a miracle; they're praying for a financial breakthrough. I say this respectfully, but often we don't really need a miracle, we just need to develop better spending and saving habits. I know some people — if God blessed them with a million dollars tomorrow, a year from now, they'd be in the same financial difficulty. They'd have the same problems. Why? They have not developed good spending and saving habits.

We need to think long and hard before we buy something that puts us deeply into debt. Do you really need that fancy car? Do you really need that extra toy? Financial counselors say that if we paid with cold, hard cash for everything we purchase, in a year we would save an average of $900. Why? When you dole out that money, one bill at a time, it makes you think, *Do I really want to give up my cash for this item?* Paying cash is a lot more thought provoking than simply swiping a credit card through a scanner.

Keep in mind, financial pressure is usually listed as one of the top three reasons why modern marriages fall apart. If you want your marriage to last, develop good spending and saving habits. It is never too late to start doing the right thing. If you'll do your part,

God will do His. He will promote you; He'll give you increase, but first you must be a good caretaker of what you have.

A young couple at Lakewood had about $40,000 in credit card debt. They were embarrassed and distraught over it. They didn't see any way out. In the natural, it looked impossible.

Then one day, they took a step of faith; they swallowed their pride and met with one of our financial counselors at the ministry. That counselor studied their finances and gave them instructions in how they could overcome their financial problems, step by step.

The couple committed themselves to getting out of debt, and for three years they didn't go out to eat, they didn't take vacations, they didn't buy extra clothes. They lived on a bare-bones budget. It was uncomfortable. It was a sacrifice.

But they were overturning years of wrong choices, forming better habits, and establishing a foundation for years of right choices. They quit using their credit cards. They learned the difference between their wants and their needs. They started practicing discipline and self-control. Three years later, that young couple is totally debt-free and God is blessing them. They're seeing increase and promotion. And it all started when they decided to form better habits. They drew a line in the sand and said, "That's it. We're not living like this anymore."

The first step to overcoming any habit or addiction is to identify what's holding you back. But don't stop there. Make a decision to do something about it. Take action. Don't be too embarrassed to seek help. People struggle with chemical addictions, sexual addictions, and all sorts of other maladies. It may be an anger addiction. You just can't control your temper. Understand that you can change. Freedom is available. Don't believe the lie that you're stuck and you'll never get any better. God already has a path of success laid out for you.

But you must do your part and be willing to walk it out. The next time that temptation comes, the first thing you should do is pray. Get God involved in your situation. We cannot defeat bad habits in our own strength. Ask God to help you. When you feel your emotions getting out of hand, and you are tempted to rudely tell somebody off, pray right then and there, under your breath, "God, I'm asking You to help me. Give me the grace to keep my mouth closed and the courage to walk away."

The Scripture tells us, "Pray that you don't come into temptation."[41] It doesn't say, "Pray that you'll never be tempted." We're all going to face temptation. God says, "When that temptation comes, ask Me for my help." In any area that you're trying to change — even small things — seek His help. "God, I'm about to walk through this kitchen and I can smell the chocolate chip cookies, so I'm asking You to help me resist the temptation to break my diet." "Father, all my friends are going out partying tonight and I know down inside, it's not right. God, I'm asking You to help me make the best choice. Help me stay on Your best plan."

"Joel, that's difficult. It's hard not to go out with my friends, hard not to use my credit cards, hard not to speak my mind."

Yes, that's difficult. But living in bondage is even more difficult. Feeling bad about yourself because you know you're living below your potential is even harder. There's nothing worse than going through the day with little things holding you back that you know good and well you can beat.

Maybe you are struggling with addictions, or you battle with your temper or impatience. Possibly, you are living in mediocrity, simply because you are allowing something small to control you. Let me tell you what you already know: You are better than that. You are a child of the Most High God. You have His royal blood flowing through your veins. Don't just sit back and settle where you are. No obstacle in your life — large or small — is insurmountable. It doesn't matter whether it's a critical spirit or an addiction to cocaine, God's power in you is greater than the power that's trying to hold you back. Fight the good fight of faith. Don't let anything or anyone on earth master you. Your attitude should be, "That's it. I'm not staying where I am. I'm moving up higher. I know I'm better than this."

Tap into God's power within you and stop saying, "I can't break that habit." Instead, start declaring every day: "I am free. I can do all things through Christ. No weapon formed against me is ever going to prosper." Remember what Jesus said: "Whom the Son sets free is free indeed." Start declaring that over your own life.

It says in Philippians, chapter 2, we have to work out our salvation. That means we have all these good things on the inside, but we must do our part to see those things brought to fruition in our lives. You have the seed of Almighty God. He's already put in you self-control, discipline, kindness, forgiveness, patience, and more. Because of your faith in

Him, these qualities are already in you, but it's up to each one of us to work it out. The good does not come into being automatically. It comes about only when we make good choices. Not once in a while, but consistently, over and over again.

My personality type is such that I am intensely goal oriented. I'm structured and organized. If I tell you I'm going to be somewhere at noon, I'm not going to be ten minutes late; I'm going to be ten minutes early. I'm disciplined when it comes to getting things done.

Even with the good in our personalities, there are always other areas that we have to work on. While I am naturally disciplined and focused, I'm not naturally patient. I don't like to wait. I like to get somewhere, get it done, and move on. It's easy for me to be impatient, so I realize that's an area I have to improve. I can't just sit back and say, "Well, I'm not a patient person; that's not the way God made me." No, I know patience is on the inside of me, but I have to do my part to work it out. Sometimes it's funny how God will use people and circumstances to try to help us come up higher.

For instance, the freeway system in Houston has taught me a whole lot about patience. I used to practice being stressed out and uptight every time traffic backed up. Now I've learned to relax, go with the flow, and stay in peace. I've worked some of that patience from the inside to the outside, to my thoughts, to my behavior, to my attitude.

Also God has used my beautiful wife, Victoria, to help me work out my salvation. When we first got married, and we were about to leave the house to go somewhere, I'd say, "Victoria, are you ready?"

She'd say, "Yes, I'm ready. I'll be right there."

With my personality type, I would get in the car and wait. After all, to me, "I'm ready" means we're leaving right now. But Victoria's personality is laid-back and easy-going; nothing's a big deal. She's the most patient person in the world. So when she says, "I'm ready," she means that as a relative term. She means, "I'm generally ready, so in the next ten or fifteen minutes, I'll begin to mosey my way toward the back door."

When this happened in the early days of our marriage, I used to sit in our car and get frustrated and aggravated. "I thought she said she was ready," I'd fume to myself. "When is she coming?"

Now, after more than twenty years of marriage, I've learned that when Victoria says,

"I'm ready," it is similar to the two-minute warning in football. The clock says two minutes to go, but if you know anything about football, you understand that it is going to be at least another ten or fifteen minutes. Now, when Victoria says she's ready, I just go sit down, look over some sermon notes, watch television, or relax for a few minutes. I stay in peace, rather than getting uptight. God has used Victoria to bring patience out of me!

How did I develop patience? By practicing it. Over time, I developed better habits.

Maybe patience is not a problem for you; you may be the most patient person in the world. But you spend half your life discouraged and depressed. You too must work the joy from the inside to the outside. You need to get up in the morning and say with David, "This is the day that the Lord has made. I will rejoice and be glad. I'm going to be happy today." Focus on what's right; not on what's wrong. Work out your salvation. Don't believe those lies that you've given birth to before: "I just can't control my temper. I'm just hotheaded." No, self-control is in you; God put it in there. The problem is you just haven't worked it out yet.

The way you work it out is by exercising your muscles in that area. If you want to work out kindness, start by encouraging people. Start giving compliments. You can't sit back and wait for God to change you into a kind, loving person. You must work it out by developing a habit of being kind to people.

Moreover, we should always keep new goals in front of us. Our attitude should be, I'm going to practice treating my family better. I'm going to come up higher in how I honor and respect my spouse. I'm going to be more loving and generous to my children. Don't just work on overcoming bad habits; work on strengthening and improving good habits.

You may have some areas in your life that you need to get under control. God is saying, "Don't put it off any longer. Today is the day to start. Today can be a new beginning." If you'll take this to heart and be willing to press past the pain of change, a year from now, you won't be the same person. You'll be free from addictions, free from bad attitudes, free from the bondage that's been holding you back.

Make sure you are practicing the right things. Starve any bad habits and feed your good habits. If you do this, you will rise higher and God will pour out His blessings and favor in your life. Friend, don't let anything master you. Develop better habits. Get rid of anything that is not producing good fruit in your life.

Remember, your habits today will determine your future. Examine your life, take inventory of your habits, and when you find something that's not right, be quick to change. In the process, you will establish the habit of becoming a better you.

CHAPTER 17
DEVELOP A HABIT OF HAPPINESS

Many people don't realize that much of the manner in which we approach life — our attitudes, and our demeanor — is learned behavior. These habits have formed by repetition throughout the years. If we've spent years focusing on what's wrong rather than what's right, then these negative patterns are going to keep us from enjoying our lives.

We acquired many of our habits from our parents or from the people who were around us as we grew up. Studies tell us that negative parents raise negative children. If your parents focused more on what was wrong, living stressed out, uptight, or discouraged, there's a good possibility that you have developed some of those same negative mindsets.

I often have people tell me, "Well, Joel, I'm just a worrier. I'm just uptight. I'm not a friendly sort of person."

No, please understand, those are habits

that you have developed. And the good news is you can "reprogram" your own "computer." You can get rid of a negative mentality and develop a habit of happiness.

The Bible says, "Rejoice in the Lord always." [42] One translation simply says, "Be happy all the time." That means no matter what comes our way, we can have smiles on our faces. We should get up each morning excited about that day. Even if we are facing difficult or negative circumstances, we need to learn to keep a positive outlook. Many people are waiting for their circumstances to be worked out before they decide to be happy. "Joel, as soon as I get a better job; as soon as my child straightens up; as soon as my health improves."

No, the bottom line is if you're going to be happy, you need to make a decision to be happy right now.

Happiness does not depend on your circumstances; it depends on your will. It's a choice that you make. I've seen people go through some of the most awful, unfortunate situations, yet at the time you would never know they were having a problem. They had a smile on their face and a good report on their lips. In spite of their dire dilemmas, they remained positive, upbeat, and energetic.

Other people in similar circumstances — and some in far less severe situations — insist on wallowing in despair; they're down, depressed, discouraged, and worried. What makes the difference?

It's all in how they've trained their mind. One person has developed a habit of happiness. She is hopeful, trusting, believing for the best. The other person has trained his mind to see the negative. He's worried, frustrated, and constantly complaining.

If you are going to develop a habit of happiness, you must learn to relax and go with the flow, instead of getting frustrated. You have to believe that God is in control, and that means you have no need to be stressed out and worried. Moreover, you have to be grateful for what you have, rather than complaining about what you don't have. A habit of happiness boils down to staying on the positive side of life.

Each day is full of surprises and inconveniences, so you must accept the fact that not everything is going to always go your way. Your plans are not always going to work out just as you scheduled them. When that happens, make a willful decision that you are not going to let the circumstances upset you. Don't allow stress to steal your joy. Instead, be adaptable and adjustable and seek to make the best of a bad situation.

One of the best things I've ever learned is that I don't have to have my way to be happy. I've made up my mind that I'm going to enjoy each day whether my plans work out, or whether they don't.

Our attitude should be, *I'm going to enjoy today even if I have a flat tire on the way home. I'm going to enjoy each day even if it rains out my ball game. I'm going to be happy in life even if I don't get that promotion that I was hoping for.*

When you have that kind of attitude, minor irritations or inconveniences that may have stressed you out will cease to be a source of frustration. You don't have to live all uptight. Understand, you can't control people, nor can you change them. Only God can do that. If somebody is doing something that's getting on your nerves, you might as well leave that up to God. Quit allowing somebody else's quirk or idiosyncrasy to get the best of you.

If your husband is fifteen minutes late coming from work and dinner gets a little cold, that ruins your entire evening. No, don't be so rigid and set in your ways. Life is too short to live it stressed out. Besides, prolonged stress can damage your health and significantly shorten your life. I don't want to die early because I got upset every time I was stuck in traffic. I don't want to live with knots in my stomach because some person is not doing what I want him to do or because my big weekend was rained out.

It's not worth it. You can choose to be more flexible and have a more easygoing attitude. Think about this. Ten years from now, many of the things that you are allowing to create stress in your life won't even matter. You won't remember the fact that your golf game was rained out last Tuesday. You won't care that you were stuck in traffic.

One time, Victoria and I had the perfect vacation planned. We had been looking forward to it for several months. It was an opportunity for just the two of us to get away together and take a break for a few days. The closer I got to the vacation dates, the more excited I became. I had my tickets and I was ready to go.

My mother had been dealing with a hip problem due to a bout with polio she had suffered when she was a child. When the doctors had done their best to treat my mother with medicine, they decided that they were going to have to replace her hip, so they scheduled her for surgery. Something came up right at the last minute, and they had to reschedule that surgery. The postponed surgery date fell on the exact same day we planned to leave for our big trip. I had a tough decision whether I was going to go on vacation or stay home and take care of my mother. We decided to stay home. At first, we were disappointed; it was a bit of a letdown, but we decided that we weren't going to let that steal our joy.

Mother had the surgery, and that week while I was at the hospital visiting her, I must have prayed for twenty or thirty other people, too. At one point, I was going from hospital room to hospital room, as one family after another asked me to pray for their loved one. At the end of that week, I felt more refreshed and more relaxed than I would have had I gone on vacation.

We could have let that stress us. We could have said, "God, it's not fair. We had this planned for a long time. Why is this happening to us?"

Instead, we simply remained adaptable and adjustable. The Bible says in Romans 8:28, "That all things work together for good when you love the Lord." I don't know why Mother's surgery fell on the exact same day as our vacation. I don't know what all the factors were, but I do know this: God worked it out for our good. I know, too, even when my plans don't work out, even when things don't go my way, because I am honoring God and striving to keep the right attitude, God will make it up to me.

He'll do the same for you. When your plans don't work out, don't get negative and sour. Don't start complaining, "I can't believe this is happening to me. God, I just can't afford this delay." God may be protecting you from an accident. How do you know God has not allowed that delay so you can meet somebody He really wants you to know? Learn to go with the flow. Don't get upset and let minor interruptions steal your joy.

Sometimes our plans may be interrupted because God has somebody He wants us to touch or something special He wants us to do. Many times we don't even realize such "behind the scenes" events are happening, but God is using us.

Recently, my son Jonathan and I went to one of our favorite restaurants to eat. A large party had arrived ahead of us, and the hostess informed us that we would have a forty-five-minute wait. We couldn't wait that long and were disappointed, since we had really been looking forward to eating there. But we decided to take it all in stride. I told Jonathan, "Let's go down to that little hamburger place and eat." I hadn't been to that hamburger place more than twice in my life. But when we went in, I noticed a well-dressed man sitting at one of the front tables; he was all by himself. As Jonathan and I passed by him, I glanced at him, nodded my head, and smiled. No big deal. We proceeded to the counter and ordered our food.

A few days later, I received a note from that man. He said that he was at one of the lowest points in his life and that he had rarely ever prayed before, but that morning he prayed, and said, "God, if You are real, show me some kind of sign." In his letter, he wrote, "When my eyes met your eyes, something on the inside of me happened. I've never felt love like that before."

Now, what is amazing to me is I didn't feel anything at all — apart from hunger pangs. I just wanted to eat. Looking back, though, I realize God changed my plans on purpose. God interrupted my plans so that I could see that man, and in some small way, so Jonathan and I could be part of the answer to that man's prayer. Sometimes God may lead you an entirely different way, just so you can give somebody a smile, just so you can say hello. Your very countenance can give people hope. God can cause people to look at you and see His love and compassion.

I don't believe any of that would have happened if I had been stressed out. I doubt that I would have carried that same anointing if I had been all upset and frustrated because one of our favorite restaurants didn't have room for us.

When you are inconvenienced, and things don't go your way, don't give in to the temptation to get bent out of shape. Not only is it going to cause you problems, but it also may prevent God from using you in the way He really wants to.

Sometimes, everything that can go wrong will. When you have one of those days, dig your heels in, make a decision you're going to keep a smile on your face, and just go with the flow, knowing that God is still in control. Victoria and I were aboard a flight recently, returning home to the United States, when, for no reason at all, they upgraded us to first class. It was simply the favor of God that allowed us to sit in the front row of that plane.

We travel a great deal, so when I get back to town, I like to hit the ground running. We were scheduled to land in Houston around noon, and I had already scheduled the rest of my day. I wanted to go eat lunch at a favorite restaurant, play with our kids, go work out, and do a few other things. I had it all planned out, and I figured that since Victoria and I were going to be the first ones off the plane, we could get through customs and immigration rather quickly.

The plane landed and just as I had planned, Victoria and I made a hasty exit. Evidently four or five other international flights had landed just prior to our arrival, because the customs area was as crowded as I had ever seen it. The line was backed up all the way to the jetways. At least a thousand people stood in that line. One look and I knew that it could take an hour or two to clear customs and immigration, and that was going to throw my plans completely off schedule.

I decided I wasn't going to get uptight, but that I was going to believe for the favor of God. I sort of joked with Victoria, saying, "Watch this, Victoria. Somebody's going to come get us, and take us right up front." I prayed, "God, please give me Your favor. God, cause us to stand out in the crowd," and on and on.

The line seemed to surge with even more people, but I remained undaunted. I was expecting God's favor, so I had stood off to the side and momentarily got out of the line so I could look up toward the front. That's when I noticed a woman coming toward me. She was dressed in a uniform, wore a badge, and was carrying a walkie-talkie. She was some sort of official, I knew. I told Victoria, "Here she comes. She probably attends Lakewood." I was so excited. I knew she was going to take me up to the front of that line.

Sure enough, the woman came right up to me. She said, "Sir."

I smiled real big. I said, "Yes, ma'am," already reaching for my carry-on bag so I could step to the front of the line.

She said, "Would you please get back in the line?"

"God? That is not what I was praying for."

My whole day went like that. Not one of my plans turned out. But thank God, I have learned to be adaptable and adjustable. I've made up my mind I'm going to enjoy every day whether I get my way or not.

Make a decision that you're going to be happy even if you get stuck in traffic, even if the waitress spills something on your new coat, even if you have to wait in that long line.

Understand, God did not create you to be a negative-thinking person. He didn't make any of us to live depressed, stressed out, worried, or frustrated. God intends for you to be happy, peaceful, contented, and to enjoy your life. God wants us to be examples of what it means to live a life of faith. When people see us, they should see so much joy, peace, and happiness that they will want what we have.

Take an honest look at your life. Are you as happy as you know you should be deep down inside? Do you get up each day excited about your future? Are you enjoying your family? Enjoying your friends? If not, what is stealing your joy and causing you to get upset? Why are you worried? Identify what it is. Take inventory and then take it one step further. Begin retraining your mind in those particular areas.

Many times, you can make a small change — a minor adjustment in your attitude, or a minor adjustment in how you treat people; a minor adjustment in how you respond to problems — and it will make a huge difference in your life and in your level of joy.

Years ago, the Russian scientist Ivan Pavlov did an experiment with some dogs. He studied their habits and how they responded to certain situations. Every time he fed them, he rang a bell. When the dogs saw the food, they became excited and started salivating. They couldn't wait to eat.

Over the next couple of weeks, every time Pavlov fed the dogs, he made sure he first rang that bell. After a while, the dogs associated the ringing of the bell with the presence of food.

A few weeks later, Pavlov decided to try something different. He started ringing the bell at odd times when he wasn't feeding the dogs, just to see what they would do. Interestingly, every time he rang the bell, even though there was no food within sight or smell, the dogs began salivating. In their minds, they were about to eat. Pavlov called this a "conditioned response."

Something similar can happen in us. We can allow ourselves to develop all sorts of negative conditioned responses. For instance, we get stuck in traffic and almost instantly our blood pressure shoots sky high. We get all upset. Or maybe at the office somebody doesn't speak to us, somebody intentionally ignores us. Instead of letting it go and giving that person the benefit of the doubt, we get offended. We've conditioned ourselves to respond in a certain way. We've allowed these negative mind-sets to steal our joy.

To develop a habit of happiness, you must retrain those negative responses. When you get up in the morning, you may feel discouraged or depressed. You may not feel like going to work. But instead of dragging through the day, thinking, *Nothing good ever happens to me; this is going to be a lousy day,* break out of that rut. No matter what those circumstances look like, say, "This is the day the Lord has made. I'm going to enjoy it. I'm going to be happy today." Speak that out by faith. Every time you do, you are retraining your mind. You're forming a new habit of happiness. Just as we can form negative habits of defeat, discouragement, bitterness, or self-pity, we can get in the habit of enjoying every single day.

Train your mind to see the good. Be grateful for what you have and get rid of any negative conditioned responses.

Friend, there's too much sadness in our world today. Many people are even sick physically because they are living so stressed out, uptight, and worried. Granted, depression may be caused by a chemical imbalance, but I see too many people dragging around defeated and depressed because they habitually focus on the negative. They focus on their problems, on what's wrong, rather than what's right; or what they lost or can't do, rather than what they can do with what they have left.

Change your focus. You can have a tiny problem, but if you stay focused on it, it will seem to get bigger and bigger. Don't magnify your problem; magnify your God. Step out of doubt and step into faith. Get out of that discouragement and come over into joy.

Make a decision that you are going to live your life happily.

I don't mean that you feel on top of the world all the time. That's not realistic. I'm talking about being content. In fact, one definition of joy is "calm delight." That means you are at peace, you have a smile on your face. You are excited about your future. Sure, you may have some problems. We all have obstacles to overcome. But we know God is in control. We know He has us in the palm of His hand.

The key is to retrain our mind to move away from negative conditioned responses. I know some people who actually get depressed every Monday morning. They don't like their jobs, they dread going to work, and every week, they develop a bad case of the Monday Morning Blues.

Oddly enough, researchers purport that we are 70 percent more likely to have a heart attack Monday morning than any other time of the week because people are more uptight and stressed out on Monday than on any other day.

In contrast, the Apostle Paul said, "I have learned how to be content no matter what state I'm in." Think about that. He said, "*I have learned* to be content." In other words, "This didn't happen automatically. I had to train my mind to stay at peace. I had to train my mind to look on the bright side. I had to train my mind to focus on the good."

We must do the same thing. Happiness is not going to fall on us. It's a choice we have to make. Being positive doesn't necessarily come naturally. We have to make that decision daily. Our mind, left alone, will often drift toward the negative. If we don't stay on the offensive, little by little we will grow more sullen; we won't smile as much. Soon, we're not as much fun to be around. We start to find fault. We start to get critical.

Instead, refuse to allow these negative habits to take hold. When you get out of bed in the morning, put a smile on your face. Set the tone right at the start of the day. If you don't set the tone, somebody else will set it for you.

"Joel, if I smile or act as though I'm in a good mood, I'm just faking it, because really I'm depressed. I've got so many problems."

You need to realize that when you smile, it's an act of faith. When you smile, you're sending a message to your whole body, announcing that everything is going to be all right. If you will develop this positive attitude of faith, you will sow a seed for God to work in your life.

I read about a young couple in college,

studying to get their degrees. They lived in an apartment complex next door to another young college couple, so the two couples soon became good friends. They had a lot in common.

The second couple, however, seemed to get all the breaks. They lived in the corner apartment, and it was much bigger and nicer than the other units in that complex were. They furnished their apartment with brand-new furniture. The other couple barely had any furniture, and the pieces they did have were old hand-me-downs. The one couple wore nice clothes, the latest fashions, while the other couple wore the same clothes again and again. At one point, both of the men were trying to get an assistant teaching job at the university. Once again, the second man got it.

The first young man was extremely frustrated that he couldn't seem to get any breaks. To top things off, at Christmastime, the second couple received a brand-new fancy sports car from their parents. The first couple drove an old beat-up pickup truck. It didn't have any air-conditioning, and they lived in a hot and humid part of the country. Many times they'd be driving to class in the morning, sweating and miserable, and they'd look over to see their friends in that brand-new sports car.

As this sort of thing continued, the young man got more negative and more depressed. He started complaining about their circumstances, and before long he was at odds with his wife. They started arguing and fighting. Ironically, they had never before had problems in their relationship, but negative attitudes will quickly spread to every area of our lives and drag us down.

One day, this young man was in his statistics class on campus. He'd spent several hours entering an enormous amount of data into his computer. He was working on this long, complicated equation. He had to get the numbers all lined up. He got them in the right order in the right column, and then he hit the "enter" key on his computer, asking it to give him the answer. As he did, he sat back and folded his arms. He thought it would take ten to fifteen minutes for the computer to analyze and calculate all that information. But much to his surprise he looked up to find that the computer was already finished. He couldn't believe it. He thought, *That is amazing! It took me hours to put this in, and the computer gave me the answer in less than one-tenth of a second.* About that time, the professor came by and noticed that the student looked perplexed and befuddled.

"What's wrong?" the professor asked.

"Well, sir, nothing's wrong. I just spent all this time putting data in the computer, and I don't really see how it could calculate it that rapidly."

The professor smiled and said, "Let me explain." He told the student how the computer takes every bit of data, and it gives it either a positive electrical impulse or a negative electrical impulse, and then stores it away. Then the computer simply recalls the information and combines it in the right order. It does it so quickly because the information has already been categorized.

Then the professor said something that really got the young man's attention. He said, "The computer works much like the human brain. Before anything ever goes into our mental computer, before any sight, sound, taste, feel, or intuition gets stored in the brain, it's first stamped either positive or negative. That sensation is permanently stored in our memory. That's why sometimes you can't remember a person's name, but you can remember how you felt about that person." The professor went on to say, "But unlike a computer, every person develops a habit of mainly programming their mind positive or negative."

The professor's words turned on a light in

that young man's mind. He realized he had gotten in the habit of making himself miserable. Without even knowing it, he had been stamping everything in his life as a "negative." When he saw his friends next door, all he could see was what they had and he didn't. "They've got a bigger apartment . . . negative. They've got a better car . . . negative. They get all the breaks . . . negative." He realized that the reason he wasn't enjoying his life was that he was categorizing everything he was putting into his mental computer as negative.

Unquestionably, what you put into your heart and mind is what you're going to get out. Sure, you may have negative circumstances. Maybe you didn't get good breaks. Maybe you didn't get the position you were longing for. Now instead of automatically stamping it "negative" and storing it away, turn your attitude around. Remind yourself, "I know God has something better in store for me. I know when one door closes, God can open another door." When you do that, you will take that negative situation, turn it around, and stamp it "positive."

You can do this even in your most difficult times. Maybe you lost a loved one. I know that can be painful, but our attitude should be, "I know where they are. They're in a better place, a place of joy, a place of peace." When we do that, we're stamping that experience as a "positive."

Pay attention to what you're feeding yourself. Are you storing away more positive or more negative? You cannot mentally brand everything as negative and expect to live a positive, happy life.

"I got caught in traffic last week, and I missed an important meeting."

No, turn it around and declare, "Father, I thank you that you have me at the right place at the right time. I am not going to get depressed. I believe you're directing my steps and you're going to turn that missed meeting around and use it for my good."

When you do that, you're turning around the negative and stamping it positive. In the process, as you grow more accustomed to this sort of mind-set, you will discover that you are developing a habit of happiness.

Our brain possesses a fascinating function known as the "reticular activating system." It's a function through which our minds eliminate the thoughts and the impulses deemed unnecessary. For instance, years ago, my sister Lisa lived in a townhome right beside the railroad tracks. Two or three times a night, a train rumbled by, loudly sounding its whistle as it passed her window. That train literally shook that place. When Lisa first moved in, the train awakened her no matter how deeply she was sleeping. But after living there for several weeks, an amazing thing happened. Those trains could pass by in the middle of the night, and Lisa would hardly even notice. Several months later, Lisa was able to sleep all through the night.

One time, I stayed at her house, and that train came by in the middle of the night. I think I jumped three feet off the bed. It sounded like the world was coming to an end.

The next morning, I asked Lisa, "How do you sleep here with that train going by in the night?"

"What train?" she asked.

The reticular activating system in her mind processed the sound of the train going by and allowed her to sleep right through it.

In a similar manner, we can train our minds in such a positive fashion that when negative, discouraging thoughts come, they won't affect us anymore. When that thought of fear comes, learn to tune it out as Lisa did. Or that depressing thought of "It's going to be a lousy day" — tune it out. If you'll keep it up, before long, your mind's reticular activating system says, "He doesn't need this information. She's not paying attention.

Don't even send the thought of fear or worry." Certainly, that is an oversimplification of the mental process, but just as Lisa was able to tune out the sounds of that train, I believe we can tune out negative messages. We can tune in to thoughts of joy, peace, faith, hope, and victory, as we learn to turn around negatives and stamp everything positive.

"Well, Joel, my children are not doing well. They've gotten off course. I'm so worried about them." No, just turn that around: "Father, thank you that my children are blessed, they're making good decisions. I declare what Your Word says, 'As for me and my house, we will serve the Lord.' "

"Well, Joel, it's my finances. Gas prices are so high. Business is slow. I don't see how I'm going to make it."

No, tune that out and start tuning in, "God is supplying all of my needs. Everything I touch prospers and succeeds. I am blessed. I cannot be cursed."

Following the devastation of Hurricane Katrina, I was watching a special news program one day as reporters were interviewing people in New Orleans who had gone through the hurricane. Person after person told his or her story, and most of them were extremely negative and bitter, blaming other people, blaming the government, blaming God.

One young woman stepped up to the microphone, and I could tell immediately that she had a different attitude. She had a big smile, and her face almost seemed to glow.

The reporter asked her somewhat sarcastically, "Okay, tell us your story. What's wrong?"

"Nothing's wrong," the woman said. "I'm not here to complain. I'm simply here to thank God that I'm still alive and I have my health. I thank God that my children are okay."

The reporter was taken back. Everyone else had been complaining about not having any electricity or water. It was more than a hundred degrees and they had no air-conditioning. The reporter probed further, "Well, what about your power? Do you have any air-conditioning?"

The woman said, "No, I not only don't have any power, I don't even have my home. It was swept away in the flood." Then she smiled as she said, "I'll tell you what I do have." She reached down and picked up her Bible. "I have my hope, I have my joy, I have my peace," she said. With a radiant countenance, she continued, "I know God is on my side."

That woman chose to take a heartrending, negative, unfortunate situation, and she chose to turn it around; she stamped "positive" on it. She refused to tune in thoughts of self-pity. She refused to allow her negative circumstances to steal her joy. She was saying in effect, "I know God is still in control of my life. He said a little sparrow would not fall to the ground without Him seeing it. So I know He's watching over me. I know He's going to take care of my children and me."

Train your mind to see the good. Get rid of any negative, conditioned responses. Everybody around you may be complaining, but you can find the good in every situation. If you'll do what the Scripture says, you can indeed be happy at all times.

CHAPTER 18
HANDLING CRITICISM

"I can't believe she said that about me!" Tera said through her anger and tears. "I don't want to work with someone that I can't trust, someone who is going to say one thing to my face and then do the exact opposite behind my back."

"She didn't really mean it," Tera's friend Bonnie tried to console her. "She's always that way. She criticizes everybody; it's her way of trying to feel good about herself."

"Well, maybe so, but she didn't win any points with me."

Every one of us will have times when we are criticized, sometimes fairly, but more often unfairly, creating stress in our hearts and minds and tension in our relationships. Somebody at work or in your social circle speaks negatively about you or blames you for something, trying to make you look bad, or blowing some minor incident out of proportion. Usually, your critics have no interest in helping you; they are simply trying to drag you down.

Certainly, constructive criticism can be helpful. An insightful point of light presented by someone who truly has your best interests at heart can illuminate an area where you need to improve. Sad to say, most criticism is not intended to build up another person; quite the opposite. It is not given in the spirit of blessing, but is more often presented with an intentional sting. The criticism that hurts the worst is frequently undeserved and unfair. Such criticism is a reflection more of the critic than of the person being criticized.

I've found that unwarranted criticism is most often based on jealousy. It stems from a competitive spirit. You have something that somebody else wants. Instead of being happy for you, instead of keeping a good attitude, knowing that God can do something similar for anyone who trusts Him, jealousy rises up in the critical person. They try to cover their own insecurity by being critical, cynical, caustic, or snippy toward others.

The more successful you are, the more criticism you will encounter. If you get that promotion at the office, don't be surprised when your critics come out of the woodwork.

"Well, he's not that talented," someone might say. "She's just a manipulator, always playing up to the boss."

Or your friends may be fine as long as you are single. Once you are married, however, they start saying things such as, "I can't believe he married her. She has no personality whatsoever."

Unfortunately, not everybody will celebrate your victories with you. Not all your single friends may jump up and down when you marry the man of your dreams. Your coworkers may not sing your praises when you get that promotion. Sadly, for some people, your success evokes that jealous, critical spirit rather than appreciation and compliments.

Here's the key to handling criticism: Never take it personally. Many times, it's not even about you, even though it may be directed at you. If the critic weren't tearing you apart, he'd be complaining about somebody else. It's something on the inside of the critical person that lashes out at others. Unless they deal with it, it's going to keep them from rising higher.

One of the most important things I've ever learned is to celebrate other people's victories. If your coworker gets the promotion you wanted, yes, there is a tendency to be jealous. Sure, there's a tendency to think, *Why didn't that happen for me? I work hard. That's not fair.*

However, if we'll keep the right attitude and be happy for other people's success, at the right time God will open up something even better for us. I've found that if I can't rejoice with others, I'm not going to get to where I want to be. Many times, God has a promotion in store, but first He sends along a test. He wants to see if we're ready. When our best friends get married, while we're still single, can we be happy for them? Or when our relatives move into their dream house, and we've been praying for years to own a home but are still renting a crowded apartment. That's a test. If you get jealous and critical, your attitude will trap you right where you are. Learn to celebrate other people's victories. Let their success inspire you. Know that if God did something so marvelous for them, He can certainly do it for you.

If you are going to become better, you will need to know how to deal with critics — people who are talking about you, judging you, or maybe even making false accusations. In Old Testament times, these people were called "slingers." When an enemy attacked a city, their first priority was to pry the stones off the wall that was protecting that city. They would then sling those stones into the city's wells. The attackers knew if they could clog the wells with stones and interrupt the flow of water, eventually the people within the walls would have to come out.

Do you see the parallel? You have a well of good things on the inside, a well of joy, peace, and victory. Too often, we let the slingers clog up our wells. Perhaps somebody speaks derogatorily about you, but instead of letting it go, you dwell on it, growing more and more upset. Before long, you think, *I'm going to get even; I'm going to pay them back. They are speaking untruths about me; let me tell you what I know about them.*

Instead, make it a priority to keep your well pure. If somebody is critical of you, trying to show you in a bad light, recognize that is a stone coming your way. If you dwell on it, or get upset and revengeful, the person who threw that stone has accomplished his or her goal. Another stone landed in your well. Now your joy, peace, and victory become more restricted. They don't flow like they should.

Truth is, we all have some slingers in our lives, people who try to bring us down with their words or actions. They may be a friend to your face, but you know behind your back, they would shred you if given an opportunity.

The way you overcome unwarranted criticism is by not allowing yourself to take revenge or even harboring an attitude that wants revenge. Don't sink down to their level and start talking badly about them. Most of all, don't get defensive or try to prove that you're right and your critic is wrong. No, the way you defeat a slinger is to shake it off and keep moving forward. Keep your eyes on the prize; stay focused on your goals and do what you believe God wants you to do.

This is what Jesus told His disciples to do when He sent them out to various towns to teach the people, to heal the sick, and to care for their needs. Jesus knew His followers would sometimes suffer rejection. Not everybody would like them or gladly receive their message. Some people would get jealous and start talking negatively about them, trying to make them look bad. Jesus knew the slingers would be out there, so He instructed His disciples, "When you go into a town, whoever will not receive and welcome your message, when you leave that place, shake the dust off of your feet."[43]

Notice, He didn't say *if* they treat you

poorly, if they start talking about you and spreading rumors; He said *when* they do these things. Jesus did not advise His disciples to become defensive or worried. Nor did He instruct them to defend their reputations and set the record straight. He simply said, "Shake the dust off of your feet." That was a symbolic way of saying, "You're not going to steal my joy. You may reject me or speak badly about me, but I'm not going to sink down to your level. I'm not going to fight with you. I'm going to let God be my vindicator."

Sometimes when you leave the workplace, you simply have to shake it off. People backbiting, playing politics, trying to bring you down — leave it; don't lug that heavy, worthless load home. Shake it off. Sometimes even leaving a relative's house, you may have to say, "I'm shaking this off. I'm not going to drink of their poison."

"I heard one of my competitors at work is talking about me," Rick said. "I'm not going to take that. I'm going to fight fire with fire. I'm going to let him have it."

"You could do that," I told him, "but that's not the way to win. Instead, let God be your vindicator. If you'll stay on the high road, God will fight your battles for you. You never really win by sinking down to your critics' level and attacking them personally. Rise above that."

When somebody is critical or negative toward you, your attitude should be, "I'm better than that. I'm not going to let their stone clog up my well. I'm not going to let their jealous spirit poison my life. I'm going to stay full of joy."

Perhaps you have not been shaking things off, and recently you have let the slingers get the best of you; you've been dwelling on their criticism, fretting about who's talking negatively about you or who has rejected you. You feel sluggish because your well is nearly clogged up. It's time to clear out the rocks and keep your inner well fresh and clean.

Once the Apostle Paul was shipwrecked on a small island. He went to pick up some firewood and a poisonous snake bit him. The people thought he would die immediately. That's what it feels like when somebody criticizes us, when somebody is talking behind your back, trying to put you in a bad light; we can feel the sting of his or her words. I love what Paul did. One translation says, "He simply shook it off." It was as though he was saying, "No big deal. I'm not going to let this thing bother me. It may be poisonous, it may look bad, but I know God is in control.

I know God can take care of me."

Miraculously, that snakebite didn't even harm Paul. Although it was dangerous and poisonous, Paul knew the secret of simply shaking it off.

Many people let negative words or other people's opinions totally ruin their lives. They live to please other people and honestly think that they can be happy by trying to keep everyone else happy. They don't want anybody to say a negative word about them.

That's simply impossible. You have to accept the fact that not everybody is going to like you, not everybody is going to accept you, and you certainly cannot keep everybody happy. Some people will find fault, no matter what you do. You can be there for them a thousand times in a row, but they will remind you repeatedly of that one time when you couldn't show up. Life is too short to try to keep people like that happy.

Yes, we should be kind and loving, but don't spend too much time trying to please somebody who is impossible to please. Until they deal with their own issues on the inside, they're not going to be happy. Say, "I'm not going to play up to them. I'm not going to try to keep them happy, because I know no matter what I do or don't do, a month later, they're going to be running me down." Tremendous freedom results when you accept the fact that not everybody is going to like you.

The Scripture says in Proverbs, "A gossiping, fault-finding tongue is like a venomous snake." A person's words can poison your life, if you allow them to do so. The longer you think about it, the more venom goes into you.

If somebody relates something uncomplimentary that another person may have said about my family or me, I try to stop them as quickly as possible. I'll say, "I don't really want to hear that. I don't want that poison to get inside me." I've found it's a lot easier to shake things off if you don't know all the details. If somebody is talking about you, don't go home and call seven of your friends and say, "What did you hear about this?" Just shake it off. Remember, most of the time, it's not really about you. It's about the fact that they haven't dealt with that jealous, critical spirit on the inside.

We can't live with an idealistic view of life thinking, *I'm a good person. I'm kind and loving. Nobody is going to talk badly about me.*

Unfortunately, sometimes, the nicer you are, the more people will talk about you. The good in you seems to stir up the bad in them. They feel convicted by the purity of your heart. You can feed the poor; you can mow your neighbor's lawn; you can take in a person who needs a place to live temporarily. You'd think your critics would be happy. But no, here comes that jealous spirit: "Well, who does he think he is? Mr. Goody Two-shoes? Why does she get to work early every day? He's just playing up to the boss. Why is she so friendly to everybody all the time? She's just trying to get something."

The best thing you can do is ignore the slingers. They won't put forth the effort to be their best, so they feel like they need to tear you down to help ease their consciences. When you hear those negative comments or false accusations, just remind yourself, "No big deal, it's just another slinger. I've already made up my mind: No more stones are going into my well. I'm going to live my life in freedom."

Slingers' comments are nothing more than distractions, trying to get you to lose focus on what you should be doing. You shouldn't waste five seconds of your emotional energy trying to figure out why somebody said something or what they really meant. You only have so much energy each day. So shake off a distraction immediately so you can use your strength positively. Otherwise, if you allow yourself to focus on the distraction, you'll go to work and not be able to give it your best. You'll come home and not really want to interact with your family, because you will be emotionally drained. You got distracted and poured all your energy into something that really didn't even matter.

RUN YOUR OWN RACE

Recognize that you cannot stop people from talking negatively. If you are trying to be the "gossip police," hoping to make sure that nobody ever says a negative thing about you, you're going to live a frustrated life. No, accept the fact that certain people are going to make cutting remarks. But you are better than that; you don't have to drink of their poison. You can rise above it. You can stay on the high road and enjoy your life anyway.

I don't have time to sit around thinking about all the people who don't like me. I realize that every day is a gift from God, and my time is too valuable to waste it trying to please everybody. No, I've accepted the fact that not everybody is going to like me and not everybody is going to understand me. You don't have to try to explain yourself. Don't spend time trying to win over your critics; just run your own race.

I start every morning searching my own

heart. I make sure, to the best of my ability, that I'm doing what I believe God wants me to do. As I follow the Scripture and I feel in my own heart that my life is on course, that's all that matters. I can't afford to let critics and negative voices distract me — and neither can you!

Some people spend more time focused on what other people are saying about them than they do thinking about their own dreams and goals. But understand that if you're going to do anything great in life — whether you want to be a great teacher, a successful businessperson, or a champion athlete — not everybody is going to be your cheerleader. Not everybody is going to be excited about your dream. In fact, some people are going to be downright jealous. They will find fault and criticize. It is crucial that you learn to shake off unwarranted criticism. Because the moment you start changing so you can please people, you will be taking a step backwards. Sure, you could say, "I'm not going to show up early at work anymore because my coworkers are starting to talk about me." Or "I'm not going to buy that car that I really want, because I know people are going to judge, people are going to condemn me." No, I've found that no matter what you do or don't do, somebody won't like it, so don't waste your time worrying about it. Do what God has put in your heart and trust Him to take care of the critics.

One thing that I'm good at is staying focused. I don't allow what people are saying to distract me. I realize that not everybody is going to understand me. I also recognize that it is not my job to spend all my time trying to convince them to change their minds. I'm called to plant a seed of hope in people's hearts. I'm not called to explain every minute facet of Scripture or to expound on deep theological doctrines or disputes that don't touch where real people live. My gifting is to encourage, to challenge, and to inspire.

I've heard people say, "Well, that Joel Osteen; he's not enough of this," or, "He's too much of that." If I changed with every critic, I would be living in a revolving door! I believe that one reason God has promoted me is that I have stayed true to who I am. I refuse to let people talk me out of doing what I know in my heart God wants me to do.

Maybe you need to get free from trying to please everybody as well. Stop worrying that somebody might criticize you. Remember that if you are criticized when you are trying to make a positive difference in the world, you're in good company. Jesus was perpetually criticized for doing good. He was even criticized for healing a man on the Sabbath. He was criticized for going to dinner with a tax collector. The critics called Him a friend of sinners. He was criticized for helping a woman in need, somebody that they were about to stone. Jesus didn't change in a futile attempt to fit into everybody's mold. He didn't try to explain Himself and make everybody understand Him; He stayed focused and fulfilled His destiny.

This truth really helped to set me free. There was a time in my life when I wanted everybody to like me. If I heard one negative comment, I thought, *Oh, no. I've failed. What have I done wrong? What do I need to change?*

One day I realized it's impossible for everybody to like me, and if someone chooses to misinterpret my message or my motives, there's nothing I can do about it anyhow. Now I don't let my critics upset me or steal my joy. I know most of the time it's not about me. The success God has given me stirs up the jealousy in them.

If you're making a difference in your family, or at the office, or in your workplace, you will always have your share of critics. Don't allow them to stress you out. Simply recognize that the higher you go, the more visible a target you will be and the more critics will want to take shots at you.

The Apostle Paul had great crowds following him. But time and time again, people became jealous; they got all stirred up, and on several occasions ran him out of town. What did Paul do? Did he get depressed and say, "God, I'm trying to do my best, but nobody understands me"? No, he shook the dust off his feet. He was saying in effect, "It's your loss, not mine, because I'm going to do great things for God. I'm not going to allow your rejection or your negative words to keep me from my destiny." His attitude was, "Sling all you want to. I have a cover on my well. I'm not going to let you poison my life." I heard somebody say, "If people run you out of town, just get to the front of the line and act like you're leading the parade." In other words, shake it off and keep moving forward.

I love the Scripture "No weapon formed against us will prosper, but every tongue raised against us in judgment, You will show to be in the wrong."[44] You may have to endure some people speaking against you, but if you can just stay on the high road and keep doing your best, you will prove their criticism invalid. Moreover, God will pour out His favor on you, in spite of your critics.

Understand that your destiny is not tied to

what people are saying about you. Some critical people in Houston predicted that Lakewood Church would never be able to meet in the arena known as the Compaq Center. They told us we didn't have a chance. In fact, at a business luncheon attended by numerous high-level city leaders, one man told the people at his table, "It will be a cold day in hell before Lakewood Church ever gets the Compaq Center."

When I heard about that remark, I just shook it off. I knew our destiny was not tied to one dissenter. I knew that remark was nothing more than a distraction. I also realized that not everybody was going to understand our decision to move the church. I heard people saying, "Why do they need to move? Why do they want a bigger church? Why are they leaving their roots?" Many times, I was tempted to get in there and try to explain it, hoping to convince them that our moving was a good idea. I knew not everybody wanted to understand. And I guess today is a cold day in hell because Lakewood Church has now been worshiping God in the location formerly known as the Compaq Center since July 2005.

Friend, your destiny is not determined by your critics. God has the final say. Quit listening to what the naysayers are telling you and stop living to please people. Shake that off and keep pressing forward in life.

Another important key is not to allow the criticism to change you. We need to be tough on the outside, but you have to stay tender on the inside. Often we become hard and calloused by criticism. If we're not careful, when critical people talk behind our backs, it's easy to let their poison get on the inside of us and start to change us. But you must keep your heart pure and stay true to who God has made you to be.

Sometimes when people see little quirks in our personality, or even something about our appearance, they make fun of it. If we learn of it, we tend to overcompensate, and it starts affecting our personality and the way we carry ourselves. But we cannot let cutting remarks and insensitive words cause us to become self-conscious.

A high school friend of mine was popular, fun, and outgoing, but he had an unusual high-pitched laugh. One day, a couple of our friends started making fun of him, going around the school imitating his laugh. They didn't mean any harm. They were just teasing, trying to have fun. I noticed how that young man started to change, though. He quit laughing as much. He became much more quiet and reserved. Where he once was gregarious and the life of the party, little by little he tucked his true personality inside a shell. He lost his confidence, became insecure, and started overcompensating. That's what happens when we don't shake things off.

You may have some distinct features or personality traits. But know this: God made you like you are on purpose. If people are making fun of you or causing you to feel overly self-conscious, just shake it off. Don't let their comments or actions stick to you.

For example, I smile a lot. In fact, I smile all the time. I can't help it. I've been doing it since I was a little baby. When I was seven years old, I was in a car accident and I suffered a severe gash on my head. Some friends came up to the emergency room to see me, and they were worried that I'd be upset and crying. When they came in, I was lying on the emergency room table. They later told me, "Joel, when we walked in there, you were smiling from ear to ear."

That's just the way God made me. Sometimes people make fun of me for smiling so much. You'd think they'd be happy that somebody is smiling instead of frowning. I've heard people say, "Why does he smile so much?" Almost as if to say, "There's something wrong with him."

A few months after my father went to be with the Lord and I began ministering, somebody started calling me the Smiling Preacher. The nickname really caught on. Shortly after that, a well-known reporter interviewed me and asked rather sarcastically, in a demeaning tone, "What do you think about being known as the Smiling Preacher?"

My answer surprised him. I said, "I kind of like it. I'm happy. I believe God wants us to be happy, so that's just fine with me." His jaw dropped open, as though he didn't know what to think.

I don't want to allow what other people say or what other people think to change me from being who God made me to be. You too should be confident in who you are.

The other day I saw a parody that somebody produced about me. It was a television clip of me speaking and every time I smiled, my front teeth would *ping,* and a star rose off my teeth, sort of like a toothpaste commercial. When I saw the parody, I laughed — probably more than the people who watched it with me. I thought to myself, *That doesn't bother me one bit. I smile a lot. If somebody doesn't like it, I'll just smile some more.* Who knows? Maybe Crest or Colgate will want to sponsor our television program!

You ought to be able to laugh at yourself. Don't let unwarranted criticism create stress in your life. Stay focused on what God has in store for you.

CHAPTER 19
KEEP YOURSELF HAPPY

One of the most important keys to a better life is to keep yourself happy, rather than living to please everybody else. It's easy to take on a false sense of responsibility, thinking that it is our job to keep everybody happy, to "fix" this person, to rescue that person, or to solve another person's problem.

Certainly, it is noble and admirable to want to help as many people as possible, and it is always good to reach out to others in need. Too often, though, we get out of balance. We're doing everything for everybody else, but we're not taking any time to keep ourselves healthy. I've discovered that when I try to keep everybody around me happy by trying to meet all their needs, I'm the one who ends up suffering.

God does not want you to sacrifice your happiness to keep somebody else happy. At first brush, that may sound a little selfish, but there's a tenuous balance here. Your first priority is to take care of yourself. To do so, you must recognize that some people are still not going to be happy no matter what you do for them, no matter how nice you are, no matter how much time and energy you give them. They have their own issues with which to deal or things inside that they need to resolve.

You should not take responsibility for someone else's poor choices. If you do, before long, that person will be controlling you and manipulating you.

Maybe you are stressed because you are allowing someone else to dull your happiness — it may be a spouse, a child, a friend, or a neighbor. They won't do right. They're always dumping their problems on you. They expect you to bail them out of every problem and keep them cheered up. Now you are frustrated because you are spending so much time and energy on them. It seems like every time you get that person fixed up, he or she is back a week later with that same problem. If you continue to help them, you're not only hurting yourself, but you are doing them a disservice as well. You've become a crutch to them. Because as long as they know they can come running to you, making you feel guilty and talking you into solving all their problems, then they will never deal with the real issues. They won't change.

Truth is, some people don't really want to be helped; they don't want to change. They like the attention their perpetual dilemmas bring them. Sometimes, the best thing you can do for somebody like that is *not* to help them.

Consider a small child. If every time that child throws a fit, you come running over and give him exactly what he wants, he will continue that pattern. The child knows what he has to do to get his way, and he will try to use that to control you. But if the child yells and screams, and you don't give in, you just ignore it or reprimand him for his behavior, it won't be long before he realizes that throwing a fit isn't working.

The same principle is true for adults. As long as you allow somebody to pressure you into doing what he or she wants, he or she will continue to do it.

But, friend, life is too short to go through it being controlled and manipulated by people who refuse to make good choices on their own. Please understand: You are not responsible for everybody else's happiness. You are responsible for your own happiness. If people are controlling you, it's not their fault; it's your fault. You must learn to set some boundaries. Quit allowing them to call you at all hours of the day and night to dump their problems on you. Quit catering to them and giving in every time they throw a fit. Quit lending them money every time they make poor choices. Let them take responsibility for their actions.

You needn't be harsh or uncaring, but sometimes we can be so good-hearted and generous that we allow people to control us. At some point we have to realize that we are not helping that person anymore. Beyond that, now they are hurting us.

Many people go around all upset, frustrated, and discouraged because they've made the mistake of taking on a false sense of responsibility for somebody close to them who won't do what is right. They carry a heavy load, trying to fix the person, or trying to keep someone else happy.

You can be free from all that if you will just give those people to God. Quit trying to be the keeper of the universe. That's not your job. You can't make everybody do what's right. You can't make your children serve God. You can't force your relative to make good decisions. Take the pressure off yourself and let God deal with them.

"But, Joel, if I don't loan them money they may lose their house," I hear someone saying. "If I don't call him every morning, he will get angry at me." Or "If I don't give in when she throws a fit, she may not talk to me for two weeks."

All that *may* be true. But do you want to live the next twenty years like that? Or do you want to help that person get free? Because you are not doing anyone a favor by allowing him or her to control you. In fact, in a sense, you are hurting that person because you are allowing him or her to take the easy way out.

I realize that at first, it may be difficult to say no to the stress-inducing controller, but if you'll put your foot down and make these necessary changes, in the long run your life and that other person's life are both going to be much better.

Linda and Troy's marriage was miserable. Linda came from an extremely negative family environment where she had endured many unfair hardships growing up. Unfortunately, she dragged her unhappiness and negativism right into her marriage with Troy. If she didn't get her way, she would pout or throw a tantrum. Sometimes, she would pout for two or three days. She was always having some kind of crisis where she needed attention. She was miserable and she did her best to make everyone around her equally as miserable.

Troy was a good man and a good husband, so he did almost anything he could to keep Linda happy. He was always encouraging her, trying to fix her problems, and letting her know she was going to be okay. For three years, he catered to her every need, giving up his own happiness in a futile attempt to keep Linda happy. Then one day it dawned on him that she was never going to change. He finally was fed up. He realized that although he had good intentions, he was not helping her anymore; he was hurting her. He had become her crutch.

Troy boldly went to Linda and said, "Honey, I love you, but I realize there's nothing I can do to keep you happy. I've done everything I can. So I'm just letting you know that I'm finished trying."

Troy's honest and heartfelt statement stunned Linda, forcing her to look inside herself and deal with the real issues. Beyond that, as Troy followed through and no longer coddled her, Linda had to take responsibility for her own actions. That wake-up call took place more than twenty years ago, and today their marriage is stronger than ever.

If you are in a relationship with somebody similar to Linda, don't allow that person to steal your joy. Do not go through life unhappy because somebody close to you is unhappy. If they insist on making poor choices, choosing to live depressed and in the pits, be kind and courteous, but don't get in the pits with them. At the right time, and in a controlled voice, tell that person, "If you don't want to be happy, that's fine, but you're not going to keep me from being happy."

Certainly, there's a very fine line here, but you are not responsible for your spouse's happiness. Nor are you responsible for your children's happiness. All of us are responsible to keep ourselves happy.

If you are on the flip side of this issue, and you are the person who is doing the controlling, pardon me for being so blunt, but it is time for you to grow up and take responsibility for your own life. Quit relying on that other person to carry you. Quit demanding that your spouse cheer you up every day and work constantly to keep you encouraged. That's not fair to the other person. Stop manipulating that person when he or she does not comply with your wishes or do what you want. No, take responsibility and learn to keep yourself happy.

I'm not talking today about being selfish or self-centered. We should be givers. But there's a big difference between giving and allowing somebody to control you and make you feel guilty until you do what they want. God has not called you to be unhappy simply to keep somebody else happy. Again, if you are allowing that, the other person is not the only one at fault. You may have taken on a false sense of responsibility and now you are allowing them to control you.

If you are in a relationship where you do the majority of the giving and always encourage or rescue the other person, that is a clear sign that something is out of balance. You've become a crutch. And unless you make some changes, the relationship will continue to flounder. You must take a stand. You can do it in love, but you need to go to that person and say, "I love you, but I'm not going to allow you to keep dumping your problems on me and making my life miserable. I'm not going to let you keep draining all my time and energy. You have to take responsibility and learn to keep yourself happy."

"Well, Joel, if I do that, they may get their feelings hurt," I hear you saying. "They may get angry."

Yes, they might. But that is between them and God. When you stand before God, He's not going to ask you, "Did you keep everybody around you happy?" He's going to ask you, "Did you fulfill the call that I placed on your life?"

Ben was thirty-one years of age and still living at home. He was lazy and undisciplined, and wouldn't go out and get a job. He just liked to sit around the house and watch television. Ironically, he didn't think that he had a problem. He didn't see anything wrong with that lifestyle; in fact, as far as he was concerned, life was great.

Ben's parents catered to him constantly because they loved their son and didn't want to be too hard on him. Occasionally, they tried to get him to go out and apply for a job, but he ignored their requests and refused to take any initiative. Why should he? He had no motivation.

The situation continued year after year. One day, Ben's parents were so distraught by their son's sluggardly behavior, they went to a professional counselor for help. The parents explained the situation to the doctor and told him how their son was extremely lazy. "Doctor, on top of all of this, our son doesn't even think that he has a problem," one of the parents lamented.

The doctor's reply shocked the parents. He said, "Well, I agree with your son. He doesn't have a problem. *You* have the problem because you have delivered him out of all his problems." He went on to say, "You have buffered him from any pain, and you have helped him avoid responsibility for his own life. If you want your son to get better, you need to give him back his problem."

The parents were too stunned to speak, so the doctor continued, "You must stop making it so easy on him. Quit delivering him out of all his trouble."

It is difficult to understand, but it is not always the best thing to rescue somebody and make his life easy. It's not always best to solve his problems for him. Sometimes you have to say, "I love you, but if you're going to live in my household, you're going to have to get up and go get a job. You're going to have to start taking some responsibility."

The Bible says, "If you don't work, you won't eat." You may need to say, "If you don't go get a job, you're about to find out what it means to go on a long, long fast!"

I heard somebody say that there are two important qualities all of our children need to have. They need to be grateful and they need to be eager. If they're not grateful, they will take everything for granted. They will expect everybody to give them what they need on a silver platter.

They also need to be eager — eager to learn, eager to serve, eager to achieve, eager to be better than they are currently. Sometimes as parents, we like to make life too easy for our children. Victoria and I have some help around the house and the easy thing is to let the housekeeper make sure our children's rooms are clean. But I know that is not the best thing. As I write these words, our children are twelve and eight, and every morning they make their own beds, get their own clothes together, and get dressed by themselves. When they come downstairs, they have their chores to do. Sure, Victoria or I could do it ourselves, or we could pay somebody to do those same chores. But I know that if we make it too easy for our children, they will develop the wrong habits and mind-sets, and our excessive kindness will actually hurt our children later on in life.

Adults, too, need to be grateful and eager. I have a tendency to want to help everybody. I want to solve all their problems. "Let me do it for you." But I have to realize that's not always the best. Several years ago, I ran into a homeless man who was about my age. He asked me for some money, and I was about to hand him a twenty-dollar bill, but I felt a check in my heart and mind, so instead of handing him some money and going on my way, I engaged the homeless man in conversation.

As we talked, he told me his story, how he had gone from city to city and had lived a rough life. He tried to hold down a job, but it just didn't work out.

I felt compassion for the man, and I really wanted to help him, so I invited him to church. I said, "Hey, I'm a pastor of a church here in town. Where are you on Sunday mornings? I'll have somebody come by and pick you up."

"Oh, no; I can't come to church," he said. "I don't have time to come to church."

I thought, *Man, what are you going to be doing? You don't have to mow your lawn. You don't have to clean your house!*

The more I talked to him, the more I realized he didn't want to be helped. He didn't want to change. He preferred to take the easy way out. He just wanted my money. Please understand, I'm not saying he didn't have a hard life, but when people don't want to change, when they don't want to be helped, we do them a disservice by delivering them out of all their problems. I could have easily given him that money and been on my way, but I didn't want to do anything to prolong his misery. Yes, we should help the needy, but there comes a point where if you continue to help somebody who refuses to try to help himself or herself, you are actually hurting that person more than you're helping.

Too often, we are controlled by others more than we realize. "I've got to work sixty hours a week or my boss will look down on me. He won't invite me to important meetings. He'll leave me out."

No, recognize what's happening. You are being manipulated and you need to set some boundaries. Go to your boss and say, "Here's what I'm able to do. I cannot work late every night. I have a family. I have other commitments. When I am here at work, I'll give you one hundred ten percent, but when the workday is over, I will leave the work here and go home."

You need to confront it. Don't allow yourself to be manipulated or coerced into doing something out of guilt. Start paying attention to why you respond certain ways and why you do certain things.

Maybe you are operating more out of guilt than out of desire or destiny. You are working late night after night because you feel guilty about leaving when others in the office are staying. Or maybe you are helping somebody because you feel guilty, you're overcommitted, worn out, and run down because you're afraid you're going to hurt somebody's feelings. This is all rooted in that taking on a false sense of responsibility, trying to keep everybody happy.

You should not feel guilty because you can't meet the demands that others arbitrarily put on you. You must change how you respond. If every time you disagree with your spouse, you get the cold shoulder and life is miserable for the next four hours, that's a form of manipulation. The next time something similar happens, you need to address it. Don't respond the same way. "Well, she's ignoring me. I'll show her. I'll go to the ball game!" Or "I'll go play golf." Or "I'm going shopping!"

No, if you'll change how you respond and not give in and not play those games, it will force the other person to change how he or she responds.

Say a person invites you to an event, so you check your schedule and realize you are too busy to attend, but you feel the pressure to acquiesce. You know the person will get upset if you decline. You may even fall out of their good graces.

You must recognize that is a controlling spirit, and you need to be able to say, "I would love to go, I'm sorry. I'm just not going to be able to accept your invitation." If they can't understand, then that's their problem.

To reduce your stress, be aware of high-maintenance people in your life. These people are almost impossible to keep happy. You have to call them so many times a week. You must respond at their beck and call. If not, they're going to get upset; they'll be disappointed in you. And they'll attempt to make sure you feel guilty about it!

I've found that high-maintenance people are usually controllers. They're not interested in you; they're interested in what you can do for them. They're interested in how you can make their life better. If you fall into the trap of trying to keep them happy, you're going to be weary and worn out, and you're going to be frustrated in your own life.

Many years ago, I attempted to help a married couple. They were fine people and I really liked them. In fact, when they moved to another state, I gave them some money and I tried to stay in touch. If they ever needed anything, I was always available. But it seemed like I was never doing enough. They were never happy.

I was being kind and generous, but they never saw any of that. They continually found some reason to complain, to find fault, or to make me feel guilty, as though I was not doing enough to help them.

One day I realized that they are just high-maintenance people and I am not responsible to keep them happy. I can't make them like me. I can't make them be grateful. I need to just run my race and not allow them to steal my joy.

I continued to be their friend, but I had to step back and let them work on making themselves happy. That made me very happy! That's a very freeing way to live.

Examine how you spend your time and check your motives as to why you do what you do. Is it out of guilt? Is it because somebody is manipulating or controlling you? If so, make some changes. If you don't take control of your life, others will, and they may take you places you don't want to go. You must be secure enough in yourself to tell people no. If you refuse a friend's invitation to dinner and he or she gets upset, understand something: He is not responding out of love or friendship; that person is attempting to manipulate you. She is using you for what she wants.

A true friend understands. A true friend doesn't get upset when you can't meet every one of his or her requests.

These days, I get numerous invitations to speak in all sorts of venues, and I'm always honored to be asked. But between my obligations to Lakewood Church and to my family, I'm not able to accept most invitations, even those from close friends or people that I've loved and respected for many years. At first, it was extremely difficult for me to say no to requests, because I don't like to disappoint people. But I've learned that I must take care of myself. That's my first priority. After that comes my family.

The first few times I declined those invitations, I was nervous, wondering what people would think. *They may think that I've gotten a big head,* I fretted, *that I think I'm too important.* But every time those people wrote back, they said, "Joel, it's no big deal. It's no problem. Whenever you can come, the invitation is always open." That is a true friend, somebody who is not merely concerned for his own interests. A true friend will not try to pressure you and make you feel guilty when you don't do exactly as she wants.

It is liberating to understand that you don't have to keep everybody happy. More important, I really believe that if you live your life just trying to please people, you will not be able to fulfill your God-given destiny.

When I went away to college, after my first year, I knew deep down on the inside that I was supposed to come back to Lakewood and start a television outreach. I felt it so strongly. But I was concerned about what my parents were going to think. After all, my brothers and sisters had all graduated from college. My brother Paul had spent twelve years or more in study and preparation to be a surgeon, so when I left school and went back home, I didn't know how my parents would respond.

I talked to my father about it one day, and he was open to the possibilities. He said, "Joel, that'd be great. Just do what you feel good about doing." Daddy was fine with my leaving school and developing the television ministry at Lakewood. My mother, however, was a different story. Mother needed prayer! She couldn't stand the thought of one of her children not graduating from college.

That was tough for me. As I said, I don't like to disappoint people, especially my parents. But I finally had to make the decision to do what I felt good about. I had to follow my own heart. Of course, my mother eventually came around. I told her the other day, "Mother, I didn't graduate from college, but I'm doing pretty well today!"

Sometimes, you're not going to be able to keep everybody happy, even your closest loved ones. Of course, we should honor our parents, respect them, and listen to their advice. In the end, you have to follow your own heart. An intriguing Scripture verse says,

"They have made me a keeper of the vineyards, but my own vineyard I have not kept."[45] Solomon was saying, "I was real good at keeping everybody else happy. I kept my parents happy, I kept my family happy. I took care of all my relatives and my friends. But in doing so, I neglected to take care of myself."

Too often, we live to please everybody else, but we neglect to take time to please ourselves. We end up allowing somebody else to run and control our lives.

If you allow them, some people will draw all the time and energy right out of you. You would see your life go to a new level if you dared to confront those people and start making the necessary changes.

I'm not saying it's going to be easy. If people have controlled you for a long time, they're not going to like your putting your foot down. Always do what you must in love, be kind and respectful, but stand firm and make a decision that you will live in freedom.

If you are the controller rather than the person being controlled, you too need to change. You're not going to be blessed by manipulating people to get your way. Quit pressuring people into doing what you want. Take the high road, walk in love, and you'll see your relationships and life become so much better.

Let this be a turning point. If you have been living to please everybody else, or constantly trying to fix everything, rid yourself of that false sense of responsibility. Yes, reach out to others. Yes, be kind and be compassionate. But make sure that you're keeping yourself happy. After God, you are your first priority.

Friend, if you will run your race and not let people control you and manipulate you, you'll not only have less stress and more time and energy, but I also believe you'll be happier, and you will be free to fulfill the best plan that God has for you.

Action Points
Part 4: Form Better Habits

1. I will examine my daily routine and identify any habits that are affecting my life negatively. I determine today that I will begin to break at least one of those negative habits and replace it with a positive habit instead.

2. I will beware of negative conditioned responses; I will train my mind to see the good. I will relax and learn to go with the flow.

3. I will not be distracted by my critics. I realize that not everyone will agree with me, or cheer me on, but I will stay focused on what I am called to do. Today, I will seek fresh ways to use the gifts, talents, and resources God has given me.

4. I recognize that I am not responsible for the happiness of everybody around me. Today I will be aware that I am responsible for keeping myself happy. I will be kind to everyone around me, but I refuse to be manipulated. I will not take on a false sense of responsibility for the actions or attitudes of others.

■ ■ ■ ■

PART FIVE
EMBRACE THE PLACE
WHERE YOU ARE

■ ■ ■ ■

CHAPTER 20
EMBRACE THE PLACE WHERE YOU ARE

Do you know someone who is not happy with where he or she is in life? She is frustrated because she is not married, and her internal body clock is sounding an alarm. Or he is upset because somebody is not treating him fairly on his career path. They are constantly worried, trying to reason things out, trying to change things that only God can change.

I believe that we create much of our own unhappiness and frustration by constantly resisting and fighting against situations and circumstances occurring in our lives. We don't understand why our prayers aren't being answered, why things aren't changing sooner. "Why has this happened to me?" Consequently, we live with unrest and uneasiness on the inside.

Learn to relax and accept the place where you are. Admittedly, it may not be a great place right now. We all have things we want to see changed, things we want to happen sooner. If we really believe that God is in control and is directing our steps, then we must believe that we are exactly where we are supposed to be. We needn't be wrestling with life and resisting our circumstances all the time.

Yes, we should resist the enemy; we should resist sickness and other robbers of joy. Now, that doesn't mean that every minute we must be fighting and struggling. Some people seem to wear themselves out, constantly praying, resisting, and rebuking. They beg, "Please, God, you've got to change this situation. Change my husband. I don't like my job. My child won't do right."

No, turn all of that over to God. Your attitude should be: "God, I'm trusting You. I know that You are in control of my life. I may not understand everything that is happening, but I believe You have my best interests at heart. I'm not going to go around resisting and struggling. I'm going to relax and enjoy my life." Friend, if you can sincerely pray such a prayer, it can take an enormous amount of pressure off you.

The Bible says to "Be still, and know that I am God."[46] Notice, you need to get still. You need to be at peace with where you are right now. Things may not be perfect. You may have some areas in which you need to improve. But as long as you are living with worry and stress, you are tying the hands of Almighty God. If you could get to a place of peace, God could fight your battles for you. He can turn your negative situations around and use them for good.

Scripture records, "Those who have believed enter in to the rest of God."[47] Being in God's rest means that although you may have a problem, you trust Him to take care of it. It means that you may have a situation that you don't understand, but you are not constantly trying to figure it out. It means you have a dream in your heart, but you are not in a hurry, you're not frustrated because it hasn't come to fruition yet. In other words, when you are really in God's rest, you know that God has you in the palm of His hand. No matter where you are, you accept it as the place God wants you to be.

I'm not saying that God wants you to stay there, but if you are truly trusting Him, if you believe He is in control, then wherever you are — in either good circumstances or bad — that is where you are supposed to be. Maybe something unfair has happened; maybe somebody is not treating you right, or you are struggling financially. Still, that doesn't give you the right to live upset and frustrated.

We have to understand that God has promised He will use whatever comes into our lives for our good. He will use that difficulty to do a work in you. What you are facing currently may not be good, but if you'll keep the right attitude, He'll use it for your good.

You may be saying, "Joel, you don't understand my circumstances. I'm doing the right thing, but the wrong things are happening to me." Or "I'm in a lousy marriage." Or "People aren't treating me right."

Please don't use that as an excuse to live your life in the doldrums or in the pits. Consider the Old Testament character Joseph. He spent thirteen years in prison charged with a crime that he didn't commit. He could have constantly fought that. He could have spent all his time trying to figure out why the horrific events happened to him. He could have easily lived his life upset, negative, and bitter, but he didn't. He simply embraced the place where he was and made the best of a bad situation. His attitude was "God, this is where You have me right now. I may not like it. I may not understand it. I don't think it's fair, but I'm not dwelling on any of that. I'm going to keep doing my best, knowing that in the end, You are going to use this to my advantage."

That's exactly what God did for him. God will do the same thing for you if you will keep your attitude positively focused on Him.

You may be frustrated because you are not yet married. You're not going to be happy until you find a mate. Instead, relax and enjoy the place where God has you right now. Being frustrated will not make it happen any sooner, and perpetually fretting about your marital status may slow down the process. You pray every five minutes, telling God what to do and how to do it. You have your ideal man all picked out — what he should look like, what kind of car he should drive, how tall he should be, how much money he should make. "God, I've got to get married. I can't take it another month."

No, you have already expressed your desire to God. Why don't you just relax and say, "God, not my will but Yours be done. I'm turning this over to You. I believe You have my best interests at heart."

It is okay to be honest and pray, "God, you know I'd like to see it happen today. But I'm going to trust You and believe that at the right time, You are going to bring the right person into my life." That's what it means to trust God. You can quit trying to figure it all out on your own.

One of my favorite Scripture verses is Romans 8:28: "All things work together for good to those who love God." [48] If you can stay in an attitude of faith, God will cause every situation to work for your good.

"Well, Joel, these people at work aren't treating me right. I'm uncomfortable. I don't like it. I want to get out of this situation."

No, we can't pray away everything uncomfortable in our lives. God is not going to remove every difficulty from you instantly. He uses those things to refine us, to do a fresh work in us. In the tough times, God develops our character. The fact is, we don't grow nearly as much when everything is easy; we grow when life is difficult, when we are exercising our spiritual muscles, in the pressure spots.

Of course, none of us enjoys being uncomfortable, but it will help you to press through difficult times if you can remember that God is going to get some good out of your discomfort. You will come out of that situation stronger than before, and God is getting you prepared for greater things.

But you have to pass the test. If you are dragging around worried, trying to figure everything out, and fighting against everything that's not going your way, you will simply prolong the process. You must recognize you are where you are for a reason. It may be because of your choices, or maybe it is merely an attack of the enemy. Whatever it is, God will not allow anything to come into your life unless He has a purpose for it. You may not like it; you may be uncomfortable. But if you'll keep the right attitude, in the end, you will come out stronger and better off than you were before.

Understand that your faith will not instantly deliver you out of every problem. Instead, your faith will carry you through the problem. If God removed some of the things that you are praying for Him to remove right now, you wouldn't be prepared for the promotion that He has in store for you. He's using what you are currently going through to get you ready for the good things to come. If you are not getting your way, it doesn't mean that God doesn't love you. If your prayers aren't being answered in the way you want, or on your timetable, it doesn't mean that God is angry with you or that He is trying to punish you.

Get a bigger vision than that. Maybe it means God has something better in store. Maybe it means He's protecting you from danger up ahead. Or maybe God is just trying to do a work in you so He can take you to a whole new level. Why don't you quit resisting everything that's going on in your life? Quit fighting against everything that doesn't go your way.

"It seems like God never answers my prayers," someone may say. "He never does what I want."

Maybe God *is* answering your prayers; He's simply saying no. Or maybe He's saying it's not the right time. Or maybe He's saying, "I'm not going to remove that obstacle until you change your attitude and quit complaining about it." Make some simple adjustments, and you will see things begin to improve.

I thank God that He didn't answer some of my prayers, because sometimes what I thought was the best for me wasn't the best at all. Nevertheless, if you push and manipulate, trying to make things happen, God will sometimes let you have your way — and you will have to learn His lessons the hard way.

I've seen people jump into a relationship or a business deal that they didn't feel good about, but they wanted it so badly. God is a gentleman. If you insist, He will back off and let you do things your way. Most of the time when we do that, though, we end up settling for second best.

If events are not happening as quickly as

you would like, or if you are not seeing circumstances change in your favor, open your grip on the situation; relax and learn to trust God. Know this: God is on your side. He is not trying to hold you back. Nobody wants you to fulfill your destiny more than Almighty God. Nobody wants you to see your dreams come to pass any more than He does. He put the dream in your heart in the first place. Let Him lead you and guide you.

I believe one of the best prayers that we could ever pray is "God, not my will, but Your will be done." I pray it in some form every day: "God, open up the right doors and close the wrong doors." If you will stay open to His direction, and follow your heart, God will protect you. It says in Proverbs, "If you acknowledge God in all your ways, He will direct your paths."[49] One translation says, "He'll crown your efforts with success."

Not long ago, some of our staff members and I were flying to another city aboard a small airplane. The aircraft had only one seat on each side of the aisle. After we took off, I wanted to get my tray table out so I could make some notes. The tray table on this particular plane came right out of the side, beneath my window. There was a little sign that said "pull," so I pulled, but I couldn't get it open. It was stuck. My friend Johnny was sitting across the aisle, so I looked over at his tray table, which he had pulled out with ease, and his window looked exactly like mine. I went back to work, trying to extricate my table, yanking on it even harder. I thought, *I'm going to get this tray table out if it's the last thing I ever do!*

I tugged and pulled, and it still wouldn't come out. About that time, Johnny came over and started pulling on the table release, and he couldn't get it out either. One of our other staff members tried as well. Nothing happened. Finally, I sat down across the aisle in a different seat. That's when I looked up and noticed right above that window where we had been pulling was a little sign in big bold letters. It read, "No tray table this seat. Emergency exit only."

I said, "Dear God, thank you for not letting me have my way. Thank you for not opening up that door." Thank goodness the people who designed that plane knew there'd be people like me on board. They put a latch up top, where you had to use both hands to open the emergency door. Otherwise, pulling that latch may indeed have been one of the last things that I ever did!

Thank God, He knows what's best for us. Thank God that He's merciful and He doesn't always give us our way.

I've learned that when my prayers aren't being answered, or when things aren't happening as fast as I would like, that either means that God is protecting me from danger up ahead, it's not the right time, or God has something better in store.

The first year I went away to college, I applied for a job at the university television studio. The school owned a large, well-known production facility, and I'd always wanted to be a part of it. Television production was my passion. The first week of school, I met with the production manager in charge of all the cameramen and hiring all the assistants. At that point, I had several years of camera experience under my belt.

The production manager went out of his way to be kind to me. He took a couple of hours to show me around, and we seemed to really hit if off. When it came time for me to leave, he said, "Joel, I'll call you later this week and I'll let you know about the job."

That week went by, and I didn't hear from him. The next week, nothing. The following week, still no word. Finally, I called him, and he was always either busy or out of town. It was the strangest thing: I didn't think I would have any problem getting that job, but the door simply wasn't opening. Worse yet, I wanted it so badly, but I could see it just wasn't meant to be. Finally, I accepted it and embraced the thought, "No big deal. I'm just going to let it go."

In retrospect, I now realize that if I had taken that position, I probably would not have returned to Lakewood Church to start a television outreach. I know my personality. I would have been so caught up in the excitement and I would have loved it so much, I'm sure I just would have stayed right there at the university TV station.

But God knows what's best for us. Although that job looked great to me at the time, I didn't know where God was taking me. I didn't know what He had in store. Had I remained there, I would have missed what God wanted me to do at Lakewood, and you would probably not be reading this book.

Too often, we're shortsighted. We can see only a little ways down the road, and even that we see through a glass dimly. God, though, can see the big picture. He knows when something is going to be a dead end. He knows when someone is going to be a distraction that will hinder us from our destiny.

Some of the things you may be frustrated about right now, ten years from now you will look back at and thank God for not answering that prayer the way you wanted or for not opening up that door. You may not be able to see it right now, but that's what faith is all about. Why don't you trust God? Believe that He has you in the palm of His hand and know that when it comes time for God to open a door, no man can keep it shut. No obstacle is too high. Your enemies may be powerful, but our God is all-powerful. When God says it's time to promote you, you are going to be promoted. The good news is that your promotion will not be one second late. *Suddenly,* God can turn any situation around. *Suddenly,* God can cause a door to open. All it takes is one touch of God's favor.

Our attitude should be "I'm not going to live upset and frustrated. I know that everything is going to be all right. I know that in the end, it is all going to work out to my advantage."

You may be going through some tough times. But remember, God has promised He will never let you go through more than you can handle.

"Joel, I don't understand why this has happened to me. Why haven't my prayers been answered? Why did I get sick? Why did my marriage not last?"

Some things you may never understand this side of heaven. If you are always trying to figure it out, it will only bring frustration and confusion. Learn to trust God, and know that as long as you're doing your best, as long as you're keeping your heart pure before God, you are exactly where you're supposed to be. It may not be easy, but in the end, God is going to use it to your advantage.

One of the most important aspects of faith is trusting God even when we don't understand. A good friend of mine contracted cancer. I called him to encourage him, and I thought he'd be all down and depressed, but I was pleasantly surprised. He said, "Joel, I'm at peace. I don't like this, but I know God is still in control. And I believe in my heart that He's going to bring me through this thing."

Even in your times of greatest difficulty, even if the bottom falls out, you don't have to be distraught and let yourself get all worked up. Sometimes we think we always must be praying, resisting, quoting the Scriptures every minute. Certainly, there's nothing wrong with that. But remaining at rest, remaining in peace, keeping your joy, keeping a smile on your face, that's all part of fighting the good fight of faith as well.

If you're in a hard place, be encouraged in knowing that God is still in control of your life. He made your body. He knows your circumstances. Don't sit around depressed and discouraged. Your attitude should be "God, I'm trusting You. I know You can do what men can't do, and I'm committing my life into Your hands." That attitude of faith pleases God. People who have a made-up mind. People who say, "God, I'm going to trust You if I get my way or if I don't get my way. I will trust You in the good times or the tough times."

Recall those three Hebrew teenagers in the Old Testament who wouldn't bow down to King Nebuchadnezzar's golden idol. The king got so upset that he ordered them thrown into a fiery furnace.

The Hebrew boys said, "King, we're not worried about it. We know that our God will deliver us. *But even if He doesn't,* we're still not going to bow down." Notice, they embraced the place where they were, even though it was difficult, even though they didn't like it.

You can do something similar. Quit living frustrated because your prayers weren't answered the way you wanted. Quit being depressed because you're not as far in your career as you had hoped, or because you have a problem in your marriage, or in your finances. No, just keep pressing forward. Keep your joy and enthusiasm. You may not be exactly where you hoped to be, but know this: God is still in control of your life. Moreover, as long as you keep passing the tests, no forces of darkness can keep you from fulfilling your God-given destiny.

You can have that heavy burden lifted off you. You don't have to fight and struggle all the time, trying to change everybody and everything. No, just embrace the place where you are and believe that God is in control. He's doing a work in you. He's guiding and directing you.

If you are currently in a storm, or if you are facing some severe difficulties, hear God speaking to your heart these words: "Rise above it. Quit fighting. Quit trying to change things that only I can change."

Believe that God has a great plan for your life. Friend, if you'll learn to embrace the place where you are, you can rise higher. You'll overcome every obstacle, and you can live that life of victory that God has in store for you!

CHAPTER 21
IT IS WELL WITH MY SOUL

Have you ever noticed that it is in the difficult times that we grow stronger? That's when we are being stretched. That's when God is developing our character and preparing us for promotion.

We may not like it; stretching can sometimes be uncomfortable. But if we can keep the right attitude, we will come out better than we were before.

The key to passing the test is to remain in peace, at rest. When you're in peace, you have power. When you're at rest, God can fight your battles for you. Many people wear themselves out, frustrated because they don't have the job they want, upset because a child won't do right, worried over a health problem. No, turn all that over to God and be willing to go through tough times with a good attitude.

In Colossians, chapter 3, Paul prayed that the people would have the strength to endure whatever came their way. Think about that. The great Apostle Paul didn't pray that God would remove every difficulty. He didn't pray that God would deliver them instantly. He prayed that they'd have the strength to go through it.

Sometimes we pray, "God, you've got to get me out of this situation today. I can't stand it any longer. If it goes on another week, I'm not going to make it." But a better way to pray is, "Father, please give me the strength to go through this with a good attitude. Help me to keep my joy. Help me to keep my peace." Our circumstances are not going to change until we change.

But you may say, "It is so difficult. I have a serious health problem. And I have this situation at work . . ." No, you have the power of the Most High God on the inside of you. You can withstand anything that comes your way. You are more than a conqueror, a victor and not a victim. Sure, we'd all love God to deliver us instantly. Most of the time, though, that's not the way He works. Make a decision to turn the situation over to God and then stop worrying about it. Don't allow it to dominate your thoughts and words; instead, move to that place of peace and rest. Even though the situation may be hard, and you may not like it, you are growing.

God has a plan and a purpose for everything. We may not be able to see it right now. But God has promised He will not allow anything to come into our lives unless He can ultimately get some good out of it. This should take all the pressure off us. That means if our prayers aren't being answered in the way we want, God must have something better in store. He knows what's best, so you can believe that all things are going to work together for your good. Don't live stressed out when the pressure times come.

Determine in your heart and mind "I'm not going to be depressed because my business hasn't grown as I wanted it to." Or "I refuse to lose heart merely because my child is not doing right. No, I'm going to stay in peace, trusting God, knowing that at the right time, God is going to turn it around and use it to my advantage." That's an incredibly liberating way to live.

You may suffer from stomach problems, headaches, ulcers, and all sorts of other ailments; possibly, you can't sleep well at night, because your mind is perpetually rerunning images of you fighting against everything that isn't going your way. You're trying to change things that only God can change. When God is not moving in the situation, either it is not the right time, or He is doing a work in you. Center your mind in that place of peace where you can truly say, "All right, Father; not my will but Yours."

When you understand this principle, it makes life so much easier. You won't live frustrated because your plans didn't work out. You don't have to be disappointed for a month because you didn't get the promotion you wanted. You don't have to get upset because somebody is being unfair to you. You know that God is in control and He has you exactly where He wants you. As long as you keep trusting Him, God is going to fight your battles for you. That's what it says in the book of Exodus, chapter 14. "If you will remain at rest and hold your peace, then the battle is not yours, but the battle is the Lord's."

Consider this: God wants you to remain at rest, to keep your peace of mind. As long as we're upset, frustrated, and all bent out of shape, God will back away and wait. To show God that we are trusting Him, we must stay in peace; keep a smile on your face; have a good attitude day in and day out. When you are consistent, when you're stable, and when you're not moved by your circumstances, you are proclaiming, "I believe that God is in complete control of my life."

I used to play basketball with my friends

several times a week. One night after the game, it was still rather early, so I asked one of the guys if he wanted to stop and get something to eat. He casually answered, "No, Joel, I've got to go up to the hospital. I'm taking chemotherapy."

"You've got to be kidding!" I said. "You're doing what?"

"This is my second bout with cancer," he replied, "so I take chemo three times a week."

I was amazed. I didn't even know anything was wrong with him. He always had a smile on his face, always was upbeat, and had an attitude of faith. He looked as if he were on top of the world.

Other people in similar situations drag around, wallowing in self-pity, defeated and blaming God. But not him. He knew that God was still in control. Even though he didn't like his circumstances, even though he was uncomfortable, he didn't allow it to get him down. His attitude was "I'm not going to sit around feeling sorry for myself. I'm not going to let this disease take over my life. I'm going to deal with it and move on." And he did exactly that. Several years later, he's cancer-free. God has totally healed him. I saw him not long ago. He's as healthy as he can be.

You may be fighting some serious battles, but the good news is, God is bigger than anything that you're facing. He can make a way even when it looks like there is no way. Don't quit living your life. Don't let that obstacle be the central focus of your existence. Keep pressing forward, trusting God, and knowing that as you believe, all things are possible. It may look dark and bleak right now, but the Scripture says, "Weeping may endure for a night, but joy comes in the morning."[50] It doesn't matter what the situation looks like in the natural, because our God is a *supernatural* God. When you are trusting in Him, you can rest. You needn't be stressed out or worried. You know that everything is going to be all right. You know that God has you in the palm of His hand. As you continue in peace, God will make sure that you fulfill every single day that He has ordained for you. The Bible says: "No man can snatch you out of God's hands." That means no sickness is too great, no enemy too powerful. If God be for you, who dare even be against you? Even when you are uncomfortable, remind yourself that you will come out better than you entered that situation. Even in the worst-case scenario — if we die — we go to heaven to be with the Lord!

Some people's faith is tied to their circumstances: When their circumstances are good, their faith is up; when the circumstances are adverse, their faith is down. You don't have to live that way. When you know that God is directing your steps, you can be consistent. No matter what comes into your life, God will use that for your good.

Sometimes God may ask us to go through things to help somebody else. He might put you in an uncomfortable place so you can be the answer to someone's prayer.

"Joel, I can't stand my job. These people get on my nerves. They irritate me. I shouldn't have to put up with them."

Have you ever considered that God may have you there on purpose, so He can do a work in them? Maybe God wants you to speak a word of hope into somebody's life; perhaps He is counting on you to let your light shine. Maybe God wants you to plant a seed of faith, so He can change their hearts.

Mary Anne endured some difficult and unfair experiences growing up. Not surprisingly, her first marriage didn't last long, so she soon married a second man and set about making his life miserable. She wasn't trying to be difficult; she was simply so wounded and hurt, she couldn't trust anybody. She was a negative and bitter person.

Curtis, Mary Anne's husband, considered

leaving her numerous times. He had every reason, and nobody who knew the couple would have blamed him. But he knew deep inside that he was supposed to stay with Mary Anne. He later told me, "Joel, it was the most difficult thing that I ever did. I was uncomfortable. I didn't like it. I didn't understand it." But Curtis stuck with her and was willing to pay the price to get her some help. Today Mary Anne is healthy and whole, and their relationship is strong.

Mary Anne realized what a gift she had been given. She said, "Joel, what if Curtis had been like my former husband and had taken the easy way out? What if he had not cared enough to stick with me? I'd be in an asylum or a cemetery today."

As much as you desire to become a better you, it is important to understand that not everything God does is about you. Sometimes God asks you to suffer for somebody else. Sometimes God takes you through challenging experiences so you can help others in need. Precisely at that point, we need to say, "God, I'm trusting You. I believe that You are in control. Even though I don't understand this and it's not necessarily something I may have chosen, I'm going to stick with it, and with Your help, I will maintain a good attitude."

You may not always feel like doing it, but do it as a sacrifice to God because you love and trust Him. God rewards such an attitude. Don't give up on that husband or wife; don't give up on those children. Don't write off your self-serving coworkers. Keep loving them, keep praying for them and encouraging them. God is keeping the records. As you sow seeds to help someone else, God sees, and He will reward you.

Sometimes we can get so focused on what we want that we let it consume us. I've known people who are not going to be happy until they get married. They're not going to be happy until their business grows or until they get out of a certain situation. No, it's imperative that we turn those situations over to God and learn to be content right where we are. When we turn loose of our will, and our way, God works wonders.

My sister Lisa and her husband Kevin desired to have a baby, but Lisa just couldn't conceive. She went through all sorts of fertility treatments, and they spent a lot of money. After several years, the doctor said, "Lisa, I'm sorry. There's nothing more we can do for you. You are not going to be able to have any children."

Lisa was so disappointed and discouraged. She had spent a great deal of time, energy, and money. She was always praying, believing, and doing everything she could. She was nearly consumed by her desire to have a baby. And now she was just emotionally and physically drained. One day she got tired of struggling and fighting. She said, "God, I'm not going to ask You another time about having this baby. You already know what I want. I'm just turning it all over to You." She later said, from that day forward, she did her best not to worry about it. She no longer begged God for a baby. Instead, anytime she thought about it, she thanked God that He was still in control. Really, she was saying, "God, not my will, but Yours be done."

A few months after that, Lisa and Kevin received a call from a friend of ours about adopting twin baby girls. Long story short, they ended up doing exactly that. A few years later, they adopted another child, a baby boy. Today they have three beautiful children. But nothing changed until Lisa turned loose of her consuming desire to have a child.

Sometimes we can get so consumed with our dreams or overcoming an obstacle, that's all we think about, talk about, and pray about, and we're not going to be happy unless it comes to pass exactly the way we want it. That leads to frustration, and if we're not careful, possibly to resentment. When you sense that happening, you must get back to that place of rest and peace where you can honestly say, "God, I trust You. I believe that You know what's best for me. And God, even if this doesn't work out the way I want, I'm not going to be unhappy. I'm not going to let this ruin the rest of my life. I'm making a decision that I'm going to be content right where You have me today."

One of my favorite stories in church history is that of Horatio G. Spafford, a wealthy lawyer and businessman who lived back in the 1800s. Spafford's story is not the success story, however, that we seek nowadays. In fact, he encountered horrendous tragedy in his life. His wife and four daughters were on a ship crossing the Atlantic Ocean when the vessel collided with another ship, and all four Spafford daughters lost their lives along with more than two hundred other people. Spafford's wife sent a telegram informing her husband of the terrible news.

Horatio Spafford booked passage across the Atlantic Ocean to be reunited with his grieving wife. At one point, the captain notified him that they were passing the spot where he believed Spafford's daughters had died. Horatio Spafford stared solemnly at the rolling waves, and that night he wrote the words to what would become a beloved hymn of the Christian faith: "When peace like a river attendeth my way, when sorrows like sea billows roll, whatever my lot, You have taught me to say, It is well, it is well with my soul."

No matter what comes our way in life, we need to be able to say, "It is well with my soul. Life may have thrown me some curves, but it is well with my soul. All my dreams may not have come to pass just yet, that's okay. I'm not in a hurry. I know in God's timing they will.

"My plans didn't work out. But nonetheless, it is well with my soul. I received a bad report from the doctor, things don't look good. But I know God has another report. I know He can do what men can't do. And whatever happens to me, it is well, it is well with my soul." That's the kind of attitude we need to have.

You may need to get a new perspective. Perhaps you have been too focused on what you don't have, what you can't do, and what's wrong in your life. Maybe you've been telling God every five minutes what to do and how to do it, and letting Him know that you are not going to be happy unless it turns out exactly like you want it.

Make a decision to turn it over to God.

Psalm 55:22 says: "Cast your burdens on the Lord. Release the weight of them and God will sustain you." No matter how dark and gloomy it looks in your life right now, if you can release the weight of those burdens, you will rise higher and you will see the sun break forth in your life.

This starts by believing that God is in control. In the following chapters, we'll look more closely at how that works out in our lives, but in the meantime, you can decide right now that you will trust Him wherever you are. When you do that, the battle is not yours; the battle is the Lord's. Ask God to give you the strength to endure. And rest assured, He will take care of you, even in the midst of life's most vicious storms.

CHAPTER 22
STAY IN PEACE

Did you know that you can have peace even in the midst of difficult circumstances? Many people are trying to get rid of their problems, hoping they will then be happy; then they can start enjoying their lives. But God wants us to learn to have peace in the midst of the storms. He wants us to have peace even when things aren't going our way — when your boss isn't treating you right, you didn't get the promotion you wanted, your child isn't doing what he should. If we make the mistake of basing our peace on our circumstances, we'll never experience God's best, because something will always upset us. You're never going to get rid of life's little aggravations. You will never get to a point where you don't have challenges or opportunities to get discouraged. We have to change our approach to life.

The Apostle Paul experienced all kinds of heartache. People had done unfair things to

him, others had lied about him. Nevertheless, he said, "In spite of all these things, we
are more than conquerors." That's the kind
of attitude we need to have. Don't use your
faith to try to get rid of all your problems.
Use your faith to remain calm in the midst
of your problems.

Jesus was asleep on a small boat when suddenly a huge storm arose. The winds were
fierce and strong, batting the boat back and
forth. The disciples got all upset and were
afraid. They finally said, "Jesus, please get
up. We're about to perish!"

Jesus got up and simply spoke to the
storm. He said, "Peace, be still." Instantly,
the wind subsided, and the Sea of Galilee
turned to a glassy calm. The reason Jesus
was able to bring peace to that situation was
because He had peace inside Himself. He
was in the storm, but He didn't let the storm
get in Him.

Peace is not necessarily the absence of
trouble, nor is it always the absence of enemies. You can have trouble and conflict all
around you on the outside, yet have real
peace on the inside.

You may be upset and worried about some
aspect of life. Perhaps you are concerned
about your finances, or there's a situation at
work that is unjust or unfair, and you are let-

ting that situation rile you on the inside. Day after day, it weighs on you, draining your joy, your energy, and your enthusiasm. You have let the storm get on the inside, and you need to make some changes.

"As soon as I get through this, then I'm going to get back to being my normal self," you may be saying.

No, you know that when this challenge is over, there will be something else that can steal your peace. You've got to change your approach and stop allowing those things to upset you. Instead, turn that situation over to God.

Understand that until you get to this place of peace, God can't really work in your life the way He wants to, because God works where there is an attitude of faith and expectancy, not attitudes of unbelief, worry, despair, and discouragement. Every day you will have opportunities to lose your peace. Somebody may be rude to you on the phone. You want to jump right down their throat. Instead, say to yourself, "No, I'm going to stay at peace. I'm not going to allow him to upset me."

Or perhaps your boss doesn't give you the credit you deserve. You didn't get the big promotion for which you were hoping. Say something such as "That's okay. I know God is in control. I know God has something better in store for me."

"Well, I'm upset because this man walked out of our relationship," Suzanne says. "It was wrong. It was just so unfair. I want to call him up and let him have a piece of my mind."

"No, hold your peace," I advised. "If you'll stay calm and at rest, God will bring somebody better into your life. He'll take what the enemy meant for evil and turn it all around and use it for your advantage. But you've got to do your part and hold your peace. Don't live life upset, worried, and frustrated."

Sometimes we lose our peace over things we can't change. You can't change the traffic in the morning. You might as well just stay calm. You can't make your spouse or your boss or your neighbor do what's right. Only God can. You might as well enjoy your life while God is in the process of changing things in the lives of people around you.

One time Victoria and I and our kids were going on vacation to Branson, Missouri. It was Christmas season and the airports were crowded. We had to change planes in Memphis, so we had a brief layover. We got off the plane and our kids were hungry, so we stopped to get them something to eat, and then we took off toward the gate. It seemed to take forever to get there. We had to catch a shuttle bus, and then we ran the rest of the way. When we got to the gate, the plane was still there, but the main door at the jetway was closed. I begged the woman behind the counter to get our family on that plane. I prayed for God's favor. I smiled real big. I was as friendly as I could be . . .

But none of that worked.

I don't want to sit in this airport for three or four hours waiting for the next flight, I thought. I could feel myself starting to get stressed. I had to make a choice right then and there: Was I going to keep my peace or was I going to give it away? I kept about half of it!

When we finally got to Branson, I got off the plane and an older couple approached me. The woman said, "I hate to bother you, but I've got to tell you, I really love you. I listen to you all the time; I just enjoy you so much." On and on she went, just heaping compliments on me. I started to feel better, and the sting of the missed flight didn't smart quite so badly. I noticed that her husband was looking at me as if to say, "Who in the world is this guy?" as his wife continued to gush. As we were finally leaving, I overheard her say, "Oh, honey, you know who he is. That's the guy that sings 'Achy Breaky Heart.'"

I thought, *It's going to be one of those days!*

We have to learn to keep our peace, even when people don't have a clue who we are, even when we get caught in traffic, even when we miss the flight, even when our plans don't work out.

How do you know that's not where God wants you to be? How do you know God is not protecting you from an accident? I love the Scripture in Proverbs that says, "Since the Lord is directing our steps, why do we try to figure out everything that happens along the way?" Just go with the flow. Quit worrying about things you can't change. Turn the situation completely over to God, knowing that He is in control of your life.

One of the best ways that we can show God we are trusting Him is by simply remaining calm. When you get to that point where the storm is raging, people are treating you unfairly, or maybe you've received a bad report from the doctor, or you just lost your job, in the natural you should be discouraged; you should be upset, but instead, you have a smile on your face. You still have a spring in your step. You are at peace. What you're really saying is, "God, I trust You. I know You are bigger than this sickness. I know You're bigger than this marriage struggle. I know You are bigger than my enemies."

Be the type of person who remains calm in the midst of the storm. When somebody is saying critical things about you, remind yourself (and others, if necessary), "That's okay, I know God is in control. I know God will fight my battles for me."

"Well, aren't you going to at least respond? Aren't you going to set the record straight?"

"No, I know God will be my vindicator. If I have been wronged, He will make things right."

Somebody may say, "I heard you got a bad report from the doctor. I'm sure you're all upset."

"No, I'm not upset," you can reply. "I'm at peace. I know my life is in the palm of God's hand."

"Well, I heard you're up against some big enemies," somebody else warns.

"Yes, that's true, but I'm not worried. I know God is bigger. Nobody can stand against my God. With men it may be impossible, but with God all things are possible."

Recently, I was waiting patiently in my car for a particular parking spot. The man was about to pull out, and I was sitting there with my turn signal blinking. I'd been there long enough that it was quite obvious I was going to pull into the spot as soon as it was vacated. When the driver backed out his car, however, he blocked me for a couple of seconds, and another car pulled in the spot right in front of me. I couldn't believe it! There was no doubt in my mind that the person who pulled into the parking spot must have seen me waiting. I had to make a decision. Was I going to lose my peace, or was I going to stay calm and overlook it? Was I going to get upset, or was I going to sow it as a seed and trust God to make it up to me?

In the natural, I wanted to blow my horn and let him know what I thought. The thought crossed my mind, *Well, I'll wait till he goes inside, and then I'll go let a little air out of each tire!*

But I decided, *This is not worth losing my peace over. I'm just going to bless him and move on.* I whispered a quick prayer for the rude driver and then pulled out to look for another parking spot.

Don't allow anyone to steal your peace. Understand that there will always be people around you who are able to aggravate you if you allow them. And usually you cannot just pray them away. Even if they did leave, God would probably send two more people to replace them! Maybe people at your office are gossiping about you, talking behind your back, or acting in some condescending manner toward you. They get on your nerves, and if you were operating under your own power, you would want to get in there and argue with them. But if you'll just hold your peace, if you'll be the bigger person and take the high road, if you will overlook those things, God will fight your battles.

Throughout Scripture, the person who truly trusts in God is compared to an eagle. The eagle has some pests, one of which is a crow. He's always squawking, always causing the eagle trouble. The truth is we all have a few crows in our life. You may have an entire flock of them, along with a few chickens and turkeys, as well!

Certain people can rub us the wrong way; they can irritate us if we allow them. We need to take a lesson from the eagle instead. When the eagle is out flying, often a crow will come up right behind him and start to pester him, aggravating and annoying him. Although the eagle is much larger, it cannot maneuver quickly. To get rid of his pest, the eagle simply stretches out his eight-foot wingspan and catches some of the thermal currents, and he rises up higher and higher. Eventually, he gets to an altitude where no other bird can live. The crow can't even breathe up there. On rare occasions, eagles have been spotted at altitudes as high as 20,000 feet, nearly as high as a jet flies.

In the same manner, if you want to get rid of your pest, you need to rise higher. Don't ever sink down to the opposition's level. Don't argue; don't try to pay somebody back; don't give them the cold shoulder. Be the bigger person. Overlook their faults. Walk in love and dare to bless even your enemies. In the long run, crows can't compete with eagles.

Friend, you are an eagle. You've been made in the image of Almighty God. Learn to live above your circumstances. Rise above the petty politics at the office. Don't let people pull you into strife and division and get you all upset or gossiping.

Always remember, the turkeys, chickens, and crows cannot live at the altitude for which you were designed to soar. God is in complete control of your life. He's promised if you will remain at rest, He'll make your wrongs right. He'll bring justice into your life. You don't have to worry, nor must you be controlled by your circumstances. You can do as the eagle and rise up above.

You won't see an eagle pecking around in the chicken coop with a bunch of chickens. An eagle lives in the high places, where he's close to God.

Moreover, when the storms come, an eagle doesn't simply go through the storm. No, he puts his wings out and catches a little more wind and he rises above it. He'll rise higher until he's completely above all that turmoil. That eagle is not concerned about the storm he's facing. He doesn't get upset. He knows he has a way out.

No doubt, he probably could fight his way through the storm, struggle and strain, and come out weary, worn, and all beat up. What a shame for him to live that way when God has given him the ability to rise above it.

Yet that is what many of us do. God has given us His peace. He's told us to cast our cares on Him. He said if we'll just remain at rest, He will fight our battles for us. Too often, though, we allow ourselves to become worried and upset. We let people steal our joy. We get bent out of shape if our plans don't work out exactly as we had hoped. Or maybe we're frustrated because our boss or our husband or wife is not doing what we want them to do.

You may not be able to change certain aspects of your life, but you can rise above them. Turn those situations over to God. Make a decision today that you are not going to allow those things to upset you and bother you anymore.

Interestingly, the crow has to flap his wings tenaciously simply to fly. He has to work constantly. The chicken can barely get off the ground; no matter how much he flaps his wings, he's not going far. Yet an eagle merely catches the right wind currents and he'll soar. He doesn't have to be like the crow, working and straining all the time. He just puts his wings out and rests in what God has given him, letting the winds carry him.

If you are always frustrated, trying to fix everything in your life, trying to straighten this person out for what he or she said about you, worried about your health, worried about your finances, you're acting like that crow. You're working and working, flapping and flapping. Friend, life doesn't have to be that way. Why don't you relax? God is in complete control of your life. He said He'd never leave you nor forsake you. He said He'd be the friend that sticks closer than a brother.

You may say, "I don't see how my business can make it." Or "I don't see how I can possibly resolve these problems."

The Scripture says that the things we see with our natural eyes are only temporary. That means they are subject to change. All it takes is one touch of God's favor, and God can turn around any situation. Suddenly, God can prosper your business. God can give you one idea or one new account that will cause your business to take off. God can bring somebody into your life who will really love you. He can cause you to be at the right place at the right time. In any situation, God can turn it around in a split second of time.

Make a decision today that you are going to enter into God's rest. You're not going to live worried anymore. You're not going to let people steal your joy. You're not going to give up on the dreams that God has placed in your heart. Perhaps you need to get a new perspective, a fresh outlook. Maybe you've been in a difficult situation for a long time. It just doesn't look like it's going to get any better. The storm is raging and you are discouraged. Life looks gloomy and you have found yourself living lower than you believe God intends. You need to do like that eagle and rise higher, above the circumstances.

At times, I have been on an airplane about to take off and the skies outside are gray and overcast, almost depressing. Then the plane races down the runway and takes off, climbing through the clouds. Finally, we break through the dismal skies, and behold, up above the clouds the sun is shining and the sky is bright blue. You can tell the air is crystal clear.

Now, here's what intrigues me: The sun was shining the whole time. I just had to get a higher perspective to see it. Similarly, the clouds in your life are only temporary. It may look dark and dismal right now, but the sun is up there, shining brightly. One of the best things you can say to yourself when you are tempted to get discouraged is, "This too shall pass. It is not going to last forever. The clouds will dissipate one day, and I will see the goodness of God again in my life."

Friend, get a higher perspective. God is on your side. There's nothing too difficult for Him. Lay aside anything that is weighing you down, so you can live free from worry, frustration, or discouragement, knowing that God is in complete control. When life gets tough and things don't go your way, don't be a crow or a chicken. Be the eagle God made you to be. Stretch your wings and rise to the level where God wants you to live. You were made to soar; you were made for more.

CHAPTER 23
REMEMBER THE GOOD

The Psalmist said, "I recall the many miracles God has done for me. They are constantly in my thoughts. I cannot stop thinking about them."[51] Notice, he said thoughts of God's goodness were constantly in his mind. That's a great way to live!

Too often, though, we remember what we should forget — our disappointments, hurts, and failures — and we forget what we should remember — our victories, successes, and the good times.

In the Old Testament, God commanded His people to celebrate certain feasts so they would not forget what He had done for them, and so they could pass on those inspiring stories to the next generation. Several times a year, the Israelites stopped whatever they were doing and everybody celebrated how God brought them out of slavery, or how God defeated this enemy, or how He protected them against that calamity. These celebrations were not optional; they were commanded, and the people were required to attend and remember God's goodness to them.

In other places, the Bible records how God's people put down "memorial stones." These large markers were to remind the people of specific victories God had given them. Every time they or future generations passed by a memorial, they would remember the mighty things God had done.

We need to do something similar. Take time to remember your victories, and celebrate what God has done in your life. Put out some memorial stones.

This is one of the best ways to build your faith and keep yourself encouraged. Remember the time that God made a way for you when it looked as if there was no way. Remember when you were so lonely, and God brought somebody special into your life. Recall how God has healed you or someone you know; think of how He protected you in the storm, guided you, blessed you. If you will get this awareness of God's goodness down on the inside, you won't go around thinking, *Well, I wonder if I'll ever get out of this mess? I wonder if God's ever going to work in my life.*

No, you'll be saying, "I know if God did it

for me once, He'll do it for me again!"

It would do you good to review God's goodness to you on a regular basis — simply thinking about the major victories in your life, the unexpected successes, or the times when you knew that God intervened in your circumstances. Remember the day your children were born. Remember how God gave you that job. Remember when God brought that special person into your life. Remind yourself how you fell in love and got married; thank God for your spouse and your family. Remember what God has done for you.

I do this often and on purpose. I think about the time I walked into a jewelry store in Houston, Texas, as a young man in my early twenties. I was minding my own business, hoping to purchase a watch battery, and out walked the most beautiful woman that I'd ever seen. The moment I saw Victoria, I thought to myself, *God, you just answered my prayers!* We dated for a year and a half and she couldn't keep her hands off me, so we got married! At least that's the way I remember it. But I don't take meeting and marrying Victoria for granted. That wasn't a coincidence or a lucky break. That was God directing my steps and causing me to be at the right place at the right time. When I remember that, it reminds me that God is in control of my life. It gives me confidence to know that if God was directing my steps back then, God can direct my steps today.

When we learn to recall the good things God has done, it helps us to stay in an attitude of faith and to remain grateful. It's hard to go around complaining when you are constantly thinking about how good God has been to you. It's hard to get negative and to veer off into unbelief when you are always talking about God's blessings and favor in your life.

"Well, Joel, if God would do something like that for me — if He'd bring me a beautiful wife, or if He'd bring me somebody great — I'd have something good to recall as well."

No, God has done something for every one of us. We merely need to go back and remember where we came from. Maybe you used to think or speak negatively. You were depressed and defeated. Today, though, you are rising higher; you know you are a victor and not a victim. Perhaps at one point you suffered with all kinds of addictions and bad habits. But God supernaturally delivered you, and today you are healthy and whole. Thank God for what He has done. Remember how He set you free. Remembering where you came from is one of the best ways to keep yourself encouraged.

Sometimes we take these things for granted. Some people don't even realize that it was God at work in their life.

One man I heard about was driving around in a crowded parking lot, trying to find a space. He finally got so frustrated, he said, "God, if You will give me a parking space, I'll attend church every Sunday."

Just then, a car backed out of the front row, and the frustrated driver pulled into the open spot. He looked up and said, "Never mind, God. I just found one."

Too often, we forget God is the Giver of all good things. God is the one who caused us get that "lucky break." He's the one who caused us to be at the right place at the right time. How many times have you been driving on a busy highway and you said to yourself, "Whew! That car almost hit me. Another split second and I would have had an accident." That was God's hand of protection. Understand that there's no such thing as a coincidence when your life is directed by God. When something good happens to you, be sensitive, recognize the work of God, and learn to recall it often.

Shortly after Victoria and I were married, I was driving on a Houston freeway by myself.

It was a Monday afternoon, and it had been pouring down rain for nearly twenty minutes. I was driving in the second lane from the left, and when I changed lanes I sloshed through a large puddle of water. My tires lost traction and the car hydroplaned. I lost control of the car and headed straight toward the concrete barrier in the center of the highway. I smashed into that median strip traveling at a speed of about fifty miles per hour. When I hit the barrier, it catapulted me back across the freeway and spun my car violently out of control.

I didn't have time to pray; I didn't have time to quote the Ninety-first Psalm. I didn't have time to call the 24-Hour Prayer Hotline. I only had time to say "Jesus!" As I spun back across that freeway, I found myself looking straight into the headlights of an oncoming eighteen-wheeler, a heavy tractor trailer truck. It looked like I could reach out and touch his front grill. I couldn't have been five or six feet away. I closed my eyes, expecting to hear the crunch of metal at any moment, assuming my life was over.

Somehow, someway, however, I suddenly found myself in the ditch on the other side of the freeway. I had crossed six lanes of traffic during rush hour in Houston, Texas, and no other vehicle had crashed into me!

After I checked to make sure I still had all my body parts, I climbed out of my car. As I did, I noticed that the eighteen-wheeler — the truck that had almost hit me — had pulled over to the side of the freeway and was backing up. It took about ten minutes for the truck to ease back to where I was.

The driver bounded out of the truck's cab and ran to where I was leaning against my car. The first thing he said to me was, "Boy, you must be living right."

I sort of laughed and said, "What do you mean?"

"I don't know how I missed you," the trucker said, shaking his head. "You were right in front of me, and I tried to swerve, but my rig is fully loaded. I couldn't do it. So, I just braced myself and got ready for the collision."

A quizzical look spread across the man's face as he said, "I know this sounds odd, but right at the last moment, I felt this pocket of wind push me into the other lane."

I thought to myself, *He may call it a pocket of wind, but I know that was the angel of the Lord. That was God's hand of protection.*

For me, that is another memorial stone that I can put out in my life. I know if it were not for the goodness of God, I might not be here today. But God showed up and made a way when it looked like there was no way. I don't take that for granted; I remember the great things God has done in my life, and I thank Him for them.

I encourage you to keep a notebook, something like a diary or a journal. When something happens in your life that you know is God, write it down. You know God opened up a door. Add that to your list. You know God spared your life or you know God spoke to you a specific word of direction; make a note of that, too. You were down and discouraged, ready to give up, when God quickened a Scripture to your heart and it lifted your spirits. Write that down. Keep a running record of the good things that God has done for you.

It need not always be something big; to others it may seem quite insignificant. But you know it is God guiding your life. You may unexpectedly meet somebody. They introduce you to another person, and that leads to you getting a new client. Write that down. Maybe you are driving down the highway, and you see a new billboard that sparks an idea that you take to the office. The bosses like it and your idea leads to a promotion. Recognize that is God at work in your life. Write that down.

Then on a regular basis, get that notebook

out and read about all the great things God has done in your life. You will be encouraged! When you recall how God opened up this door for you, protected you over here, restored you there, healed you there, your faith will increase. Especially in times of difficulty, when you are tempted to get discouraged, get that notebook out and read it again. If you do that, you will not go through the day discouraged and defeated. You will know that God is in control of your life. He is holding you in the palm of His hand, and He will take care of you.

CHAPTER 24
GOD IS IN CONTROL

To truly become a better you, it is imperative to believe that God is in control of your life. Too many people go around worried and upset. They're always trying to figure everything out. How am I going to get out of this problem? How can I change my child? When am I ever going to get married? Why won't my dreams come to pass?

But that's not the way God wants us to live. When we truly trust Him and believe that He's in control, we can rest. There's a peace in our hearts and minds. Deep down on the inside, we know that everything is going to be all right.

Many times, the reason we lose our peace and begin to worry is because we don't see anything happening in the areas we are praying about or believing for. Everything looks the same month after month, year after year. But we have to understand that God is working behind the scenes in our lives. He has already prearranged a bright future for you. And if the curtain were pulled back so you could peer into the unseen realm, you would see God fighting your battles for you. You'd find your heavenly Father getting everything arranged in your favor. You'd see how God is getting ready to open a door and bring an opportunity across your path. I'm convinced that if we could really see how God is orchestrating everything behind the scenes, we wouldn't worry. We wouldn't live stressed out anymore.

The fact is we all have difficulties; we all have things in life that can steal our joy, steal our peace. We have to learn to turn them over to God and say, "Father, I'm trusting You. I believe that You are in control. And even though I may not see anything tangible happening, I believe You are working in my life, going before me, making my crooked places straight, and causing me to be at the right place at the right time."

You may be trying to figure everything out, trying to solve every problem. But it would take so much pressure off you, and you would enjoy your life so much more, if you could just learn to relinquish control and start believing that God really is directing your steps.

The Bible reminds us, "For it is God who

is all the while at work in you." Notice, God doesn't work for a while, then go off on a two- or three-year vacation, and then come back and work a little more. God is constantly at work in your life. That means that although you may not be able to see it, God is arranging things in your favor. He is getting the right people lined up to come across your path. He is looking years down the road and getting everything perfectly in order, lining up solutions to problems you haven't even considered yet. He has the right spouse for you and the right spouse for your child. He has the best opportunities, the best doors He plans to open for you. God is constantly working behind the scenes in our lives.

"Well," you say, "Joel, I've been praying for my child for two years, but I don't see anything happening." "I've been believing for my finances to improve, but they continue to dwindle." Or "I've been praying for the right person to come into my life, but it's been four years."

No, you don't know what God is doing behind the scenes. Don't get discouraged just because you don't see anything happening. That doesn't mean God is not working. In fact, many times God works most when we see it the least.

When we're in one of those dry seasons

and we don't see anything happening, that is simply a test of our faith. We have to dig in our heels and show God what we're made of. A lot of people get negative and discouraged. "Well, I never get any good breaks. I knew nothing good would ever happen to me." "I knew I'd never get out of this problem."

No, you've got to zip that up. If you want to pass the test, you need to put a smile on your face and say, "I may not see anything happening, but I know God is working in my life."

"My child may not be doing right, but I know it's only a matter of time. As for me and my house, we will serve the Lord."

"My finances may look the same, but I'm not worried about it, I know I am blessed. I cannot be cursed. I know in my due season at the exact right time, things are going to change in my favor." When we have this attitude of faith, we will see God do great things in our lives.

Many times God is working and we may not recognize it. We need to be more aware of God's goodness. When you get a good break, when things change in your favor, when you find yourself at the right place at the right time, recognize that this is not mere coincidence; that is God directing your steps; that is God at work in your life. If you'll be aware, it will encourage you and build your faith.

Every one of us can look back in our lives and see critical moments that had to be the hand of God. It's almost as though we can connect the dots. I can see how I met this person over here and I got this break and it caused me to get this job and that's where I met my spouse. And if I had not been at this exact place, I'd never have gotten this other promotion and on and on.

That's not a lucky break; that's God's hand of favor. All the while, God is working behind the scenes.

I remember as a young couple, Victoria and I found a home that we really liked. It was a run-down house but on a nice piece of property. And we knew it was for us. In the natural, it didn't make a lot of sense. We were leaving a beautiful townhome. Yet we knew that's what God wanted us to do. So we took a step of faith and we bought the run-down house. The day we closed on it, we were standing out in the front yard and a Realtor stopped by and offered us much more than we had paid. We thought, "What's going on?" We didn't understand it. Come to find out, they were in the process of changing the deed restrictions in that neighborhood. And several years later, we sold that property for twice as much as we paid for it. That was God causing us to be at the right place at the right time.

Understand that the Creator of the Universe is working in your life. You may be doing the same thing you've done month after month, year after year, but then all of a sudden, you bump into a person who offers you a new position; you get one idea that takes you to a new level. You are at the right place at the right time, and you meet the man or woman of your dreams. God could have been working on that ten years earlier, getting everything lined up, and then suddenly it all comes together. Suddenly your due season shows up.

Here, years and years before, you could have thought, *Nothing's happening in my life. I'll probably never get out of this problem.* Yet, the whole time, God was at work. Things were happening behind the scenes.

I'm asking you to not fall into that trap of dragging through life with no joy, no enthusiasm, and thinking nothing good is happening. You've got to shake that off and start believing that right now — not two weeks from now, but right now — God is working in your life. Right now, God is arranging things in your favor. Right now, God is fighting your battles for you. Right now, God is making your crooked places straight. And you may not see it come to pass today, but here's the key: Every day you live with faith and expectancy brings you one day closer to seeing it come to pass. If it doesn't happen today, your attitude should be "No big deal. I know it may happen tomorrow. If it doesn't happen tomorrow, it may happen the next day. But whenever it does or doesn't happen, it's not going to steal my joy; I'm not going to live frustrated. I know God is in control and at the exact right time, it's going to come to pass. And in the meantime, I'm going to relax and just enjoy my life." You've got to believe God is in control. Believe God is working behind the scenes in your life.

The Scripture says, "God is effectually at work in those who believe."[52] Notice, His power is activated only when we believe. God can work in your behalf your whole lifetime and you never really get the full benefit of it because you didn't believe. Sure, you may get a break here or there, but when you really believe, when you really get up every day expecting good things, you're going to see more of God's favor. You're going to see what He's been doing behind the scenes.

And even when we have problems, even when things come against us, we have to believe that God already has the answer. In other words, that problem is no surprise to God. That child who won't do right. That financial difficulty. Being lonely. That doesn't have God baffled. God already has the answer. He knows the end from the beginning. God knows every trial we're ever going to face in the future. He knows every difficulty we're ever going to go through. The good news is God already has the solution. He has already made a way of escape. That tells me we don't have to live life worried. We don't have to go around all stressed out. God has it all under control.

When we're tempted to get negative and start complaining, we need to just turn it around. Our attitude should be "I know God is working on this problem. I know He's in the process of changing things, getting the right people lined up, softening the right hearts. And I believe God will not only bring me out, but He will bring me out better off than I was before." When we have this kind of attitude, it takes all the pressure off us. We can relax and enjoy our lives. We know God is in control. We know as long as we believe, God is all the while working for our good.

It's encouraging to look back over your life and see the things that had to be God. I know a young woman who met her husband on the side of the road. She had a flat tire on the freeway during rush hour, and he stopped to help change it. They started dating, and today they're happily married.

Now, think about the chances of those circumstances coming together. That had to be the hand of God. God was saying to that woman, "It's your due season. You've been faithful. You have passed the test. Now, let me show you what I've been doing behind the scenes all these years." He had that young man move from another city. He gave him the right job and worked the details of his life so he was coming down the freeway at the exact right time. Only God can orchestrate that.

Take the pressure off yourself and start believing that God is in control of your life.

When we were negotiating to get the Compaq Center, we needed ten votes from the city council members. We had worked for two years and had gone through several other votes. When it came down to the final vote, we had exactly ten votes — the minimum that we needed. But unfortunately, just a few days before the vote, we received word that one of the council members had changed his mind. He wasn't even going to show up at the last vote, equating to a vote against us — a vote we sorely needed.

We were terribly discouraged. The situation looked hopeless. It seemed that all our hard work and prayers had been in vain. But we decided to go back and meet with another council member to see if he might change his mind. He's a young Jewish man, a fine gentleman, but he had staunchly opposed Lakewood's acquiring of the Compaq Center for more than two years. Nevertheless, we thought, *What can it hurt to ask him to reconsider?*

At the last moment, the man with whom we met changed his mind. It was his vote that gave us the number we needed to secure the Compaq Center as the new Lakewood Church facility.

I talked to the man later and I asked him, "What was it that really changed your mind?"

He said, "Joel, I received a call from an old friend of mine. She's an elderly Jewish lady. I hadn't talked to her in years, and I really respect her. But she told me in no uncertain terms that I was to vote for your church." He went on to say, "Even though thousands of your church members called my office encouraging me to vote yes, and even though you and your team were very persuasive, it was that lady that changed my mind."

Now consider this: As far as I know, I have

never met that woman. I didn't ask her to call. To this day, I don't know who she is. All I know is that while we were doing all that we could do, God was working behind the scenes in a way we could never have done on our own. What we couldn't do in our own ability and strength, God caused somebody else to do for us.

God knows who can influence your life. He knows who should put in a good word for you. You may not ever even know how or why it happened. Why was somebody good to you? Why did you get that break? That was God ordering your steps. For years, He was working behind the scenes, but in a moment of time, it all came together.

Don't go through the day thinking, *My situation is probably never going to change. I'll never get out of debt. I'm going to have to live with this disease for the rest of my life. I don't think I'll ever get married.* No, when you do that, you are tying the hands of Almighty God. And when you are tempted to lapse into negative thoughts and attitudes, turn it around and say, "I know God is working in my life. I know my due season is on its way and one day, I'm going to see all that God has been doing behind the scenes on my behalf." Then go out each day, expecting good things, knowing that the Creator of the Universe is directing your steps.

A while back, I talked to a gentleman who designed the freeway entry and exit ramps for parts of downtown Houston near the Compaq Center more than thirty-five years ago. He told how he had drawn the exit ramps so people could pull into the parking lots with ease. Recognizing that large crowds would be drawn to the downtown arena, he worked with the city to time all the traffic lights in the area to make it easier, more convenient, and the most beneficial for people wanting to attend events at the Compaq Center.

I thought, *That's another sign of God's goodness. Over thirty-five years ago, God was working behind the scenes, prompting people to make it easier to get to our church, so people could find hope and help.* As the engineer and I talked, I laughed and told him, "I would have thanked you back then, but I was only three years old!"

Certainly, over the years, the arena has been used for basketball games, concerts, and other events. But I believe those were all secondary. I believe God had it planned out a long time ago that Lakewood Church would be sending out hope to the world from that location.

In the same way, I believe God is working

behind the scenes in your life. He is doing things that are going to thrust you to a whole new level. You may not see the culmination of it for years, so you must learn to trust Him. Stop worrying, don't allow yourself to become frustrated because your dream is not happening as quickly as you would like. In God's perfect timing, His plan for your life will come to fruition.

LOOK FOR GOD'S HAND IN EVERYDAY LIFE

Trust God even in the small things in your life. About six months ago, I received some disappointing news about a certain situation. It was going to be a pain to deal with, and I didn't know how it was going to turn out. At first, I was tempted to worry and try to figure it all out. In stressful situations such as that, if we're not careful, we can allow our minds to conjure up all the worst possible scenarios. Negative voices will tell you, "You're going under. You're not going to be able to pay your bills. You may lose your house."

You may have a pain in your side, and your mind frets, "Oh, no! That's serious; you'd better get to the doctor."

No, we must choose to control our thought life. We have to believe God is still working in the situation.

When I received the disappointing news, I was at the office, about to get on the elevator, but just then, off stepped a woman I've known since I was a little boy. She has always loved me and prayed for me. Yet because of our schedules, I probably hadn't bumped into her for four or five years. We greeted each other with a hug and before she opened her mouth, I knew what she was going to say. She said, "Joel, I still pray for you every single day."

I thought, *This is not a coincidence.* That was God ordering my steps to be at the right place, just so He could encourage me. That was God's way of saying, "Joel, everything is under control. Everything is going to be all right. Just stay at peace. Stay at rest."

If we will pay attention, we will often detect God's activity; we'll know that He is speaking to us, guiding us, directing our steps.

The den of the townhouse in which my parents once lived had large windows that looked out onto the courtyard. Birds flitted back and forth between the trees in the yard. One bird in particular became a favorite of my mother's. Every day a beautiful little cardinal would perch on one of the branches right by the window. My mother enjoyed having it there. She got to the point where she looked forward to seeing it each day. Like clockwork, the little bird showed up and spent the afternoon in the courtyard. This went on for five or six months, but eventually the friendly little bird quit coming by. I tried to give my mother my pet hamster to console her, but she didn't want that!

About a year later, my father went to be with the Lord. Now Mother was at home by herself. She had to make some adjustments. I'm sure at times she was tempted to be lonely, tempted to get down and discouraged.

Then one day, the little cardinal came back. To some people, that may have been coincidence, or merely an explainable function of nature. But to my mother and our family, that was God saying, "I still have a plan. I'm still in control."

Throughout life, if we will be sensitive, if we'll be aware, we will see the hand of God even in little things. That's God letting us know He's still working behind the scenes.

A friend of mine has what the doctors say is terminal cancer. They're not giving him any hope. But the other day, his four-year-old son came in with his Bible. He opened it up and said, "Daddy, I want you to read this Scripture right here." The little boy can't read yet, so he didn't know what passage he was pointing to, but when the father read the Scripture, it spoke right to his heart. It was John 11:4, a passage where Jesus said, "This sickness shall not end in death. But it is for the glory of God."

My friend took that to heart. He felt that was God saying, "I know what you're going through. I've seen every tear you've shed. It may not look possible to you, but remember, I'm the God of the impossible. Keep believing. Keep trusting. I'm still in control."

These little signs are simply glimpses that God gives us to build our faith. They are reminders He is working behind the scenes. Our responsibility is to be sensitive to His leading, to be on the lookout for His hand moving in our everyday circumstances. If you are tuned in to God, you will soon recognize that most of the time, you don't simply bump into somebody. You didn't just get a lucky break. You don't just happen to be at the right place at the right time. God has been directing your steps.

The last weekend that Lakewood Church met at our Northeast Houston location proved to be an emotional experience for me. I had attended services on that campus with my family my whole life. I had grown up there. Although I was excited about moving downtown, in a way it was sad leaving that place. Memories of so many marvelous things that had happened there flooded my mind as I drove to the final Saturday evening service. I was reflecting on all that God had done, when I looked up in the sky and saw a beautiful rainbow. It looked as though one end of it was literally touching the church on the northeast side, and the other was reaching out across the city of Houston toward downtown. It was almost as if God was putting His stamp of approval on our move, saying, "I'm pleased. Your work here is done. It is time for a new beginning."

You may say, "Well, Joel, I've seen rainbows before, and they never meant anything to me."

That's because this promise is for believers! You must believe God is at work in your life, and then be on the lookout to see His hand shaping the events. It may be that a Scripture jumps out at you one day while you're reading. Perhaps it will be a small bird in your backyard. Or maybe you will see a rainbow in the sky and know that it is your time to step into a fresh start. God gives us these little glimpses to build our faith, to let us know that He is still in control and working behind the scenes.

Even in our dark times, God is still working in our lives. Some young parents told me about their daughter who is now in heaven. When she was three years old, she contracted a serious illness that confined her to bed as death ominously approached. The parents were distraught and in so much pain. They rarely left their daughter's side at the hospital.

Toward the end, the little girl drifted in and out of a coma. The parents knew they were about to lose her. But just before she died, she smiled with the most peaceful look on her face, and said, "Look, Mommy. Look, Daddy. Jesus is saying it's okay to come." She closed her eyes and breathed her final breath.

Even when we don't think that we'll ever smile again, God is there. He is the friend who sticks closer than a brother. He has a new beginning for you. The Bible says, "Weeping may endure for a night, but joy comes in the morning."[53]

Dare to trust Him today. Dare to believe that even in your disappointments, heartaches, and pains, God is right there with you. He said He would never leave you nor forsake you.

You don't have to figure everything out. You may not know what your future holds. But as long as you know who holds your future, you're going to be okay. God has been working behind the scenes in your life over the years.

I don't know what He has in store for my future, but I know I'm excited about it. It puts a spring in my step to think that the God who created heaven and earth and flung the stars into space cares so much about you and me that He is constantly working for our good. To know that God is bigger than anything you will ever face, and to know that He is already lining up answers for problems that you may not even encounter for ten or twenty years should give you incredible confidence as you enjoy your life today.

Whatever your circumstances are — whether good or bad — you need to know that God already knows about them, and He is working behind the scenes to arrange future events in your favor. Learn to trust Him. Quit worrying about it. Reject anything that hints at frustration or impatience. Remember, when you believe, you activate His power. And keep in mind that just because you don't see anything happening, that doesn't mean God is not working. Why don't you relinquish control and say, "God, I'm going to trust You. I know You have a great plan for my life."

When you do that, you will feel an enormous weight lift off you. And you'll not only enjoy your life more, but you will see more of God's blessings and favor. You will become a better you!

ACTION POINTS
PART 5: EMBRACE THE PLACE
WHERE YOU ARE

1. I know that God works where there is an attitude of faith and expectancy. I will turn my situation over to God. I will not allow myself to worry or become frustrated. I will recognize that God is working behind the scenes, even when I cannot see external evidence of positive change.

2. I will look for glimpses of God's goodness in the little things of my life. I will recognize His blessings in nature, and I will be more aware of His work in the ordinary areas of life — a kind word from a stranger, a rainbow in the sky, a bird perched on my windowsill, a flower blooming in a field.

3. Today I will declare God's favor in my life. I will speak aloud statements such as:
"Thank you, Father, for working in my life. Although I cannot see it yet, I know you are arranging things in my favor."
"I know the clouds will dissipate, and I

will see the favor of God in my life again."

"I am looking for one touch of God's favor that can turn my circumstance around to my advantage and for His honor."

4. I acknowledge that God has me right where I am for a reason. He is directing my steps; I'm where I am supposed to be, and even if it is not a good place, God is giving me the strength to be here, and I know there will be good days ahead. God has me in the palm of His hand, and He will protect me and guide me to His best. Today I choose to be a positive influence on someone else by the way I handle my situation.

■ ■ ■ ■

PART SIX
DEVELOP YOUR
INNER LIFE

■ ■ ■ ■

CHAPTER 25
RISING HIGHER

God's plan for each of our lives is that we continually rise to new levels. But how high we go in life, and how much of God's favor and blessings we experience, will be directly related to how well we follow His directions.

Throughout life, God will deal with us and bring areas to light where we need to improve. He often speaks to us through our conscience, or through a still, small voice. He knows the things that are holding us back. He knows our weaknesses, faults, and the inner secrets that we keep hidden. When He brings these matters to our attention, if we want continued success and blessings, we have to be willing to face the truth about ourselves and take the corrective measures God commands.

Many people don't realize the importance of dealing with such issues. Consequently, they remain stuck in a rut — a rut in their marriage, or in their finances, or in their careers. They casually sweep the dirt under the rug as if it doesn't matter, hoping that nobody will notice. All the while, they ignore the still, small voice.

Sometimes we think, *It's too hard to obey. I know I should forgive that person, but he hurt me so badly. Or, I know I need to get in shape, but I don't really have the time. I know I need to quit working so much, but I need the extra money.*

It is important to understand that everything God tells us is for our good. God never holds us back from His best. Nor does He purposely make our lives more difficult. Quite the contrary, your heavenly Father is waiting for your obedience so He can release more of His favor and blessing in your life.

Are there things in your life that God has been dealing with you about that you have been putting off? Maybe you keep procrastinating or ignoring His leading about getting your finances in order, being less judgmental, keeping strife out of your home, or making peace with somebody at work. Pay attention to what God is saying to you.

Perhaps God has been dealing with you about your close friends, the people you most frequently choose to be around. Maybe you know some of your friends are not a good influence and they are pulling you down, but you keep making excuses. "I don't want to hurt their feelings. Besides, if I didn't hang around them, I may not have any other friends." But the fact is, if you will do what you know is right, God will give you new friends. Not only that, He'll give you *better* friends — people who will lift you up rather than drag you down. Yes, you may go through a season of loneliness as you make the transition, but I would rather be lonely for a little while, knowing that I'm rising higher, knowing that I'm going to fulfill my destiny, than let people pollute me and keep me from being all God created me to be.

Anytime you obey, a blessing will follow. Why? Because you are sowing a seed to grow and rise higher. It may not happen overnight, but at some point, in some way, you will see God's goodness in your life to a greater measure.

My question to you is: How high do you want to rise? Do you want to continue to increase? Do you want to see more of God's blessings and favor? If so, the higher we go, the more disciplined we must be; the quicker we must obey. If we're hanging around people who compromise and cheat on their spouses and have no integrity, we're just asking for trouble.

"Well, Joel, they are good people, and their

conduct doesn't affect me. It doesn't seem to hurt me one bit."

No, you don't know how much your association with them is holding you back. You don't know what God wants to release, but He cannot and will not until you get away from those negative influences. If you will do as He says, you would see God's favor in a new way, and your entire life would rise to a higher level.

Understand, the longer we delay dealing with a character issue, the more difficult it is to do later on. You'd be far better off if you'd learn to obey God's promptings quickly. The moment you feel the uneasiness, the moment an inner alarm sounds and something says, "This isn't right," take the proper steps to move away from that action, comment, or attitude. That may well be God talking to you — trying to keep you on His best path for your life.

God has given us our own free will. He will not force us to do what is right. He won't force us to make good decisions. It's up to each one of us individually to pay attention to the still, small voice; at the same time, we mustn't get so busy or self-directed that we miss what God is trying to tell us. Learn to act on His leading.

God's directions often affect the most

practical aspects of our lives. Recently, a young woman told me that she felt a strong urge to go to the doctor to get a medical checkup. She looked as healthy as could be, and she was active, energetic, and exercised regularly. Nevertheless, the feeling persisted: "Go see the doctor. Go get a checkup." That still, small voice was speaking to her. For several weeks, she ignored it and put it off. "Oh, I'm fine. That's not a message for me."

But she couldn't get away from it. She finally decided to schedule an appointment with her doctor. During a routine checkup, the doctor discovered a small cyst in her body, and found that it was malignant. Thankfully, he was able to remove it completely, because it hadn't spread. The young woman required no further treatment. But after the operation, the doctor told her, "It's a good thing you came in when you did, because a couple of years later, this could have been a major problem, possibly even life-threatening."

The young woman was so grateful. She later told me, "Joel, I know that was God. I would not have gone to the doctor for that checkup had it not been for God's promptings."

We need to listen to the still, small voice. God knows what's best for us.

I've had people come to me with tears in their eyes, saying, "Joel, I knew I should have kept the strife out of my family; I knew I should have spent more time with them. I knew I shouldn't have been so hard to get along with."

Isn't it amazing that we can know the right thing to do, yet still ignore it? Don't let that be you. Be obedient now, so you won't have regrets later on.

Victoria and I were married in 1987 and for the first few years, like any young couple, we were trying to learn how to live together as one. The problem was that she wasn't learning the way I wanted her to. We didn't have major difficulties, just minor irritations. I'd argue over things that didn't matter, always wanting to have my way, not willing to compromise. I'll never forget — God spoke to me back then, not aloud, but deep inside. He said, "Joel, if you don't make changes and do your part to keep the peace in the family, you're not only going to change the beautiful girl you married, but it's going to cause you major problems in the future." That was all the warning I needed. Thank God, I was smart enough to heed that warning, and we stopped arguing over little things and were willing to make compromises and adjustments in our marriage. Today, we're as happy as could be and have a great relationship.

God may be dealing with you about your words, cautioning you against saying so many hurtful, sarcastic, critical things. You've developed a bad habit, and you know down inside, it is destroying your relationship. Don't be hardheaded. Don't wait till the sirens go off before you do something. In most instances, God will not hit somebody over the head with a baseball bat and say, "Hey, you're ruining your marriage. You're going to end up hurt and lonely."

No, He whispers it in a still, small voice. We have to be sensitive and pay attention to His leading and then do whatever it is that He tells us to do to make life better.

Too often we make excuses. "Well, I know I should treat my spouse better. I know I can be disrespectful, but she's disrespectful to me. I know I have a chip on my shoulder. I know I'm hard to get along with, but I've been through a lot in life. It's just not fair."

Those excuses will cause us to remain stuck right where we are. The way to rise higher is by staying open and dealing with issues as God brings them to light. It may be something as simple as how you speak to your spouse, your tone of voice, body language, or facial expressions. If you come across as harsh or short or too direct, you can hurt someone with your words — especially someone who loves you.

On the other hand, if you will listen to that inner voice of conviction when it says, "That's not right. You can do better. You can be kinder," and make some simple adjustments, you will see that relationship go to a new level.

I know some people who are extremely jealous. They see somebody who is blessed and prospering, and rather than being happy for that person and rejoicing, the jealous person seeks to find fault. Interestingly, that person could have enjoyed the same success and fulfillment, but he or she was unwilling to pay the price. That person wasn't willing to obey his or her conscience, to discipline himself or herself, or to make the sort of sacrifices the successful person made to get ahead.

Any one of us can rise higher. There is no limit to what God will do in your life, if you will learn to obey quickly and deal with the issues He brings to light, even the small things.

Some time ago, I was watching a minister on television. He's a fine man and he has a great ministry. As I was watching, though, I began to critique the production of the program. My background involves television production, so I naturally thought, *Why did they put the camera there? That background doesn't look good. He shouldn't be wearing that. And that light is not adjusted right.*

Within minutes, I'd found a dozen things that I would have done differently. About that time, I felt that still, small voice saying, "Joel, don't be critical. Look for the good. Look what they're doing right. Look at all the people they are helping."

I felt that conviction, and I could have easily blown it off and ignored it. Nobody would have known. But I've learned to quickly say, "Father, forgive me. Help me to never be critical. Help me to do better. Help me to always see the good."

That was an opportunity for me to come up higher. God showed me something, although small, that held the potential to keep me from being my best. I'm not perfect, but I've learned to deal with things like that. I've learned to stay open and look for ways that I can improve. I know God always has more in store, so I don't want to compromise or live in complacency.

You can do a lot in life and get away with it. You can run with the wrong crowd and still get to heaven. You can treat people disrespectfully or be sloppy in your business affairs and still live in relative comfort. But I'm talking about rising higher. I'm talking about being the very best that you can be.

For instance, perhaps God is dealing with you about your finances. Maybe you are living above your means, spending more than you can afford.

Too often, we made a purchase that we didn't feel good about. We bought a house, a car, or a boat that we couldn't afford or didn't really need. The alarm was going off even as we signed the papers, but we ignored it, and now we're in a financial bind.

It is much better to obey all along the way, and then you won't have to deal with many of these issues. This is one of the most important principles you can ever learn. Follow peace; listen to your conscience; deal with the issues God brings to light. Don't put it off. The longer you put it off, the more difficult it will be.

Many people wonder why they're not happy, why they are not blessed and increasing in influence, why they can't sleep well at night. Often it is because their conscience is not clear. We cannot bury things in our subconscious minds and expect to rise higher and enjoy God's best.

When King David committed adultery with Bathsheba, he tried to cover it up. Making matters worse, he sent Bathsheba's husband to the front lines of the battle and then ordered his general to pull back, resulting in certain death. For one full year, David pretended that everything was okay; he went on with life and business. No doubt, he thought, *If I don't deal with it, if I ignore it, it won't bother me; it won't affect me.*

That year was one of the worst of David's life. He was miserable. The Scripture says he was also weak; he grew sick physically and had all kinds of problems. That is what happens when we refuse to deal with things. We step out of God's protection and favor. When we live with a guilty conscience, we don't feel good about ourselves, so we take it out on other people. Many times, just like David, we're weak, defeated, living in mediocrity. It's because of the poison on the inside.

But, friend, none of us needs to live that way. Our God is a forgiving, merciful God. When you make a mistake, you don't have to hide it. When you do wrong, don't run away from God. Run to God.

After a year of living in denial, King David finally admitted his sin and his mistakes after a prophet confronted the king about his misdeeds. David said, "God, I'm sorry. Please forgive me. Create in me a clean heart. Restore the joy of my salvation." When David sincerely did that, God restored him. That's how David got his joy, peace, and victory back, and although he had failed miserably, he went on to do great things.

Now think about it: David could have been stuck right there in defeat, in mediocrity for the rest of his life had he refused to deal with that issue. But he chose to change, and God helped him to do it.

Are there things in your life that you are refusing to deal with? When you ask for forgiveness, God can restore you. That's when He'll put you back on your best path. That's when He'll give you a new beginning.

Keep in mind, God deals with each of us individually. We are all at different levels, so we should never compare ourselves to others. Too often, when we compare ourselves with others, we tend to make excuses for ourselves. For instance, maybe all your friends are going to see a movie, but you read the review and don't feel good about it. You know it would not be God's best for you. Your inner alarm goes off and your conscience cautions you, "You are better than that; don't willingly take dirt into your mind."

Right there is an opportunity for you to rise higher. Sure, you could attempt to quiet your conscience and say, "Oh, it's not going to hurt me. I'm strong and besides, all my friends love God. They attend church. They're good people. They are going to see that movie."

No, maybe your friends are at a different stage in their spiritual walk than you. Or perhaps they are ignoring God's voice speaking to them; maybe they would be much more blessed if they would quit giving in and living at such a low level. You must do what you feel good about in your own heart. It may cost you a few friendships. It may mean that you spend a few lonely nights. Or maybe you can't play on a team that parties after every game.

Remember that anything God asks you to do is for your benefit. It's so He can ultimately release more of His favor in your life.

Moreover, anything God asks of us, He always gives the grace to do it. If God asks you to forgive somebody, you may not think you can, but if you will take that step of faith, God's grace will be there to help you. You don't get the grace unless you step out. You have to make the first move. God will see that step of faith and He'll give you supernatural strength to help you overcome any obstacles standing in the way of doing the right thing.

Friend, God has great things in store for you. Don't get stuck in a rut and settle for mediocrity, bad habits, or bad attitudes. Pay attention to the still, small voice on the inside. Deal with the issues God brings to light and learn to obey quickly. Remember: How high you go in life will be directly related to how obedient you are.

The Scripture says, "To whom much is given, much is required."[54] God is preparing you for greater things. He's going to take you further than you thought possible, so don't be surprised when He asks you to think better of yourself and to act accordingly.

CHAPTER 26
DEVELOP A TENDER CONSCIENCE

Your conscience is often called the compass of the soul. It works like an inward monitor, similar to an alarm. When you're about to do something that is not beneficial or something that will get you into trouble, your conscience causes you to feel uneasy. Don't ignore that warning. That's your conscience helping you to know what is right and what is wrong. One of the best friends you can ever have is your own conscience.

We could avoid a great deal of trouble and heartache if we would maintain a more tender conscience. I hear people say all the time, "I know I shouldn't do this, but . . ." Or "I know I shouldn't say this, but . . ." Or "I know I shouldn't buy this, but . . ."

They know what they should do. The alarm is going off. They can feel that sense of disapproval, but they choose to disobey their own conscience. Someday they will look back and recognize how God tried to

519

warn them again and again.

Don't make the mistake of overriding your conscience. Respect it. Just as you respect your boss or someone else with authority over you, learn to treat your conscience in the same way. God will use your conscience to help lead you and keep you out of trouble. Perhaps you are in a conversation with your spouse and things are heating up. You can feel yourself getting aggravated, wanting to continue the argument more forcefully, when suddenly, that inner alarm goes off. Something down inside says, "Let it go. Drop it. Bite your tongue. Walk away. Keep the peace."

That's your conscience trying to keep you out of trouble. That's God trying to warn you. Too many times we ignore it and choose to do our own thing. We end up having a big argument and getting all upset, ruining the rest of the evening. It could have been avoided if we would have paid attention to what our conscience was trying to say to us.

Learn to be sensitive. Stop when your conscience says stop. Quit having to have the last word. Pay attention to what you're feeling inside, and don't override your own conscience.

One time, my father was driving down the road, about to get on the freeway. He was in a big hurry, running late to a meeting. Traveling well over the speed limit, he came up to a big curve in the road. Just then, that alarm went off inside. Something said, "You'd better slow down. A policeman is around the corner."

My father later told how that word came to him so distinctly. He felt it strongly, but he was in a hurry so he ignored it and didn't pay any attention. Sure enough, when he got around the corner, a police officer stood there holding out his radar gun. The police officer flagged my dad over. When the officer approached my father's car window, Daddy had a big smile on his face. He said, "Officer, you are never going to believe this, but God told me you were up here."

The officer looked at my father as if he were from another planet. He took my father's license and returned to his patrol car. He came back a few minutes later, shaking his head. He said, "Listen here, preacher, I'm going to let you go, but the next time God speaks to you, you'd better listen."

Don't override your own conscience. When you feel uncomfortable down inside, pull back and pay attention to what God is trying to say to you. You may be in the middle of a conversation. All of a sudden, the alarm goes off, and you know you need to button your lip or walk away. Don't ignore that warning from your conscience. You may be ready to buy something or about to eat something or about to make some less than noble plans when that inner siren goes off. If you will learn to be sensitive and listen to your conscience, God will keep you out of trouble. He will help you make good decisions. He can protect you from danger.

I recently encountered Peter, a young man who did some contract labor for us, and when I saw him, I almost didn't recognize him. He looked as though he had been in some type of accident. His face was bruised, and the skin around both his eyes was black and purple. He had some stitches on his arm. I said, "Peter, what in the world happened to you? Were you in a wreck or something?"

"No, Joel," he said. "A couple of nights ago, I was carjacked."

"What?"

"Yeah, I was on my way home from work, and I stopped at the traffic light, and these guys came up to me and pulled me out of my car. I didn't have a wallet, so they just beat me up and left me there."

"That's awful, Peter."

"Yes, but, Joel, the funny thing was, on my way home that night, something told me to not go that way. Right down in here as distinct as it could be" — Peter pointed to his chest — "something said, 'You'd better go another way.' It was so strong that I even debated it in my mind. I said to myself, 'I always go this way. This is the quickest way. Why should I go another way?' "

This young man was not a religious person, but he said, "I know that was God trying to warn me. I know that was God trying to protect me." He paused and looked at me, and said, "Joel, if I had only listened, I could have avoided this pain."

Before you step into trouble or make a poor decision, God will always provide a warning for you. An alarm will sound inside. The caution may not be as dramatic as Peter's, but if you'll be sensitive and pay attention, God will lead you and will help you to avoid unnecessary turmoil.

Most of the time, deep down inside, we know what we should do, but too often, we simply choose not to do it. Understand, every time you ignore your conscience, the next time that voice will speak more softly. Unfortunately, you can get to the place where you have totally drowned out the voice of your conscience.

For instance, maybe you're about to say something rude to someone and all of a sudden that check goes off inside. You feel that sense of uneasiness as something tells you to bite your tongue. But if you ignore that prompt and choose to override it, you will feel guilty as a result. If you don't go back and make things right and apologize, then the next time you're in that situation, the alarm won't be quite as loud. The voice won't be quite so strong. You can get to the place where you have overridden your conscience so often that it becomes desensitized. That's why we need to pray every day, "God, help me to develop a tender conscience. Keep me sensitive to Your voice."

Recently, I met a man whose family lives in another country while he has been in the United States for several years working with his company. He told me how he came to be intimately involved with another woman. They have been in a relationship for a couple of years, but he feels guilty about it. He said, "Joel, I just feel terrible. I know that this relationship is not right. I really want to change, but I just can't seem to do it."

"You are in an interesting situation," I told him. "You are the exception to the rule, because most people who have been overriding their consciences that long no longer care. They don't feel anything. They're not concerned."

"Really?" he asked. "What do you think I should do?"

"First of all, you should thank God that you still have a tender conscience and be grateful that you still have that concern." I then challenged him to make the necessary changes before that uneasiness wore off.

Any insensitivity to God's voice should concern us — especially when we have been willfully doing wrong for so long that it no longer bothers us, or we no longer regard it as wrong. We've grown numb in that area. Again, that is why we should pray every day, "God, help me to stay sensitive to Your voice. Don't let me get calloused, cold, or numb in any area of my life, in my attitude, or in how I treat people, or in what I say or what I do. God, help me to have a tender conscience."

Friend, God rewards obedience. Get into God's best path. Don't keep overriding your conscience. If you will be honest with yourself and have the desire to change, God will help you to do it. It is better to go through a little pain of change than it is to go twenty or thirty years stuck in mediocrity.

I have found that the more obedient we are, the easier it becomes. Obedience breeds obedience. Unfortunately, the opposite is also true. Disobedience breeds more disobedience. Consequently, you can increase the sensitivity of your conscience or you can decrease it. Every time you obey, your conscience becomes more tender. When you obey, you're letting in a little more light. Your heart will be a little softer and you'll respond more quickly. You can get to the point where you are so sensitive that when you first feel that uneasiness, it will get your attention and cause you to make changes. Really, that's the kind of people God wants us to be. When we hear the still, small voice, when we first feel that little nudge, we are quick to take action.

Understand this: When you live an obedient life, God's blessings will chase you down and overtake you. When you obey, you cannot outrun the good things of God.

God does not expect you to change overnight. He is not going to be disappointed with you or write you off if you don't turn your life around in one week's time. No, all He asks is that you keep making progress. He doesn't want you to be at this same place next year. He will lead you in His own special way, and if you will be sensitive and do your best to keep your own conscience clear, God will be pleased, and He'll release more of His blessings in your life.

God meets us at our own level. I don't have to keep up with you, and you don't have to keep up with me. I just have to be true to my own heart. I know the areas in which God deals with me most frequently, and I do my best not to go against my own conscience. That's what I'm challenging you to do as well.

A young man with whom I attended college had a habit of being short with people. Sometimes, he was downright rude. One day we were at a restaurant together with a group of guys from the school, and the waiter mixed up my friend's order. My friend jumped down the waiter's throat. I mean he let him have it and embarrassed him in front of all of us.

After we got back to the dorm, my friend came into my room about an hour later and asked if he could borrow my car. I said, "Sure you can, but where are you going at this late hour?"

"Joel, I feel terrible," he said. "I treated that waiter so badly, I can't even sleep. I'm going to go back there and apologize to him."

That young man changed over the course of that year. He went from being hard, cold, and rude to being one of the kindest, most considerate people you could ever meet. God will help you to change, if you will simply work with Him.

None of us is perfect. We all make mistakes, but we can learn to obey our own consciences if we can be big enough to say, "I'm sorry, I didn't treat you right, I'll do better next time." If you will be sensitive and maintain a clear conscience, there's no limit to what God will do in your life. In contrast, when you have a guilty conscience, you don't feel good about yourself. You're not happy; you can't pray with boldness; you feel condemned. You don't expect good things, and you usually don't receive them.

At that point, the best thing you can do is go back and make things right. Like that young man, swallow your pride and be quick to obey. Apologize to the people you have offended. Don't live with a guilty conscience.

Or maybe you need to say, "God, I'm sorry; please forgive me for having such a critical attitude toward that person."

When you do that, your conscience will relax. That heavy burden will be lifted off you; you'll be able to sleep well. Not only that, but God will help you do better next time.

Years ago, one time after a service, my father came back into the television production area. Four or five crew members and I were gathered there, and when my dad walked in, we were all laughing and having a good time. Something really funny had just happened. For some reason, my father thought that we were making fun of someone in the service, but it didn't have anything to do with that.

Now, ordinarily, my father was a very kind and compassionate person, but this incident seemed to set him off. He began to chew us out, letting us know that we should not be making fun of people, and on and on. I said, "Daddy, it had nothing to do with that; it was totally unrelated," but he didn't accept that.

He left, and, of course, the guys on the crew and I felt bad about the misunderstanding. When I got home that night a couple of hours later, my father came into my room. "Joel, I've got to talk to you," he said. "I blew it tonight. I know I was wrong. I know I made a mistake, and I'm asking you to forgive me please. I want to apologize." Before I'd gotten home, my dad had called each of those other young men as well and apologized to them. It must have been close to midnight, but he would not go to bed with that heaviness on his heart.

What an impression that made upon me! What an impression it made upon those other young men. My father was the boss, but he was not too proud to admit that he had made a mistake and needed to apologize. See, my father had a tender conscience. No wonder God blessed him. No wonder God used him in a great way.

If we can learn to have that kind of sensitive, pure heart and be quick to obey, quick to forgive, quick to apologize, quick to change our attitudes, we will be pleasing to God.

Live your life with a clear conscience. Get into God's best plan. The Scripture says in Matthew 6:22 that the lamp of the body is the eye. Your "spiritual eye" is your conscience. Jesus goes on to say that if the eye is clear, the whole body will be filled with light. In other words, if your conscience is clear, life is good. You're going to be happy. You will have a positive vision and will enjoy God's blessings.

Then the next verse describes many people today. It says in the *Amplified Version,* "If our conscience is full of darkness, then how dense will that darkness be." Many people are living with a heaviness hanging over their lives. They have some nagging feeling, something's always bothering them. They're not happy. The problem is they don't have a clear conscience. They've ignored the warnings for too long. They've gotten hard and cold in certain areas.

That insensitivity won't change until you make the proper adjustments. If there are things that you are doing that you know you should not be doing, then make some adjustments. Or if there are things that you *should* be doing and you're not, then make those changes. As I've said, it may not be something big. You may not be living in some sordid sin, but maybe God is dealing with you about having a better attitude, about spending more time with your children, about eating healthier. Whatever it is, make a decision that you're going to pay more attention to your conscience and that you are going to be quick to obey. That's when the heaviness will leave. I like what the Apostle Paul said in Acts 23. He said, "I have always lived before God with a clear conscience."

That should be our goal as well. When our conscience is clear, condemnation flees. When we have a clear conscience, we can be happy. Other people may try to judge us or condemn us, but that negative input will bounce right off us.

Sometimes people say, "Joel, why don't you do more of this or more of that?"

I know I'm not perfect, but I also know this: My conscience is clear before God. I know that I'm doing my best to please Him.

That's why I can sleep well at night. That's why I can lie down in peace. That's why I have a smile on my face. Friend, keep your conscience tender, and you will discover that life keeps getting better and better.

CHAPTER 27
DEALING WITH THE ROOT ISSUES

I heard about a man who owned a bunch of horses, and one day one of the horses kicked a wood fence and scraped his leg badly. The owner took the horse to his barn, cleaned the wound, and bandaged the animal's leg. A few weeks later, the man noticed that the horse was still bothered by that bruise. The owner called a veterinarian to come examine the horse. After checking the animal, the vet prescribed some antibiotics.

Almost immediately, the horse responded positively to the medication and began to do much better. A month or two went by, however, and the owner noticed that the injury still had not healed; it actually appeared to be worse than ever. So the vet put the horse back on antibiotics.

Once again the animal responded and was fine for a few weeks, but then the process repeated itself. The wound simply would not heal. Finally, the owner loaded up the horse and took him down to the veterinarian's clinic. He knew he had to find out why this wound wouldn't heal. In the clinic, the veterinarian put the horse under anesthesia and began to probe the injured leg. Once he got deep enough, the vet discovered a large sliver of wood that had gone far below the skin when the horse had hit the fence many months previously. The vet realized that every time the horse went off the antibiotic, the infection caused by that foreign object returned. They had been treating the symptoms rather than treating the true source of the horse's pain.

We do something similar many times. We fix the surface things. "Let me clean up my behavior. Let me just turn over a new leaf. I'm going to try being more friendly, more loving and kind. I'm not going to spend so much money, or use credit cards to get into debt. I'm not going to manipulate people anymore. I won't get so angry and upset." It's good that we're trying to improve, but so often we are not dealing with the real source of the problem. No matter how much we want to be better, that issue just keeps coming back, and we can't seem to get free.

It is usually easier to make excuses for our behavior, to pass the blame and try to justify our behavior. But if we want to experience

God's best, we must learn to take responsibility for our thoughts, words, attitudes, and actions.

Too many people never really look inside and get honest with themselves. They don't get down to the root of the problem. Instead, they simply deal with the fruit, the surface issues. They may be negative, or they can't get along in relationships. Perhaps they have low self-esteem, severe financial problems, or some other chronic problem. They try to improve their behavior, and that is admirable, but many times their efforts produce only temporary results because they refuse to deal with the bad root. Consequently, they continue to produce bad fruit.

The Bible teaches that we should not let a root of bitterness spring forth and contaminate our whole lives. It's like having a weed out in your front yard. You can pull that weed, but if you merely clip it off at the surface, you are not really getting down to the roots. A couple of days later, you look out in your yard, and you have that same weed to deal with again.

For lasting, positive change, you must go deeper and not merely look at what you do, but ask yourself, "What is the root of this problem?" "Why do I act this way?" "Why am I out of control in this area?" "Why am I always so defensive?" "Why do I feel that I must repeatedly prove myself to everybody?"

Only as you get to the root and start dealing with the source of the problem can you realistically expect positive changes.

We need to examine carefully the areas in which we constantly struggle. Is our spouse really at fault? Is it really our circumstances, upbringing, or environment? Or could it be that we have something buried deep within that is causing us to "be infected"?

This is especially important in the area of your relationships. Many people have a root of rejection — they have been through hurts in the past. Somebody did them wrong, and rather than letting it go, they hold on to it. That bitterness poisons every part of the person's life.

I know people who have a root of insecurity that causes them to feel defensive. They're always trying to prove to somebody else who they are. As long as they have that bad root, they're going to continue to produce the wrong kind of fruit.

So often we can't seem to get along with a particular person, and we're sure it must be his or her fault. We're sure it's our spouse. We're sure it's our boss or coworkers. But wait. Could the problem be you? Could it be that you have a root of pride that is causing you to withhold forgiveness or is blinding you to somebody else's opinion? We can try to correct all these things on the surface, but that's similar to merely putting a fresh bandage on that horse's leg. The problem will keep coming back until we get to the real source.

Shawna and Andy were always having problems in their marriage, especially in the area of communication. When they engaged in conversation, if Andy didn't agree with Shawna, she would get extremely defensive. She'd get all upset, lose her cool, and they'd end up having an argument. "Why can't you just let me have my opinion?" Andy said. "Why do you have to get so upset when I don't agree with you? Haven't you ever heard that if two people agree on everything in a marriage, one of them is unnecessary?"

Shawna didn't have a good answer, but she obstinately opposed Andy's opinions when he disagreed with her. This went on year after year, and the tension created by this situation tore at the fabric of their marriage.

One day Shawna decided to get honest with herself. She looked deep down on the inside, and as she did, she realized that the reason she became defensive so easily was that she was intensely insecure. She had been through a lot of hurt and pain in her lifetime. She had experienced a devastating dose of rejection from a previous relationship. Now every time Andy didn't agree with her, Shawna felt that he was rejecting her. Rather than agreeing to disagree on some matters, Shawna took it personally. She tried to control and manipulate Andy to keep that tension from sprouting in their relationship.

Shawna realized that the true source of the problem wasn't that they couldn't communicate; it was her own insecurity. It didn't happen overnight, but as Shawna began to deal with these feelings, asking God to help her, little by little things began to change. Slowly, Shawna and Andy's relationship improved, but the key was she got to the root. Once she took care of the bad root, eventually the fruit took care of itself.

We have to understand that most of our problems have deeper roots. We might be amazed at how many things affect us negatively, and we are trying to solve the problem simply by dealing with the fruit — often treating surface issues for years on an endless treadmill.

The children of Israel were doing something similar. They wandered around in the wilderness between Egypt and the Promised Land of Canaan for forty years — a trip that should have been a mere eleven-day journey.

The root cause of their problem was that they had developed a victim mentality. Granted, they had been treated horribly during the last portion of their time in Egypt; they had been through many painful, unfair experiences while in slavery. The inner pain followed them, even after God had miraculously delivered them from bondage. Out in the desert, they blamed Moses for their lack of food and water; they blamed the past, complained about the food, and fretted over their enemies. It never dawned on them that they were a part of the problem. Because of their lack of faith, they kept going around the same mountain year after year, never making any real progress.

Perhaps you have been stuck at the same place in your life for far too long. Maybe you are stuck in a sour marriage or a dead-end career. Or maybe you are stuck in a quagmire of debt or negative attitudes; you are often hard to get along with, defensive, or critical.

It's time to get up and get going. Our prayer should be, "God, please show me the truth about myself. I don't want to be at this same place next year, so if I have things holding me back, show me what they are. Help me, Father, to change. Help me to get to the root of my problems."

God is knocking on the door of new rooms in our hearts, maybe rooms that we haven't let Him enter previously. The only way He'll come in is if we invite Him. The doorknob is on the inside. I have discovered that I can allow God in some rooms of my heart, yet keep Him out of other rooms. Some of those rooms can be painful or embarrassing. Hidden in some of those rooms are hurts and wounds from the past. It's where our weaknesses and shortcomings are tucked away. Rather than dealing with the issues and cleaning the crud out of those dark corners, we keep those rooms locked. We make excuses for our behavior; we blame other people. Sometimes, we even blame God.

"That's just the way I am," someone might say.

God continues to knock. If we want to get to the source, then we must look inside; we must allow God to shine the floodlight of His Word in every room of our heart. When we have feelings that we know are wrong, rather than hiding them and trying to bury them away in one of these rooms, the best thing we can do is to be honest and ask, "God, why do I feel this way?" "Why can't I get along with my spouse?" "Why do I try to manipulate everybody?" "God, why do I always have to have my way?" "Why do I get upset so easily?" If you will be honest and willing to face the truth rather than hiding behind excuses, God will show you some answers to those questions. As you begin to act on that truth, you can come up higher.

If you're impatient, be honest enough to say, "God, show me why I'm so impatient. And then please help me to deal with it."

When you feel resentment toward another person, tending to be critical or finding fault, the first thing you should do is to pray, "Please, God, show me why I don't like this person. What's wrong on the inside of me? God, am I jealous of her position, jealous of his money, jealous of their talents? God, please show me the truth about myself. I don't want to go around that same mountain another year. I want to come up higher; I want to enter my Promised Land."

Make sure that you're not carrying around excess baggage. If you have areas in your life in which you constantly struggle and you can't seem to get free, then you need to ask God to show you what's holding you back. Ask God to show you if you have any bitter roots that you need to get rid of. If God brings something to light, then be bold enough to deal with it.

You *can* be happier, you can have better relationships, you can break free from anything that's holding you back, but you have to do your part. Be honest and face the truth about yourself. Let's not do as the children of Israel did in the years following the Exodus, thinking our lack of progress is somebody else's fault.

I know digging out those roots can be painful. The easy thing is to concentrate on surface issues, to maintain the status quo. The easy thing is to avoid change. There is a pain associated with coming up higher. It's uncomfortable to be honest and really deal with these issues. It can be uncomfortable to have to forgive an offense when it was somebody else's fault. It's hard to admit sometimes, "I'm holding on to the bitterness." Or, "I'm defensive because I'm so insecure." Or "I'm hard to get along with because I'm dragging all my baggage from the past." Moreover, don't be surprised if, as you shed the superficial layers and really get honest, you feel a little pressure. Please understand that this discomfort is only temporary. It's a growing pain, and once you get past that point, you're going to move up to a new level of victory. The pain of change is much less than the pain of staying in mediocrity.

Perhaps you have been spinning your wheels, going around in circles year after year, and are not really happy. You need to be honest enough to say, "God, show me what it is. Am I relying on other people to make me happy? Do I have unrealistic expectations? Am I going to be happy only if I get married? Am I allowing my circumstances to keep me down? God, show me the truth about myself."

Not too long ago a man told me that whenever he took time to enjoy his life, he felt guilty about it. He felt condemned, as though he were doing something wrong. Over the years, he engrossed himself in his work. He became a workaholic, not taking any time for himself, not taking any time for his family. Ironically, his overworking was all because of these feelings of guilt. His life was out of balance. This went on year after year until one day he decided to get honest and let God in that room of his heart. He said, "God, why do I feel this way? Why do I feel guilty when I just want to go out and have fun, to enjoy being with my family?"

He realized that as he was growing up his father was extremely strict. He came from a military family, and his dad didn't allow any fun in the house. Everything was serious. He didn't really know what it was like to have a normal childhood. He was taught to work, to be serious, with little to no playtime. Now an adult himself, he realized that he had become just like his father. Those thoughts, those attitudes, those habits were what he had learned early on — not that they were right, but that's all that he had known. Once he recognized what the source was, he was able to break that heaviness and really start enjoying his life.

You may have come out of an abusive situation. Maybe somebody else caused you a lot of heartache and pain; perhaps the people who raised you were unkind, or somebody with whom you shared a relationship used or abused you. They made poor decisions, and now you are dealing with the ramifications of those decisions. But please don't let that be an excuse. You can come up higher. You can set a new standard.

Understand that if you want to get to the source of the problem, you cannot just sit by idly and remain passive. You've got to come to the point where you say, "I am sick and tired of being sick and tired. We may have been this way a long time, but I'm not going to dance around this issue. I'm going to get to the source, and I'm going to start making better decisions for my family and for me."

One of the first things we must do is to stop making excuses. We have to quit blaming the past. You may have been through a lot of heartache. That may be the reason you struggle with bad habits or why you have trouble in relationships. Perhaps you suffer from low self-esteem. That may be the reason, but don't use that as an excuse to stay the way you are. Take responsibility. Many people have had unfair things happen, and they go their whole lifetime allowing that experience to poison them. They're angry. They've got a chip on their shoulder, they are hard to get along with. "Well, Joel, if you'd been through what I've been through, you'd act this same way."

No, that may be the reason you act that way, but thank God, you don't have to stay that way. You can come up higher, but you must take responsibility. You have to be willing to face the truth and say, "This is not right. I refuse to live upset and angry. I don't want to be hard to get along with. God, I'm asking You to help me to change." If you have that attitude, God will always help you.

A woman came up to me in the church lobby one time. She said, "Joel, I wish you would pray for me. I'm about to get married again for my fifth time." She continued in a pious tone, "I want you to agree with me in prayer that this man will be the one who finally starts treating me right."

I wanted to ask her, "Have you ever thought about what the common denominator is in all these marriages? It's you! Something's wrong on the inside."

After we prayed, I asked her, "Does anybody else in your family struggle with these same kinds of difficulties?"

"Oh, yes," she said. "My mother has been married four times and she's just about to get another divorce."

I thought, *The enemy loves us to perpetuate those negative cycles, passing them down from one generation to the next. If we don't take responsibility and do something about it, it will keep repeating itself. Our children, grandchildren, and great-grandchildren will all have to deal with it.*

If I have bad habits, if I have insecurities, if I have wrong thinking, I want to be honest and open enough to deal with it and not make excuses, not blame my past, my parents, my circumstances, or my spouse. I can't change any of that, but I can change me.

"But if you knew my family, you'd realize that we are so dysfunctional. We have so many bad habits. We're so messed up."

I say this respectfully: Almost every family has some dysfunction. Don't use that as an excuse. We all have things to deal with and overcome.

Some people say, "I'm depressed because my parents were so depressed," or "I'm hot-tempered just like my father." "I'm a worry-wart, because my mother always worried."

No, you can change. You are a child of God, so you have the greatest power in the universe inside you. You can break any addiction and overcome any stronghold. You can defeat any bondage. The Scripture says, "Greater is He that's in you than he that's in the world."[55] That means there is no obstacle on this planet that you cannot overcome. You can fulfill your God-given destiny. You can accomplish your dreams. You may have had a negative history, but please understand, you don't have to have a negative future. What's important is not where you've come from. What matters is where you are going.

One of the main ways we can honor God is by taking responsibility for our actions, not blaming our past, not blaming our circumstances. We must get down to the root, so we don't go through life trying to pick off the bad fruit. Take responsibility. Rise up and do something about it. You can experience the good things of God. I know if you will face the truth about yourself, get to the source of your issues, and make the adjustments God asks, I can promise that your inner life will improve, you will have better relationships, and you will be happier and more fulfilled.

Action Points
Part 6: Develop Your Inner Life

1. Today I will be aware of the issues God brings to light in my life, and I will be quick to obey and make the necessary changes so I can move up higher.

2. I will pay more attention to my conscience, listening to the still, small voice within. I will do my best to keep my conscience tender by being quick to respond to His leading.

3. I refuse to make excuses for myself; I will look inside and deal with the root, not simply the fruit. I will probe beyond the surface symptoms and get down to the source of my problems. I choose to overcome any unfair experiences by looking for the good God is bringing out of them.

■■■■

PART SEVEN
STAY PASSIONATE
ABOUT LIFE

■■■■

CHAPTER 28
PLAN FOR BLESSING

If you want to become a better you, it is important to put the right actions along with your faith. It's not enough to believe, as important as that may be. We have to take it one step further and start expecting. While we are expecting good things from God, we should be making plans. We need to talk as if what we are praying about is going to happen. We should dare to step out in faith and act like it's going to happen.

When a couple is expecting a baby, they make all sorts of preparations. Why? Because they know a child is on its way. The fact is, in the early stages of the pregnancy, they haven't seen the baby or touched it. Yet they have faith in the doctor's report, so they start making preparations.

God has put dreams in every one of our hearts. We all have things for which we are believing — perhaps you are believing to overcome an illness, believing to get out of debt, or believing to accomplish your dreams. Here's the key: We have to go beyond believing. True faith puts action behind it. If you're sick, you need to start making plans to get well. If you're struggling in your finances, start making plans to prosper. If your marriage is on the rocks, start making plans to see that relationship restored. Lay your faith on the line.

Too often, we say that we are believing God for good things, yet with our actions, we're doing just the opposite. Understand that your faith will work in either direction, positively or negatively. I know some people who plan to get the flu. At the grocery store, I hear them predicting their future: "Well, it's flu season. I had better pick up some of this flu medicine just in case. After all, it was bad last year. I got lucky and didn't get it. But I'll probably get it this year." They talk as though it is sure to happen. They take it even further and put actions behind their negative faith, by purchasing the flu medicine. Not surprisingly, a few weeks later they come down with the flu. Their faith worked, albeit negatively. They expected the flu, made plans for it, and they got it. Remember, your faith will work in either direction.

Please don't misinterpret what I am saying. It is prudent to take precautions; we have medicine at our house. However, I don't think we should run to the pharmacy every time a television commercial announces that flu season is here.

Funny, sometimes we put more faith in those commercials than we do in what God says. I love what it says in Psalms: "A thousand may fall at my side, ten thousand at my right hand; but it will not come near my dwelling."[56] Everybody at work may be getting the flu, everybody at school may have it, but I believe God has put a hedge of protection around me, and I'm going to stay in faith and not make plans to get it.

If we read the news long enough, and watch all the studies, they'll nearly talk us into having heart disease, high cholesterol, diabetes, and all sorts of ailments. "Well, you know what they say, one in four people gets cancer," a pessimistic friend points out.

Maybe that's true, but let's believe we will be among the three who don't get it instead of one of those who do. It is just as easy to believe for the positive as it is the negative. Start making plans to live a long healthy life. When you face sickness — and we all have things come against us from time to time — don't just give up and start making plans to live with it. I've had people tell me, "Well, Joel, I'm learning to live with my arthritis.

I'm learning to live with my high blood pressure."

No, that's not *your* high blood pressure; that's not *your* sickness. Quit taking ownership of it and start making plans to get well. Our attitude should be, this sickness didn't come to stay, it came to pass. Say things such as, "I know with long life, God is going to satisfy me. So I declare it by faith, I'm getting better and better every day in every way."

Don't quit dreaming. Keep the vision in front of you. A friend of mine was in an accident where both of his knees were crushed. The doctor told him he would be fortunate to walk, but he would certainly never run or play sports again. My friend was so disappointed. After being in the hospital for over three months, the first thing he did when he was discharged was to join a health club. He took a step of faith. The fact is, he couldn't go to the club for over a year. He was too weak, but he made up his mind he was not going to sit back and plan on staying in that wheelchair; he was making plans to be up walking again. That was more than five years ago, and today that young man can outrun me. He defied the odds. What happened? He started making plans to rise up out of that injury. He could have easily let the doctor's negative words sink in, convincing him to give up, and settle for mediocrity. Instead, he believed God and began making plans to be well.

Maybe you've had some negative things happen to you or some negative comments spoken over you. Don't allow those negatives to take root. Keep believing for good things. And remember, faith is always in the now. Get up every morning saying, "Father, I thank You that right now You are working in my life. I thank You that right now I'm getting better. Right now things are changing in my favor."

Stay in the now; faith is always in the present.

Avoid Planning for Defeat

We frequently prepare for the wrong things. A man told me that when his father got up in years, he had a terrible time with his eyesight. He got to the point where he couldn't read anymore. This was a common malady for the older members of their family. This man was already making plans to have poor eyesight. He said, "Joel, I love to read. So I've started buying all of my books on CD now. That way I can listen to them just in case something ever happens to my eyesight."

That's planning for the wrong things. That's putting your faith in the negative, allowing — even welcoming — it to come to pass. I told him, "You need to keep buying regular books that you always read. And even when you get older, don't start buying these large-print books just because some of your friends are, or it makes it a little easier for you. No, if you don't need it, don't take the easy way out. And even if you do need it, put that off until you cannot read the smaller print anymore. Don't give up any ground."

Victoria has always had good eyesight, twenty-twenty vision. But over the last couple of years she's developed some difficulty in reading print up close. I've tried to get her to go see the eye doctor, but she wouldn't do it. She could not stand to think about the fact that her vision might be impaired a bit.

Finally, I talked her into it. She went to the optometrist, and he said her eyes were strong. She needed the lowest-power reading glasses, the kind you can buy over the counter at the grocery store. Still, it has been like pulling teeth for her to give in to wearing those things. I love the fact that she's not going to just sit back and accept it; she stands against it. She has put it off and put if off and put it off. We'll go to a restaurant and she'll have to hold the menu eighteen inches away just to see it! It's like my dad used to say: "God, You're either going to have to heal my eyes or lengthen my arms." Victoria refuses to sit back and say, "Well, I guess I'm getting older." Or "I guess my vision is going downhill." No, she will not make plans for defeat.

I read a study the other day. It included a chart that showed how at different ages, certain parts of our bodies start to decline. According to the research, when we get to be thirty years old, our hearing diminishes so much every year. We lose so much muscle mass every year. Our brain cells decrease by a certain percentage each year. If you start believing all those reports and acting on them, no wonder your body is falling apart! The other day someone told me, "Joel, I just turned sixty and I can't hear as well as I used to. I knew this day was coming. Everybody told me my hearing would go down."

I told the person, "You are agreeing with the wrong voices. Quit putting your faith in the wrong places, and start agreeing with what God says about you. It says in Deuteronomy 34, verse 7, that when Moses was a hundred and twenty years old, his eye was not dim and his natural strength was not abated. That means he could still see clearly, he could hear clearly, he was strong and healthy. I don't know about you, but I'm going to believe to live out my days like Moses. Instead of listening to all these negative reports, let me give you a different report. Let me give you a study found in God's Word. It says in effect, 'At sixty, you're still supposed to hear well. At seventy, your mind is supposed to be as sharp as it was when you were twenty-five. At eighty, you're supposed to be full of joy, full of life, full of energy.' Why don't you start making plans to live a long, healthy, satisfied life?"

Back in the early 1990s, we were remodeling the old sanctuary at Lakewood Church, especially the platform area. At that time, my father was more than seventy years old. One of the architects I was working with said, "Joel, your dad's getting a little older. Don't you think we should put a wheelchair ramp up to the side of the platform, just in case he ever needs a wheelchair?" The architect was a nice man, and he meant well. But I thought to myself, *You don't know my father. If he heard you say that, he would chase you out of this county.* My dad was never planning on being in a wheelchair.

Don't make plans to get old and bent over and not be able to do anything. Keep your faith out there. Speak words of health over yourself. Talk about the long life God is giving you, then put some actions behind it.

I know a man in his nineties who still lives in his own home alone, and his bedroom is on the second floor. That means several times every day he goes up and down those stairs. His children and grandchildren have tried to talk him into moving into one of the empty bedrooms downstairs, but he won't do it. His mind is made up. He said, "Joel, I know if I give in, I'll never be able to go back up those stairs."

He's probably right. Certainly, we should use common sense; we have to be realistic. What I'm saying is don't make plans for defeat. Everybody around you may be getting old and cranky, complaining that this part of his body doesn't work or that part of her body is failing, but you can be the exception. Believe to live a long, healthy life.

My father wanted to preach for as long as he lived. He didn't want to retire. He used to tell me, "Joel, I will never have a stroke." He was saying that by faith because he struggled with high blood pressure his entire life. He would say, "I'll never be incapacitated. I'll never come to the place where I cannot preach."

And true to his faith, my father preached just eleven days before he went to be with the Lord. God gave him the desires of his heart, because he was bold enough to put his faith out there. He believed he was going to be productive right up until the day that he died, and he was.

It's easy to think, "Well, the law of entropy is setting in: Everything is moving toward disintegration. So of course my body is debilitating. That's just a part of getting older. This doesn't work. That doesn't work. Can't see. Can't hear. Cranky."

No, don't fall into that trap — especially not the cranky part. There are enough cranky people in the world already! Make plans to be healthy, to be full of joy, to be productive right up to the day God calls you home.

In the Old Testament, when Caleb was eighty years old, he said, "God, give me another mountain." He was saying, "Give me something else to do. Give me another assignment." Notice, he was planning on living out his life in victory. He could have said, "God, just let me retire. My back is hurting. I can hardly see anymore. Medicare wouldn't pay for that latest prescription. I'm so aggravated."

No, he was strong, energetic, and ready for the next challenge — even at eighty years of age. You are never too old to do something great for God. You can be sure that regardless of your age God has important plans for you to fulfill. You are not just taking up space, waiting to go to heaven. Get your joy back; get your enthusiasm back. Don't wither up like a prune; instead, make plans to live every day joyfully, vibrantly alive, healthy, and productive.

An older couple came to one of Lakewood's leadership conferences, and during a question-and-answer session, they stood up and the man said, "Joel, we're not real sure what we're supposed to be doing at our age."

He said that they were in their nineties. This man was dressed to the nines; his skin looked great. His eyes sparkled with life. His wife was the epitome of grace and beauty. They were a sharp, striking older couple.

I told them, "One thing you need to do for sure is to go around and let other people see you. Be an example. Your joy, your health, your peace, your victory is an inspiration to others." I said, "You need to let the younger generation — which, in your case, is anyone under eighty — see how you can be up there in years and still be healthy, joyful, and peaceful."

That elderly couple inspired me! I tell Victoria every week I'm believing for at least forty more good years of strong, productive ministry. Forty years of sharing God's Word, encouraging people, building the kingdom. Not thirty good years, and then the last ten, my back's hurting, this doesn't work, that doesn't work, no joy, no peace. No, I've got my faith out there. I'm believing that at eighty years old, I'm going to be just as vibrant as I am right now. I will still have my hair, still be telling my jokes, still be teasing my brother Paul. I'm making plans to live a long, healthy, prosperous, joy-filled, abundant life. Why don't you do the same thing?

I know a lady who went through an extensive medical checkup when she was about seventy years old. After the doctors compiled all of her information, they gave her an average life expectancy. Based on their findings, her health, her genetics, and her family history, they estimated that she'd probably live to be around seventy-five years old.

The doctors might as well have told her that she was going to die the next day. She got so depressed that she wouldn't come out of her house. She lost her joy and her peace. Basically, she just gave up living her life. This went on for a while, until one day, her family brought her to see me. I told her, "Don't make plans for the worst. Don't let the negative take root. God can do what man's human intelligence and medical science can't do. And I found sometimes these experts, even though they're fine people, they can be wrong." We talked further, and I tried to encourage her. I could tell by the expression on her face that she was filling up with faith. Today, that woman is eighty-one years old and as healthy and vibrant as can be.

When I saw her recently, she said, "Joel, I've already beaten it by six years."

I laughed and said, "Yeah, and when you make it to ninety, we're going to have a real party around here!" And we will.

While it is important that you don't let negative thoughts and declarations take root, it is equally important to set high goals for your life. My father always believed that he would live to preach into his nineties. He didn't quite make it, but he used to say, "I'd rather shoot high and miss it than shoot low and make it." Keep a high goal.

I used to play basketball with a gentleman who was in his seventies. He was in great shape and could run up and down the court with the twenty-year-olds. One day he said, "Joel, it's funny. When I was forty, my doctor told me that my knees wouldn't hold up playing this much, but I just kept playing. At fifty, he told me my back would start hurting if I kept running and jumping like this. But I just kept on. At sixty, he told me I could never keep up physically, but I can still run with the young guys." He said, "I went back at seventy, and finally the doctor told me to just keep playing as much as I want."

I laughed and asked him, "How long are you going to play?"

He smiled and said, "I'm going to play until I get old."

I like that. Old is a state of mind. Your body may age, but if you'll stay young in your spirit, your body will age even better. This man had the heart of a twenty-five-year-old. He was always grateful and happy, always in a good mood. You could tell that he wasn't making plans to get old and worn out. He was planning on living out his life joyfully, vibrantly, and in good health.

Maybe you have a history of serious illnesses in your family. You must stand against those diseases and believe God for good health. You can be the exception. You can be the one to start a new standard for your family. Here's what you have to do: You must think differently, and you need to take a different tack, take different actions. You cannot prepare for defeat and expect to live in victory. Keep your faith working for you, rather than against you.

Grandmother Osteen, my grandmother on my father's side, was a feisty woman. She stood only about five feet tall, but she had a big faith. One time, when she was older in life, she went to see her doctor. He said, "I'm sorry, Mrs. Osteen, but you're in the beginning stages of Parkinson's disease."

Well, Grandmother Osteen didn't know what that was, but she was sure she didn't want to have any part of it. She bristled back and she got real stern. She said, "Listen here, doctor, I'll not have that. I refuse to have it. I'm too old to have it."

She went home and never did come down with Parkinson's disease. She just kept doing what she'd always been doing, planning on living a long, healthy life. She didn't let the negative words take root.

I realize that we can't just wish things away; sometimes we can't even pray them away, but we *can* decide what we're going to plan for. We can plan to get old and lose our health, or we can plan to live a long, healthy, blessed, prosperous life.

What are you planning for today? Sickness or divine health? To barely get by or to be blessed? To stay where you are or to rise higher and accomplish your dreams? According to our actions or lack of action, we are making plans for something.

There's an interesting story in the Bible about a widow. Her husband died and she didn't have enough money to pay her bills.

The creditors were coming to take her two sons as payment. The only thing she had of any value was a small pot of oil. Elisha the prophet showed up at her home and he instructed her to do something rather unusual. He said, "Go out to all your neighbors and gather up as many large empty containers that you can find, big jars that can be used to hold oil." Elisha told her specifically, "Don't get just a few; get as many as you can possibly find."

No doubt, in the natural, it seemed like the woman was simply wasting her time. Elisha knew he had to get her faith going in the right direction. She had been sitting around long enough preparing for defeat. Now he was trying to get her to start preparing for victory. So she gathered up all sorts of empty containers, brought them home, and Elisha told her to pour the oil that she had into one of the other containers. At first, it looked as though she was merely going to transfer it from one container to another, but the Scripture says her oil never ran out. She kept pouring and pouring and pouring. God supernaturally multiplied it until every single container was completely full. If she would have gotten a dozen more containers, they would have been full as well. Friend, we are the ones who limit God; His resources are unlimited. If you will believe Him for more, regardless of your circumstances, He can provide — even if it takes a miracle to do so!

Let me challenge you. Have a big dream for your life. Make provision for abundance.

"I'd love to pay my house off," I hear you say. "I'd love to get out of debt, but I don't see how it could happen for me. I've gone as far in my career as I can go. I'd love to send my children to college, but it's so expensive these days."

No. Are you making provisions? Do you have a savings account opened up? Do you have any containers? "Well, Joel, that'd be kind of foolish to have an account and not have anything to put in it."

The woman in Elisha's day did precisely that. She took a step of faith. It's not enough just to believe. Put actions behind your faith. Do what you can. Are you being your best on the job, showing up early, going the extra mile, doing more than expected? Are you dressing for success? You may have only one suit. Clean it up, press it, and wear it like you own the place. Are you talking successful talk? "Well, everybody gets promoted except me. They're talking about laying off people at my job, and last week my washing machine broke. If it's not one thing, it's another."

No, dwelling on that sort of talk will only prepare you for defeat. Change your attitude and change what you're saying. Start saying, "This is going to be a blessed day; I'm having a good month. This is the best year of my life. I know great things are in store. Goodness and mercy are following me. God's favor is surrounding me. I am expecting increase, promotion, and abundance." Don't stop there; start making plans to prosper. Prepare to succeed, not to fail.

When my father went to be with the Lord back in 1999 and I stepped up to pastor the church, one of the first things I did was to cancel our weekly television time. I thought, *I've never preached before and I'm sure not going to get on television and preach.* So I called our representative from the main national network on which we were broadcasting at the time. He was a good friend, and I told him what had happened and how we were going to have to cancel our broadcast. What was I doing? I was making plans for defeat. I was making plans to do poorly. I didn't think I could preach; I couldn't imagine that anybody would want to listen to me, so I put actions behind my faith. But I was stretching my faith in the wrong direction.

When I got home that night, I casually mentioned to Victoria what I'd done. She said, "Joel, you need to get that time back. People all over the country are waiting to see what's going to happen to Lakewood."

When she said that, something resonated within me, and I knew that it was right. We immediately took steps to get the broadcast time back, and today the broadcast goes out all over the world. Many times, with our own actions, we are limiting God. Had I not taken a step of faith in the right direction, I don't know if we'd be on television today. We cannot prepare for defeat and expect to have victory.

Maybe you are preparing to fail, preparing to barely get by or to lose your health. Start preparing for good things; prepare for success, prepare for abundance. Prepare for victory. Prepare for a long life. Prepare for good health. Get your faith going in the right direction. Start making plans to live a blessed, prosperous, healthy, joy-filled, abundant, long life. If you do this, God will do more than you can even ask or think. He will pour out his blessings and favor and you will become a much better you!

CHAPTER 29
KEEP SINGING YOUR SONG

One of the secrets to becoming a better you is to keep singing the song that God has put in your heart — even if you can't carry a tune in a bucket! Let me explain. Too many people go around negative and discouraged, allowing their problems and circumstances to weigh them down. They live stressed out, dragging through each day, not really excited about life. I've had people tell me, "Joel, I've got too many problems to enjoy life." Or "The reason I'm discouraged and not happy is because I have all these things coming against me."

The fact is, God has put a well of joy on the inside of each one of us. Our circumstances may be negative; things may not be going our way. But if we can learn to tap into this joy, we can still be happy. We can live with enthusiasm in spite of what comes against us.

One of the keys is found in Ephesians

5:18. It says, "Ever be filled with the Spirit." Notice, you don't just get filled one time and then you live happily ever after. The Scripture says to be ever filled. That means we can be filled on a continual basis. How can we do this?

The next verse reveals the secret: "By speaking to yourselves in psalms and hymns, by making melody in your heart, and by being grateful." In other words, the way to keep your life full of joy and the way to overcome the pressures of life is by keeping a song of praise in your heart. All through the day, we should be singing, if not aloud then at least silently allowing a song of praise to dance through our minds. You may not actually vocalize words and music. You may simply express a grateful attitude. In your thoughts, you are thinking about God's goodness. Or maybe you go around humming a tune to a song. Maybe it's something as simple as whistling while you work, but throughout the day, you're making melody in your heart. Under your breath, you're saying, "Lord, thank You for this day. Thank You that I'm alive and healthy."

When you do that, you are filling up on the inside; God is replenishing your strength; He's refilling your supply of joy and peace. The very things that so often become depleted through the stress, disappointments, and rigors of the day, God wants to refresh in your life. When you keep singing that song of praise, you can be continually refilled, filling up faster than the depletion caused by life taking a toll on you. That's how we stay full of the Spirit.

"Well, I went to church on Sunday," Mike said. "I read my Bible before I went to work. Isn't that enough?"

No, this is an ongoing process. To be ever filled means we have to get in a habit of being refilled throughout the day — especially on those tough days.

Think back to when somebody gave your child some helium-filled balloons on her birthday. For the first few days following the party, the balloons remain bright and beautiful. They fly high at the end of their strings, bobbing in the wind. If you let go, the balloons would take off into the air. In a couple of days, though, the balloons begin to shrivel and shrink, sinking down, lower, smaller, weaker. Day by day, the balloons drop lower and lower. Finally, they land on the floor, totally deflated. The balloons have lost their life and attractiveness, not to mention their potential to rise higher.

Ironically, all you'd have to do to replenish those balloons and give them a fresh new start and appeal is to fill them back full of helium. If you did so on a regular basis, those balloons would last for months, bringing happiness and joy to all who saw them.

The same principle is true regarding our lives. Throughout the day, no matter how filled we are at the start, we "leak"; we get pressured or stressed; life happens. You get stuck in traffic, and a little helium goes out. You find out you didn't get the contract you were hoping for, and a little more escapes your balloon. You get home at the end of a hard day only to discover that your child is not feeling well and you must deal with that. The dog got into the trash, you have to clean up that mess, and your balloon loses a little more of its shape. The only way to stay full and to keep your joy and peace is to have this song of praise in your heart.

Understand, I'm not saying that you have to burst out in song, but I am suggesting that in your thoughts, you continually express a grateful attitude. Under your breath, throughout the day, you are thanking God for all He has done for you and your family. When you are working around the house, instead of complaining, you're whistling a tune. While you are cleaning up the dishes, you have some good praise music on in the background. You're humming along with it.

What's happening? You are making melody in your heart, and when you do that, you are continually filled up with God's love, joy, and peace.

Everywhere my father went, he was either singing or praying or whistling. Sometimes, when he would whistle incessantly, it would get on my mother's nerves. She'd say, "John, would you quit whistling? Can we have some peace around here?"

He'd say, "Oh, Dodie, I'm just happy. I'm just giving God praise."

She'd say, "John, you are whistling the tune to *The Andy Griffith Show*. You are not giving God praise."

The song didn't matter to my dad; what mattered was his attitude. My father was joyful when he was whistling. In his mind, he was saying, "God, I'm happy. God, I love You. I'm grateful to be alive." He always had a song of praise in his heart.

When you are doing the dishes, you can stand at the sink and complain, "Nobody appreciates me; all I do is work around here." Or you can choose to hum a song of praise and thanks. It's up to you.

"Well, I'm not musically inclined," you might say. "I can't sing very well."

Neither can I. But this isn't merely about music; this is an attitude. In our thoughts, we are grateful. We are excited about the future. We are expecting good things from God, so we allow a song to play continually in our minds. Any of us can do that. And yes, if you choose, you can sing in the shower or while driving to work. When you do this, you're making melody in your heart.

Not long ago, I woke up in the middle of the night and I could hear myself singing a song that I've known since I was a little boy. The words were right out of the Scripture: "You, oh Lord, are a shield unto me. The glory and the lifter of my head." Over and over, not out loud, but deep inside me, a song of praise was gushing out. As it did, God was filling me up anew.

When you're driving to work, play an inspiring praise CD. Make use of that time. At your house, put on some good uplifting music. Pay attention to what's going into you. Be aware of what you're feeding yourself.

A while back, I was driving and scanning the radio dial at the same time. I came across a station that plays oldies. When I turned it on, the first thing I heard was, "You're no good, you're no good, you're no good. Baby, you're no good."

I thought, *I don't need to hear that! I have enough things to deal with each day without putting that junk into me.*

Talk about leaking! If you listen to negative material like that, don't be surprised when you find yourself feeling totally deflated.

That's what many people do today. In their thoughts, they have no song. They dwell on negative issues, the people who hurt them, how much work they have to do, how unfair life is. Then they wonder why they don't have any energy, why they don't enjoy raising their children, why they dread going to work. It's because they've lost their song. They're not replenishing what's being taken out of them. You must stay on the offensive and make sure you have more positive input than negative.

It's interesting how little children — even toddlers — become invigorated if you put on some good music. They start swaying, dancing, and clapping. The music energizes them. Interestingly, you don't have to teach them to do that. You don't have to say, "I'm about to turn on the music; get ready to move."

It comes naturally to them because God has put a song in their heart. In the same way, God has put rhythm in every one of us. Too often, we allow the pressures of life to weigh us down. We had this song when we were children. We were happy, carefree, excited about life. But over time, we've developed new habits: being sour, dragging through the day, not really being excited about life. We need to rediscover childlike faith, and when we do, we will also discover the song within us.

One day, our seven-year-old daughter Alexandra came in early in the morning. She was dressed and ready to go to school, so happy, so enthusiastic. She smiled real big and said, "Daddy, guess what? I've already sung two songs, and I've already done two cartwheels."

I looked her in the eyes and I said, "Sweetheart, I love your enthusiasm. No matter what comes your way, keep singing those songs and keep turning those cartwheels."

Interesting to me, Victoria and I never asked Alexandra to sing. She just sings. I can hear her all through the day. It's because God has put a song in her heart. Start the day by making melody in your heart unto God, singing a song of praise. That's what I do. In the shower, I sound great! I don't know what happens when I step out! I like to start my day with a song of praise. Even if you don't do it out loud, at least do it on the inside. You may even want to try a few cartwheels, as well!

Whatever you do, get your song back. If

you need to change some of your habits and quit dwelling on the negative, do it! Things may not be perfect in your life, but it could be a whole lot worse. Stop dwelling on what's wrong and start being grateful for what's right. Throughout the day, thank God for His goodness. Meditate on His promises. If you'll get your song back, you'll not only enjoy life more, but you will see things change in your favor.

My grandmother learned how to do this. Growing up, my siblings and I used to go over to my grandparents' home a lot. Every time I saw Grandmother, she was humming a tune. You couldn't hear her unless you were right next to her, but while ironing the clothes, she was at peace; she had a smile on her face, just humming along. In everything she did — doing the dishes, cooking dinner, traveling with my grandfather — she was constantly making melody in her heart. I cannot remember one time that I ever saw my grandmother upset, frustrated, stressed out, or worried. She was one of the most peaceful, joyful people that I've ever known. Even when things didn't go her way, her attitude was, "I'm not going to worry about it. I know that everything is going to be all right."

One time, my grandparents came over to

our house for Thanksgiving dinner, and my grandmother forgot the turkey — the main dish. But it did not ruin her day. It did mine, but not hers. She stayed in peace. She just laughed and said, "Can you believe I did that?" Nothing took away her song. No wonder she lived a long, healthy life. She was always making melody in her heart unto God.

IT STARTS IN YOUR HEART

I wonder how much more you and I would enjoy our lives if we'd be a little bit more like her. How would our attitude change if we did not take everything so seriously, and refused to allow every setback or disappointment to depress us for two weeks. How much better our lives could be if we'd simply keep the song of praise in our hearts!

Maybe lately you have noticed that you don't smile as much as usual; you don't laugh much anymore. You have allowed the burdens of life to weigh you down. Perhaps you have settled into enduring your life and not really enjoying it. You don't have the fire and enthusiasm you once had.

This can all change, but it requires a decision on your part. You must develop some new habits. Number one: Develop a habit of smiling on purpose. "But I don't feel like smiling. I have a lot of problems, a lot of things coming against me," you might say.

No, sometimes you have to smile by faith. If you'll smile by faith, soon the joy will follow. Smiling sends a message to your whole body that everything is going to be okay. When you smile, chemicals are released throughout your physical system that make you feel better. Beyond that, when you smile you'll have more of God's favor. It will help you in your career. Smiling will help you in dealing with people. Numerous studies show that people who smile and are friendly, people who have a pleasant demeanor, get more breaks than other people who are solemn and unfriendly.

I read where a major corporation planned to hire five hundred new employees. They interviewed five thousand people and they automatically disqualified any candidate who smiled fewer than four times during the interview.

Somebody has said your smile is a million-dollar asset. If you're not using it, you're doing yourself a disservice. "Well, Joel, I don't think it matters whether I smile or not."

God is concerned about your countenance. Fifty-three times in the Scripture, He mentions it. When you smile, it's not only good for yourself, but it's a good witness to others. They will want the sort of happiness that you have. It's one thing to talk about our faith, but it's a far better thing to live it out. One of the best witnesses we could ever have is simply to be happy, to have a smile, to be friendly and pleasant to be around.

Some people always seem to look as though they've lost their last friend. Even when they go to church, they look as though they were attending God's funeral!

Somebody asks, "How're you doing?"

"Oh, I'm just trying to hold on till Jesus comes," the starched-faced person replies.

No, we're not supposed to be merely holding on or dragging through life. Get your song back. Quit allowing the burdens of life to weigh you down.

Sure, sometimes you think, *I have a lot coming against me. I'm dealing with some difficult issues.* But the truth is, we all have tough times, hard things to handle, or heavy loads to carry. Don't allow your problems and circumstances to steal your joy.

And don't allow someone else to rob you of God's best. Too many people are being dragged down because somebody in their life is negative. Somebody else won't do right. Maybe you work around people who always complain. Or you live with somebody who seems perpetually discouraged and wants to wallow in self-pity. Don't get into the pit with them. Keep your song.

Several years ago, I was walking through a large field covered with brown weeds. Everywhere I looked, I saw nothing but dried-up, dead, unattractive weeds. As I came to a certain point on the path, however, I noticed one beautiful flower, colorful and radiant. It had bloomed right there in the midst of all those weeds. I immediately thought, *That's the way we're supposed to be.* We may have a lot of problems; you may have a lot of negative people around you. But don't sink down to their level; just bloom right where you are. You may be married to an old weed, but you can still bloom. You may work around a bunch of weeds — people who complain, gossip, bad-mouth the company, the boss, or one another.

You may not be able to change them, but you can bloom right there amidst all the weeds. Put a smile on your face and have a grateful attitude. Don't let anyone else drag you down. Instead, by your example, pull them up; make them want what you have.

Declare today, "I'm not allowing another problem, another circumstance, or another person to keep me from giving God praise. I'm going to bless the Lord at all times. I'm going to get my song back."

I recognize that our problems are real, and at times, life is extremely difficult. But after you get through this problem, after you overcome this challenge, there will always be another challenge to overcome. There'll be something else to deal with. If you are waiting for all of your problems to go away before you decide to get your song back, you will miss the joy of living.

The Apostle Paul had all sorts of difficulties, all kinds of challenges. But he said, "In all these things we are more than conquerors." Notice, he didn't say, "When these difficulties are done, I'm going to be happy." No, he said, "In the middle of this adversity, I'm going to enjoy my life anyway."

Number one: Get in a habit of smiling on purpose. Number two: Check your posture. Make sure you stand up tall, put your shoulders back and hold your head up high. You are a child of the Most High God. You are not supposed to go around slumped over, feeling sloppy, weak, inferior, and thinking that you're unattractive.

The Scripture says, "We are ambassadors of Christ."[57] That means you represent Almighty God. Represent Him well. Even many good, godly people have gotten into a bad habit of slumping and looking down. When you do that, subconsciously you are communicating a lack of confidence, a lack of self-esteem. You need to put your shoulders back, hold your head up high, and communicate strength, determination, and confidence. Subconsciously, you're saying, "I'm proud of who I am. I know I'm made in the image of Almighty God. I know I am the apple of God's eye."

Much of communication is nonverbal. When I first started ministering publicly, and I really wanted to make a point, I'd stick my neck out and lean over. I was trying to be real emphatic and demonstrative. But a friend of mine who deals in communication suggested, "Joel, you're doing just the opposite. When you stick your head out and you're all bent over, that's a sign of weakness. You would communicate much more effectively if you'd put your shoulders back and hold your head up high. That's a position of strength and confidence, and people will receive more of what you have to say."

Our body language is communicating constantly, so make sure yours is saying what you want to say. Your countenance, smile, posture, and how you carry yourself may make a world of difference in becoming a better you.

As a young man, I noticed this quality about a friend of ours, an older gentleman.

He looked like a statesman; his posture was perfect, his manner of dress impeccable. He was always kind, compassionate, and considerate. He is now in his eighties and he carries himself exactly the same way. When I see him, I think of a prince or a king. He looks like royalty. That's the way you and I should be. Not in arrogance. I'm not saying to be proud and puffed up. I'm talking about living with a calm, quiet confidence. We know we are representing Almighty God. Let's learn to walk tall.

Certainly, your personality plays a part in this. Some people are naturally more confident. Some people naturally smile more often. I probably smile in my sleep. You may be just the opposite. But don't use that as an excuse to go through life sour and unfriendly. I've had to make changes, too. While I smile a lot naturally, I am by nature rather quiet and reserved. I have had to train myself to be more confident and to speak up.

You may have a lot of confidence, but you're too serious, you don't smile nearly enough. You can train yourself to smile more often. The best smile, of course, starts on the inside. In fact, the Scripture implies that our joy can overflow. That means we should have so much joy that when other people get around us, it rubs off on them. When they leave, they should be happier, encouraged, inspired, better off than they were before.

Notice when you get around people, are you always taking and never giving? Are you counting on them to cheer you up? It should be the opposite. You need to start making melody in your own heart. Maybe you received a bad report from the doctor, and it takes the wind out of your sail. That's when you have to dig your heels in and say, "God, I know you're still in control. I'm going to keep a smile on my face and I'm going to give You praise anyway."

The Scripture tells us to offer unto God the sacrifice of praise,[58] but that doesn't mean it is always easy to do so. Nevertheless, our attitude should be, "God, I know when I keep my song and stay grateful it not only activates your power, but it also replenishes me. It fills me up. So despite my circumstances, I choose to give you praise anyway."

Friend, you can choose what kind of song you're going to have. Don't be lazy in your thought life; speak to yourself in psalms and hymns. You talk to yourself throughout the day. Perhaps you have been talking to yourself in the wrong way. You need to start declaring, "This is going to be a good day. Thank you, Lord, for your strength. Thank you, Lord, for my health."

Get your song back. Say things such as, "Father, thank You for this day. Thank You that I'm alive." Every time you do that, God will fill you afresh with His joy, His peace, His strength, His victory, and His favor. And when you're full of God's love and power, a natural by-product is that you start looking for the good things of God in your life. Let's look at that more closely in our next chapter.

CHAPTER 30
FROM BELIEVING TO EXPECTING

I hope that by now you are making preparations for the good things God has in store for you. God has put dreams and desires in every one of our hearts. We all have promises that we're standing on, things that we believe will come to pass. But almost always there's a time of waiting involved. Maybe you're waiting for a relationship to improve, waiting to get married, waiting for a promotion, or perhaps you are waiting to overcome an illness.

Much of life is spent waiting. There's a right way to wait and a wrong way. Too often when things don't happen on our timetable we get down and discouraged. Even though we have the promise in our heart, we give up and settle for the status quo. I believe it's because we're not waiting the right way.

The Bible says, "Be patient as you wait." [59] Notice, it doesn't say *if* you wait, it says *as* you wait. The passage goes on to say, "See how the farmer waits expectantly." That's the key: We have to wait with expectancy. We're not supposed to sit around thinking, *My situation is never going to change. I prayed, I believed. But I don't see how I can ever get out of this mess.*

No, to wait with expectancy means that we are hopeful and positive. We get up every morning expecting good things. We may have problems, but we know this could be the day God turns it around. This could be the day I get the break that I need.

Waiting should not be a passive thing. Waiting the correct way means you are on the lookout. You talk as if what you believe is going to happen. You act as though it's going to happen. You are making preparations.

If you are expecting someone for dinner, you don't wait until the guest shows up at your door before you prepare for the meal. Most likely you start early in the day. You make sure the house is clean. You may go to the grocery store the day before; perhaps you will buy some flowers for the table and swing by the bakery to get your favorite dessert — low-fat, of course. You make all these preparations. Why? Because you're expecting someone.

We need a similar attitude while we're waiting for God's promises to come to pass.

It's not enough merely to pray. We must put actions behind our prayers. The Scripture says: "Faith without corresponding actions is dead."[60] In other words, we can believe one way, we can talk one way, but if we're not putting the right actions behind our faith, it's not going to do any good.

I talked to Scott, a young man who has a dream to go to college. But nobody in his family has gone beyond high school. He immediately began listing all of his obstacles. "Joel, I don't know if I can afford it. I don't know if I'll make good enough grades. I don't know if they'll accept me. I don't know what my other family members will think." He was about to talk himself out of his dream.

Finally, I stopped him and said, "Scott, why don't you take a step of faith? Put some actions behind your prayers and at least fill out an application. Go tour the campus. Talk to the counselors. Make preparations to succeed. If you'll do what you can, then God will do what you can't."

Too often, we're believing one way, but actions are demonstrating the opposite — we're actually preparing for defeat. Maybe you come from a long line of divorce in your family. Instead of being afraid of ever getting married or worrying that your marriage will end in divorce, you need to start planning what you're going to do on your first wedding anniversary, and on your fifth anniversary, and on your twenty-fifth anniversary. Speak words of vitality and life regarding your marriage. Don't say, "I'm not sure our marriage is going to survive this strain." Not any of this, "If we make it, maybe we'll go on a cruise next year." Get rid of the "if" and start saying, "*When* we make it!"

I tease Victoria that I have already planned our fiftieth wedding anniversary. The way I figure, after sticking with me for all those years, I'm going to take that girl to Dairy Queen!

Seriously, though, stay hopeful and positive, and make preparations to succeed. We must understand there's a difference between believing and expecting. You can believe to have a child and not even be pregnant. But once you go from believing to expecting, you kick into a different gear. When you are expecting, you'll go furnish the nursery. You'll buy clothes for a baby that's not here. You'll call your friends and relatives and let them know the good news. "Mom! Dad! A baby is on its way." Even in the early stages of pregnancy, you start making all sorts of preparations. It affects your attitude, what you eat and drink, how you exercise, talk, and think.

Interestingly, you may go several months and say, "I look the same. I don't feel all that different."

It doesn't matter what you see or feel. You received a report from the doctor that says a baby is on its way. That's all you need to know to start making preparations.

You need to do something similar when God puts a dream in your heart. Maybe one of His promises comes alive in your heart and mind, and for the first time, you dare to believe that your family can be restored. You know you can be healthy again. You know you can accomplish your dreams. The first thing is you have to let the seed really take root. But you can't stop there. You must move on from believing to expecting.

"I'm doing that," you might say, "but I don't see anything happening. My finances aren't improving. I don't see any doors opening. My health is slipping rather than improving."

Scripture teaches, "We walk by faith, not by sight."[61] If you can see everything happening, you don't really need any faith. But when you have nothing to stand on in the natural — and you start acting as though God's Word is true, being positive and hopeful — you are putting actions behind your faith. That gets God's attention. That's what causes Him to work supernaturally in your life. What happened? You went from believing to expecting.

That's what the leadership of Lakewood Church did when we were negotiating to move our congregation to the Compaq Center, former home of the National Basketball Association's Houston Rockets. I announced to the congregation that we were going to raise funds to renovate the center before we really knew for sure that it was going to be ours. After we won the main city council vote, a company filed a lawsuit to try to keep us from moving in. Our attorneys told us there was no guarantee that we would win, and even if we did, the case could be tied up in the courts for up to ten years through various appeals.

From a logical business standpoint, I should have waited to see how everything was going to turn out. But down inside, I knew God wanted us to go forward. So I went from believing to expecting, and we started making preparations. Just like a young couple preparing the nursery, we started drawing the new plans, doing the studies, putting the vision out there.

It wasn't always comfortable or easy. Many times, I'd wake up in the middle of the night in a cold sweat. Those negative voices would pummel my mind, saying, "Joel, what are you going to do if you don't get that building? You're going to look like a fool! You've already encouraged people to donate their money to the cause. You're going to have to give their money back." And on and on.

I'd say, "God, I know You're in control, and I'm not going to be moved by what I don't see. I know You are bigger than our obstacles. And God, I believe at the right time, You will change things in our favor."

A year and a half later, that's exactly what happened.

How does the farmer wait? Expectantly. How does he take care of his seed? By watering it, by pulling the weeds, by keeping the soil soft.

How do we water our seeds? By staying full of praise. By getting up every morning and thanking God that the answer is on the way. When negative thoughts threaten that it's never going to happen, you're never going to get well; you're never going to get out of debt, pull those weeds by simply saying, "God, I know You are faithful. My trust and confidence is in You. I know You have great things in store for my life." You protect your seed by having a grateful attitude of expectation.

Are you believing or are you expecting?

"Well, Joel, I'd like to get out of debt," you might say. Or "I'd like to have a nice house one day. But my business is so slow. And the cost of living is so high. I don't see how it could ever happen for me."

That kind of thinking will keep you right where you are. Decide to wait with expectancy. Declare, "God, I know You can do what men can't do. You are my provider; my job is not my source, the economy is not my source. But God, I know You are my source."

Get a bigger vision; get rid of that limited mentality and start making preparations for God's blessings, even if it's in some small area.

Years ago, I went to the apartment of Peter and Becky, some friends of mine. It was a small place, and even though they were happy and content, they knew God had put bigger things in their hearts. As an act of faith, when the young couple bought furniture for their den, they bought pieces that were much too large for the size of the small room. The couches were crammed against each other, with tables on each end. I could barely step by them.

Naturally, I didn't say anything about it, but it looked odd to me. A few minutes later, Becky said, "Joel, you'll have to excuse our den. We bought this furniture for our *new* house."

I didn't know they were moving, so I said, "Really, where are you going?"

They laughed and Peter replied, "We don't know yet. We just know we're not staying here. This is only temporary."

They were saying, "This is not our destiny. We're not going to sit back and accept this. God has put bigger things in our hearts and we're making preparations to rise higher."

They stayed in that apartment for several years, and when I'd see them in passing, I often asked, "Have you moved yet?"

"Not yet."

"When are you moving?"

Their answer was always, "Soon!" I never heard them speak out discouraging words. I never saw them down and defeated. They stayed hopeful and expectant.

One day, Becky got a huge break at work, resulting in a promotion and a sizable increase in her salary. Suddenly, things started falling into place.

Can you guess where that oversized furniture is now?

No, it's not in their new home. They gave it to another young couple who are believing for their dream home, and Becky and Peter purchased brand-new furniture for their new home.

You get God's attention when you put actions behind your faith. Why not take a step of faith, plant a seed, do something that indicates to you and others that you are planning to succeed?

You may be facing sickness and disease. Maybe you got some bad news concerning your health. Well, don't start planning your funeral. Don't sit around depressed thinking about all the other people who have died from that same disease. Start making plans to get well.

When my father was preparing for open-heart surgery, it was an extremely serious situation. The doctors gave us no guarantees that it would turn out okay.

Instead of moping around in defeat, my father had us bring his tennis shoes and his running suit up to the hospital and put them right beside his bed. The facts said that he would not be up running anytime soon. But every day as he recovered, he'd look at those tennis shoes. In his mind, he was saying, *One day soon, I'm going to be running again. One day I'm going to be healthy. One day I'm going to be strong.* He was watering his seed, living expectantly, and that is what gave him the strength to carry on.

The Scripture says, "Those who wait upon the Lord"[62] will have their strength renewed. The Amplified Bible expands what it means to "wait on the Lord." It says, "Those who expect, who look for, and hope in Him." What might happen if we were to live with expectancy, stay hopeful, and make preparations for the goodness of God?

This Scripture goes on to say, "We will mount up with wings like the eagle. You will run and not get tired. You will walk and not faint." In other words, you will not stay down; you will overcome life's challenges.

If you can just get up every morning expecting God to turn your problems around for good, if you can stay positive and hopeful, then God promises He will give you a supernatural strength that will cause you to soar like the eagles.

PUT SOME ACTION BEHIND YOUR PRAYERS

Remember, though, you need to put some actions behind your prayers. You may already be praying and believing; that's good. But don't stop there; keep pressing in closer to God. Move deeper to not only believing God can do something in your life, but expecting that God will do great things in, for, and through you.

A minister I know had a dream to go all over the world and share God's Word. But at the time, he didn't have a single open door, not one invitation.

Instead of getting down and discouraged, thinking, *I must have missed it. This must not be for me,* he took a step of faith. He went out and bought a brand-new set of luggage. He had hardly traveled more than a few miles beyond his hometown, and in the natural he had much better things on which he could have spent his money. But deep down, he knew that one day, God was going to open doors of opportunity for him. The minister kept his faith fresh and strong.

About six months later, he received his first invitation to speak outside his church. He was so excited that he brought it up and showed it to my father. Today that man travels all over the world. He has more invitations than he could ever possibly accept. He went from believing to expecting to receiving. Notice how he put action behind his faith. We cannot be passive and have God's best. When we're really expecting, we're on the lookout for opportunities. We're doing everything we can to make our dreams come to pass.

When my sister Tamara was about seven years old, she decided she wanted some rabbits. We lived out in the country and we already had a couple of dogs, and even some chickens. But Tamara wanted some rabbits, too. She went to my father and said, "Daddy, would you please get me some rabbits?"

My father was generous and good to his children, but he had endured enough problems with our chickens. They frequently escaped their pen or the yard, and we had to go round them up from our neighbors.

Daddy said, "Tamara, I love you, but we are not going to get any rabbits." Well, he might as well have told that to a tree for all Tamara heard him; she paid no attention. Instead, she kept acting like she was going to get those rabbits.

It reminded me of a time when Jesus was walking down the road on His way to pray for a little girl who was sick. Along the way, though, he encountered several delays and interruptions. Finally, the people came up and said to his disciples, "Tell Jesus not to bother coming. It's too late. The little girl has died."

The Scripture says, "[Jesus,] overhearing but ignoring."[63] Now, there's a principle: Sometimes, to stay in faith, you must ignore a negative report. Sometimes people will try to talk you out of your dreams. Sometimes medical science will tell you there's nothing more they can do for you. Sometimes our own thoughts can even try to convince us of all the reasons why our dream, goal, or prayer request is not going to happen.

Jesus heard the bad news, but He chose to ignore it. He chose to not allow it to influence Him. That's what my sister Tamara did. Every two or three days, she went back to my father and asked him again, "Daddy, have you thought any more about those rabbits? I really would like to have one."

"Tamara, I don't have to think about it," Daddy said. "We are not getting any rabbits."

A couple of days later, Tamara asked again. "Daddy, I'd still like to have a rabbit." This went on for two or three months. Tamara was determined that one day she was going to have those rabbits.

At one point, I could tell she was wearing my father down. He said, "Tamara, even if I wanted to get you rabbits, I have no idea where to get one."

"I do!" Tamara responded. "I know exactly where they are. I've already seen the place."

He said, "Show me." They got in the car and drove about fifteen minutes down the highway. About two hundred yards off the main road, way back in the woods, was a small sign. On it in handwritten letters were the words: "Rabbits for Sale."

Tamara was on the lookout. And when you have a dream in your heart, you'll see things that other people don't see. My family and I had traveled up and down that road hundreds of times, yet none of us had ever seen that sign. Finally, my father said, "Tamara, I'd love to get you rabbits, but we don't have any place to keep them."

She said, "Yes, we do. I've already had Paul make me a cage."

Needless to say, Tamara got her rabbits.

A lot of times, we are waiting for God to do something. "God, just give it to me on a silver platter."

But we must do our part by making preparations. Do some research, sow some seeds, and then stay expectant.

"Well, Joel, what if I do that and it doesn't happen?"

What if you do this and it *does* happen? Even if it doesn't turn out the way you had hoped, you'll still be better off to live your life positively and hopeful.

Many people are waiting for their situation to change, and while they're waiting to get the break they need, they get all sour. "Nothing good ever happens to me." "When am I going to get married?" "When am I going to get out of this problem?"

No, you need to turn that situation over to God.

In the Old Testament, David said, "God, my times are in your hands." He was saying, "God, I don't know when it's going to happen, but I know You know what's best for me, so I'm going to expect good things. And even if it doesn't happen today, I'm not going to go to bed disappointed. I'll keep trusting that I am one day closer to seeing it come to pass."

Start making preparations to live a blessed life. Keep your vision in front of you and don't believe the "never" lies: I'll never get well. I'll never see my dreams come to pass. No, shake that off, and stay positive and expectant.

You may say, "I did this. I prayed, I believed, I expected. But my loved one died. I just don't understand it."

No, God still has a great plan for your life. You cannot let one setback or even a series of disappointments keep you from pressing forward and believing for God's best.

John and Karen had become estranged from their son. Some things had happened, causing them to be at odds with each other. The young man wouldn't talk to his mother or father, wouldn't come visit them, and wouldn't have anything to do with them.

This went on month after month, until it looked as if they would never be reconciled.

But John and Karen refused to give up on their son. They took a step of faith and bought their son a Bible. They even had his name engraved on the front of it. The young man had never had anything to do with the things of God, so by all outward appearances, it seemed that his parents were wasting their money. They put the Bible on their coffee table anyway, and every time they walked by it, they thanked God that one day their son would be back home. One day, he would get back on the right course.

A few years later, they got a phone call from their son. "Mom and Dad," he said, "I want to come home." God supernaturally restored that relationship and today, I see that young man in church all the time, and he's carrying a Bible — but not just any Bible. He's clutching that Bible with his name engraved on it, the same one that sat on that coffee table all those years.

John and Karen waited expectantly. They made preparations for their son to come back home, and today their entire family is reaping the benefits.

Stacey was so tired of being overweight. She had tried every diet that came along, yet nothing seemed to work. Finally, she gave up and resigned herself to being overweight, even though she knew that wasn't God's best for her.

In any area of life, it is easy to settle for mediocrity. But one day, Stacy got fed up. She put her foot down and started applying actions to her prayers. She went to the mall and purposely bought a new outfit that was two sizes too small for her. She knew she couldn't wear it.

What was she doing? She was preparing to lose the weight. She went from believing to expecting. She later told me that she put that outfit in her closet right by her mirror so she could see it every day. It inspired her. Every time she saw it, she'd say, "Father, thank You that I'm going to lose this weight. Thank You that every gland, every organ, every cell in my body functions normally. Thank You that I have discipline and self-control."

When I next saw her, she was wearing her new outfit. She said, "Joel, I not only lost thirty pounds, but I feel better today than I've ever felt before."

God rewards people like that — people who keep the vision in front of them. Stay determined. Tamara would have never gotten those rabbits if she had not already had the cages built. Lakewood Church would never have been able to secure our new building had we not pressed through those obstacles.

Stretch your faith. Put some actions behind what you are believing God to do for you. Maybe you've just about given up on what God has put in your heart. You think your life is never going to get any better.

It can, but you must rekindle that fire.

"Well, Joel, it's been a long, long time . . ."

The Scripture says, "Though the vision tarries, wait earnestly for it." Notice, we can't wait passively; we must wait earnestly and expectantly. What will happen when you do that? The Scripture passage goes on to say, "The vision will not be one second late." That means when we stay in faith, positive, expectant, and hopeful, then all the forces of darkness cannot keep God from bringing those promises to pass.

You may remember Gavin MacLeod, the actor probably best known for playing the captain on *The Love Boat,* a popular television show years ago. He and his wife Patti had been married for seven years. They hit some bumps along the road and Gavin left.

He later told how he got caught up in his career and wasn't making good choices. He and Patti divorced and Patti was devastated. She never wanted the breakup of their marriage.

Instead of just giving up and accepting their divorce, every day she started thanking God that one day Gavin would be back home and their relationship would be restored. She took it one step further and started putting actions behind her faith.

Patti later told how every night at the dinner table, instead of setting one place setting, she would set two place settings. She was making preparations for Gavin to come back home.

Three years later, Patti heard a knock on the front door. She opened it and there stood Gavin. She smiled and said, "Come on in. Your dinner is getting cold." They remarried shortly thereafter.

How are you waiting for the good things of God? Learn to wait with expectancy. Get up every morning and water your seeds by thanking God that the answer is on the way. Then take it one step further and start making preparations for the dreams God has planted in your heart. Talk like it's going to happen, act like it's going to happen. Keep the right attitude. If you will go from believing to expecting, God promises that in due season, at the right time, He will bring you the desires of your heart.

CHAPTER 31
STAY PASSIONATE
ABOUT LIFE

If you want to become a better you, it is imperative that you appreciate the good things that God has done for you. Too many people have lost their passion for life. They've lost their enthusiasm. At one time, they were excited about their dreams. They got up every day with purpose and with passion. But now because of the time that's passed, the disappointments they have experienced, and the pressures of life, they're not excited about them anymore. They've lost their fire.

At one time maybe you were excited about that person to whom you are married. You were so in love and so passionate, but now that relationship has become stale. You are going through the motions of life, getting up, going to work, coming home. But God does not want us to live that way. We should get up every day with enthusiasm, excited about that day. We should be grateful that we're alive, grateful for the opportunities in front of us, grateful for the people in our lives.

Understanding that most of life is rather routine, anything can become stagnant if we allow it to do so. You can have an exciting job, but it can become boring. Or you can be married to a fine, loving, caring person, but if you don't nourish that relationship and put something into it, over time, it is likely to get stagnant. We have to work at it if we're going to stay fresh. It doesn't automatically happen.

We need to stir ourselves up every day. The Apostle Paul told Timothy, "Fan your flame." He was saying, "Timothy, don't let your fire go out. Stay passionate about your life. Stay enthusiastic about your dreams."

Maybe right now, you are having difficulty being excited about your life, but keep your hope alive. You may have just a tiny flicker, and that fire is barely burning. You're about to give up on one of your dreams. Or maybe in that relationship, you're not excited about it anymore. But the good news is the fire is still in there, and if you will do your part to fan the flame, it can burst forth into passion once again. That means instead of dragging around finding every reason you can to be unhappy, you must change your focus. Quit looking at what's wrong in your life and start being grateful for what's right in your life.

Your attitude should be: "I am not going to live my life defeated and depressed. My dreams may not have come to pass yet; I may have some obstacles in my path, but I know God is still in control, I know He's got great things in store for me, so I'm going to get up each day excited about my life."

Everything may not be perfect in your life, but if you don't learn to be happy where you are, you will never get to where you want to be. You may not have the perfect job, but you should thank God that at least you are employed. Some people would love to have your job. Fan your flame and go to work with a new enthusiasm. Don't drag into the workplace with a long face and then waste half the day playing on the Internet. Instead, give your employer 100 percent. Do your work with all your heart, to the best of your ability. Stay passionate about it. Everybody else may be slacking off; everybody else may have a sour attitude. But you are not everybody else; you are a child of the Most High God. Don't be part of the problem; be part of the solution.

Enthusiasm is contagious. If you go into your workplace with a smile on your face, full of life, full of joy, full of victory, before long, you'll rub off on others. That whole place will come up to a higher level, thanks to you.

The Bible says to "never lag in zeal, but be aglow and on fire serving the Lord."[64] Do you get up each morning passionate about your dreams? Are you grateful for the home in which you live?

"Oh, I'm living in a tiny apartment," you may say. "I can't stand it. I want a bigger house."

No, you must learn to be happy right where you are. Understand that it dishonors God for us to go around complaining and thinking about everything that's wrong in our lives. You may not be living in your dream house, but you should thank God you have a roof over your head. Thank God you're not homeless, living out there in the elements.

"My husband and I don't have anything in common. We don't get along anymore."

Well, he may not be the perfect husband. But you can thank God that at least you have somebody to love. Do you know how many people are lonely today? Believe it or not, some woman would be glad to have your husband. Be grateful for that man. Be grateful for that woman.

We need to recognize that every day is a gift from God. What a shame to live any day in a negative and defeated mind-set.

Certainly, we all have obstacles in our path and challenges to overcome, but our attitude should be, "Thank God, I'm alive. I live in a great country. I have family. I have opportunity. So I'm going to make the most of this day and give it my best."

"Well, Joel, I would do that, but I just found out I have to work late next week. I have to go on a business trip. I've got to take care of these kids all day."

No, you don't *have* to do anything; you get to do it. God is the One who has given you breath. You wouldn't be able to work late next week if God hadn't opened up that door of opportunity. You need to change your perspective. Don't do things out of obligation or because you have to — do them with an attitude of gratitude. In other words, "I don't have to go to work today; I get to go to work." "I don't have to take care of these children, they're a blessing; I get to take care of them." "I don't have to give; I get to give."

The Scripture says, "When we are willing and obedient, we will eat the good of the land."[65] It's one thing to be obedient. That's good. That's better than not doing it. But if you really want to experience God's best, you need to be more than obedient; you have to be willing. You have to do it with the right attitude.

For instance, it's one thing to give because you have to. It's another thing to give because you want to. It's one thing to go to work to pick up a paycheck. It's another thing to go to work to be a blessing to somebody else. It's one thing to stay married to that person because it's the right thing to do. People may look down on you if you don't. But it's another thing to stay married to that person and to treat him or her with respect and honor and help your partner reach a higher level. That's being willing and obedient. When you do the right thing with the right motives, there's no limit to what God will do in your life. It is important that we get beyond mere obedience. That's easy, anybody can do that. To become a better you, take the next step and be willing to do the right thing with a good attitude.

Roger was down and discouraged so he went to see his minister for some advice. "Nothing's going right in my life," Roger said. "I don't have any reason to be excited."

The minister thought for a moment and then said, "All right, let's do a simple exercise." He took out a legal pad and drew a line right down the center. "On the left side, we're going to list all of the good things in your life, everything that's going right. And on this other side, we'll list all your problems and all these things that are bothering you."

Roger laughed skeptically and said, "Okay, but I'm not going to have anything to put on the asset side."

The minister said, "Fine, let's just go through the exercise."

Roger put his head down.

The minister said, "I'm so sorry to hear that your wife passed away."

At that, Roger snapped to attention. "What are you talking about?" he asked. "My wife didn't pass away. She's alive and healthy."

"Oh, really?" The minister wrote on the asset side: "Has a wife, alive and healthy." Then he said, "I'm so sorry to hear that your house burned down."

"What?" Roger cried. "My house didn't burn down. I have a beautiful house."

"Oh, really?" the minister said, as he wrote on the asset side of the ledger: "Has a beautiful house." Then he said, "I'm really sad to hear that you lost your job. You got laid off."

"Where are you getting all this nonsense?" Roger asked incredulously. "I've got a great job."

"Oh, really?" the minister said, as he raised his eyebrows and wrote down, "Has a great job."

About that time, Roger caught on. He said,

"Give me that list." The minister passed the yellow legal pad to Roger, who proceeded to list several dozen more good things in his life. By the time he was finished, he left the minister's office with a different attitude. His circumstances hadn't changed, but his perspective was completely different.

It's so easy to get focused on what's wrong and to take for granted what's right, what is going well. When you focus on the good, that's when you bolster your enthusiasm and passion. If you struggle with staying excited and passionate about your life, you too need to make a list of all the things for which you can be grateful. Write down all the things God's blessed you with. If you have your health, write it down. "I'm healthy." If you can see, write it down. "I can see." If you're good-looking (like me!), write it down. "I'm good-looking." If you have a job, write "I've got a job. I've got family. I have several close friends. I have great children." Make that list and every day before you leave the house, read over it two or three times. It is important to get your mind going in the right direction, because your life will follow your thoughts.

At the first of the day, set the tone. If you can go out with a grateful attitude and a positive frame of mind, you'll not only feel better, but you also will draw in the good things of God. We attract what we continually think about. If you get up thinking, *My life is dragging; nothing good ever happens to me. I know my marriage isn't going to last,* you attract defeat, failure, and mediocrity. However, if you can learn to turn it around and go out with a grateful attitude, thinking about how blessed you are and how good God's been to you, then you will draw in the goodness of God.

Sometimes we lie in bed in the morning thinking, *I don't want to go to work today. I've got so many problems. I'm sick and tired of cleaning this house.*

Unfortunately, you just paved the way to have a lousy day. You made preparations for defeat.

When those negative, discouraging thoughts come, you must turn them around. Get your list out and read over it again. Remind yourself, "I'm alive. I'm healthy. I've got a great spouse. I have beautiful children. I have so many good things." Put that list on your bathroom mirror, on your desk, or some place where you can see it throughout the day. Read over it occasionally as you go about your normal routine, and it will help you to stay excited about your life.

Another important key to fanning your

passion is to keep fresh goals before you. Some people have lost their passion for life simply because they're not pursuing anything. But understand that God created us to be always reaching for something beyond where we are presently. If you live with low motivation, few dreams, and no realistic goals, you are bound to become stagnant. On the other hand, if you will continue to pursue a new goal, it will keep you fresh and excited about life. Your goal needn't be lofty or grandiose. It may be a goal to finish school, or to be a better parent, or to increase your income. Still, have something out in front of you. Always be growing and never allow yourself to become complacent. After you accomplish one goal, immediately set another. Keep moving; keep looking for new challenges.

If you're not healthy, have a dream to get healthy. If you're in debt, let your dream be, "I'm going to get out of debt and be a blessing to others as well." Then get up each day knowing that you're pressing toward that goal.

"Well, Joel, I'm retired," you might be saying. "I'm just kicked back, taking it easy." No, even though you are retired from your job, you never retire from the life of service God has for you. It is unhealthy to not have something to pursue every day.

Years ago, my father and I met Jacques Cousteau, the famous underwater explorer. Daddy and I were on a flight down to the Amazon jungle and Mr. Cousteau was on the same flight, so we engaged in conversation. He was probably in his early eighties, yet he was incredibly passionate about his life. He began telling us about a new project he was working on, excitedly explaining it in great detail. As we were about to leave, he told us about his ten-year plan and all that he hoped to accomplish. I thought, *Most people his age are not thinking ahead much more than a week or a month. But Jacques Cousteau is still thinking ten years down the road.* No wonder he was so vibrantly alive.

If your assignment right now is to raise your children, do it with passion; do it with enthusiasm. Maybe you have a dream to start a business, a dream to own your own home, a dream to be in the ministry. Keep it in front of you and keep pressing toward it.

The Scripture says in Proverbs, "Where there is no vision, the people perish." My dad kept a globe everywhere he worked — at his chair at home where he studied and on his desk at the office. Daddy's passion was to share God's love all over the world, and that globe reminded him of that. Even later in my father's life when he had to go on dialysis, he asked us to check to see if they could do dialysis in India. Although Daddy never made it back to India once he started dialysis, that didn't keep him from dreaming. In fact, that was one of the things that helped him to get up every day with enthusiasm in spite of his adversity.

Maybe you have some obstacles or challenges in your path as well. That's fine, but don't give up on your dreams. God still has something important for you to do. However, if you make the mistake of dwelling on the wrong things, before long you'll be planning your own funeral. No matter what the situation looks like in the natural, keep your dreams alive. You may be a mother raising small children and you're facing a serious illness. Keep a picture of your children in front of you. Get up every day and say, "I'm going to be here to raise my children. I'm going to live and not die."

Or perhaps you are struggling financially, but you have a dream of owning your own home. Keep that dream alive. Put up a picture of the home you would like to have. Keep it in front of you. You need something to be striving toward, then work and save and make wise financial choices, and you will be surprised how your dream can become a reality.

REMEMBER THE MIRACLE

Sometimes we lose our enthusiasm because we let what once was a miracle become too common to us. We get used to it and it becomes routine. For instance, maybe at one time you were excited about your job. You prayed and believed and you know God opened up that door for you. God supernaturally gave you that position, and you couldn't wait to get to work every morning. You got there and gave it 100 percent. Now, a few years later, the newness has worn off. It's become routine, and you don't really enjoy going to work anymore, and you have become discouraged. Do you know what has happened?

You let your miracle become common. You need to go back and remember how God brought you to where you are. You need to fan your flame.

I'm not saying that we never want to move on, but too many times we are taking things for granted that we should still be excited about.

A friend of mine complained incessantly about his job. He told me how the company wasn't treating him right. He wasn't being paid enough money. He couldn't stand his boss. On and on it went. One day, the company announced that they were going to downsize and lay off about half of the employees and it looked as though he was going to get laid off. Amazingly, my friend really started liking his job. At the last minute, his company decided to keep him on, and you would have thought he'd just won the lottery! It's interesting how things like that can change our perspective. You may be a lot more excited about your job if you realize that you may not always have it.

Or maybe you would be much more excited about your marriage partner if you thought you were about to lose that person. At one time, you were so excited that you couldn't keep your eyes off him or her. But over the years you've allowed yourselves to grow stale, stagnant, and apart. You don't enjoy each other like you should. You don't have time for hugs and kisses and compliments. You're too busy to talk at night. You might miss your favorite TV program.

No, don't take that other person for granted. Do whatever you have to do to get that spark back and rekindle the relationship that brought you together in the first place. Bring some freshness to your marriage. Get out of your normal routine and do something different.

I am a person of habit, and I have to make myself get out of my normal routine. For instance, Victoria and I have a date night every Friday night. Usually we simply go out to eat, take some time to talk, and enjoy being together. But we've also done more adventurous activities for our date nights as well. Not long ago, we went and rode go-karts. Another time, we took our bikes down to the park and rode them around.

It takes a little creativity, but with effort you can do something to bring some freshness to your relationship. Don't lose that enthusiasm for the other person. Don't let that miracle, that relationship with the person God has brought into your life become so commonplace that you take it for granted.

Maybe at one time, you were excited about that house God's given you. You prayed, you believed, and you know God opened up the door. But now you think, I have to clean this place, my gutters are messed up, my dishwasher quit working. Taxes are so high.

You are focused on the wrong things. God blessed you with that house. No doubt, at one time it was a dream come true. Don't allow it to become commonplace.

We should never lose the amazement of what God has done. Every time I drive by Lakewood Church, I am amazed. And I've made up my mind that twenty years from now, I'm still going to be amazed. As I drive into Lakewood's parking lot, I say, "God, You've done more than we could ever ask or think."

God told some people in the book of Revelation, "I'm not happy with you because you've left your first love." In other words, you're not excited about what I've done for you. Too often, we do the same thing. We let something that was so great at one time become routine and we don't appreciate it as we should.

I heard a reporter ask a famous heart surgeon how he kept his excitement. This man had developed a certain procedure and he had performed it more than a thousand times. By now, the operation was considered routine and ordinary.

The reporter asked the surgeon, "Do you ever get tired of doing it?"

"No," he said, "because I act like every operation is my first one."

He was saying, "I don't take for granted what God has allowed me to do. I don't want to let it become so common that it doesn't excite me anymore."

Maybe God has done great things in your life. He's taken you further than you could dream. He's brought great people into your life. He's opened up great doors. Don't get so accustomed to those things that they don't excite you anymore. Choose to remain passionate, living every day with enthusiasm.

Sometimes I hear people complain about their children. "Well, I'd be more enthusiastic if I didn't have to stay here and take care of my children all day."

No, you're missing the point. Your children are a miracle, and if you want evidence of that, simply think back to the day they were born. No doubt you had tears running down your cheeks. You were so overjoyed. You knew each child was a gift from God. Don't allow that sense of awe to disappear with time.

Recently, I was in a hurry to leave the house and trying to get the family rounded up and out the door. Somebody had given us a label maker — a little machine that prints out labels — and our children loved to play with it. Jonathan had the label maker out and was typing a message.

I said, "Jonathan, put that thing away. We've got to go."

He said, "Daddy, just give me a few more seconds. I want to finish this up."

"No, Jonathan," I said. "Put it up. We have got to go right now." He and I bantered back and forth and I was getting all uptight. Finally, he got finished and printed out the label. It read: "BEST DADDY IN THE WORLD."

I thought, *Well, maybe we can stay here a little longer and print a few more of these labels!*

Sometimes we get in such a hurry that we miss the miracles all along the way. Take time for your children. Look in their eyes every day and tell them how much you love them, how proud you are of them. Think of the joy and the fulfillment they bring you. That alone should be enough to cause us to get up each day with enthusiasm. And when you're tired of cleaning up after them or tempted to have a bad attitude, learn to turn it around. Say, "Father, thank You for these children. Thank You for each of these gifts that You've given me."

Miracles are all around us. The people in your life, the doors God has opened, the things that have happened along the way are not by accident. It was God's favor that caused you to be at the right place at the right time. You met someone and fell in love. Or you qualified for that home and you know that by all usual means you would not have done so. Or you got that promotion unexpectedly. These are not coincidences. God was directing your steps, so don't take it for granted.

What are you focused on today? Are you becoming a better you? Is there peace in your home and in your heart and mind? Are you happy, at rest, and enjoying life? We need to realize that this day is unique and irreplaceable. We need to make the most of it, and live like it could be our last.

An elderly couple I knew were tremendous role models, always smiling and encouraging other people, and everyone loved them — especially the young people. Moreover, after decades of marriage, they still treated each other with honor and respect.

In her mid-eighties, the woman went home to be with the Lord. At the funeral, her husband, also an octogenarian, told an interesting story. He said, "About fifteen years ago, I had a heart attack. When my wife came to the hospital, she said, 'Honey, this just shows us how fragile life really is. You could have died.' She said, 'From now on, every night before we go to bed, I want us to kiss seven times just to show how much we love each other, just to show that we're not taking each other for granted.' And so, for these last fifteen or twenty years, we never went to sleep without kissing seven times."

Don't you love that? That woman lived every day like it could be her last. She went to be with the Lord on a Tuesday, but Monday night, she kissed her husband seven times. Monday night, she told him how much she loved him. And when her life was over, she had no regrets. She made every day special. The last day of her life, she lived it loving, caring, at peace, and enjoying every moment. That's the way I want to live.

Friend, this day is a gift, so make the most of it. Shake off anything that hints of self-pity or discouragement and find some reason to be grateful.

Becoming a better you is all in how you choose to view life. I heard a story about two men who were patients in the same hospital room. Every day, the man closest to the window shared with his friend what he saw outside, describing it in great detail, so his roommate could enjoy the view, even though he was confined to his bed.

"Today, I see a beautiful sunrise," he'd say. "The kids are out there playing. The trees are blooming," and on and on. Each day, the bed-ridden patient looked forward to hearing his roommate's report on the outside world. It was the highlight of his day.

One day, the patient next to the window became so excited. "Oh, you should see it! There's a parade coming by, with a marching band, kids and adults celebrating something and having such a good time."

After several weeks, the patient next to the window passed away, so his friend asked the nurse if he could have the bed by the window, so he could see all the great scenes of activity outside.

"Why, certainly," the nurse replied, as she and an orderly moved the patient to the bed next to the window. But when the man looked out the window, much to his surprise, all he could see was a brick wall. About fifteen feet away stood another wing of the hospital. The patient called the nurse back in, and said, "Hey, wait a minute! What's going on? My friend who passed away described all those beautiful scenes for several weeks, and I can't see anything but a wall!"

The nurse smiled and said, "Sir, didn't you realize that your friend was blind? He chose to see a beautiful life from the inside out."

No matter what twists and turns life takes, you can find the good if you look for it. If we have the right attitude, we can see the sun shining even when it's cloudy. We can stay full of joy and keep getting better, even when things don't go our way.

My prayer is that God would give us a spirit of gratitude, that we'd always focus on the good and never take life for granted. If you will trust God each day and live according to His plan for your life, you will be happier, healthier, and you'll rise higher than you ever imagined possible.

Make a decision that you're going to live every day with enthusiasm. Get up each morning and think about all the things for which you can be grateful. If you need to, make a list. Keep it in front of you and then go out each day pursuing your God-given dreams.

The Bible says, "To set your mind and keep it set on the higher things." [66] I believe the higher things are the positive things, so first thing every day, set your mind in the right direction. Set your mind for success and victory. Set in your mind that you are going to enjoy this day. Then rise higher and get into the jet stream of God!

Remember, friend, you have seeds of greatness in you. You weren't made to be stagnant; rise out of complacency; keep growing, keep reaching for new heights. Your best days are still out in front of you.

You have not seen, heard, or imagined the great things God has in store for you. As you keep stretching to the next level, improving your life, and reaching for your highest potential, you will not only give birth to your dreams, but you will become a better *you,* better than you ever dreamed possible!

1. Today, I will look for tangible ways that I can stay passionate about life. I will develop a habit of smiling on purpose. I will keep singing a song of joy in my heart, despite the circumstances. I will have a grateful attitude, recognizing this day is a gift.

2. I will exercise my faith in a positive direction, preparing for success, and expecting God's best in my life. This week, I will tell someone close to me that I am planning to live a long, healthy, prosperous life. I will take action to fill my life with healthy activities, while eliminating any unhealthy actions, attitudes, or lifestyle issues.

3. I choose to move from believing to expecting. Today I will reach for something beyond where I am presently. I will actively pursue new goals, keeping them out in front of me, and expecting to meet them.

4. I will be continually aware that becoming a better me is all in how I choose to

view life. I will constantly look for ways to improve my life; I will choose to be kind to people; I will seek more vibrant relationships with the people closest to me, and I will actively pursue a deeper relationship with God.

5. I choose to live this day passionately as a positive reflection of God in our world. I will put actions behind my faith and leave a lasting legacy for my family and the world.

WE CARE ABOUT YOU!

I believe there is a void in every person that only a relationship with God can fill. I'm not talking about finding religion or joining a particular church. I'm talking about developing a relationship with your heavenly Father through His Son, Jesus Christ. I believe that knowing Him is the source of true peace and fulfillment in life.

I encourage you to pray, "Jesus, I believe You died for me and rose from the dead, so now I want to live for You. I am turning away from my sins and placing my trust in You. I acknowledge You as my Savior and Lord, and I'm asking You to guide my life from now on."

With that simple prayer, you can get a fresh, clean start, and establish a close relationship with God. Read the Bible every day; talk to God through prayer, and attend a good Bible-based church where you can find friends who will lift you up rather than pull you down. Keep God in first place in your life and follow His principles; He will take you places you've not yet imagined!

For free information on how you can grow stronger in your spiritual life, we encourage you to contact us. Victoria and I love you, and we will be praying for you. We'd love to hear from you!

To contact us, write to:

Joel and Victoria Osteen
P.O. Box 4600
Houston, TX 77210–4600

Or you can reach us online at www .joelosteen.com.

NOTES

1. See Romans 11:29.
2. Psalm 30:5.
3. See Isaiah 28:16 and Romans 10:11.
4. See Psalm 139:16.
5. See Revelation 12:11.
6. See 2 Corinthians 5:17.
7. See Genesis 2:7.
8. Galatians 3:29.
9. See Isaiah 61:7.
10. Galatians 3:13.
11. John 8:36.
12. Proverbs 26:2.
13. James 5:16.
14. See Ephesians 6:12.
15. 1 Chronicles 4:40.
16. See Romans 7:19.
17. See Ephesians 6:14.
18. See Philippians.
19. Hebrews 4:16.
20. Luke 15:20.
21. Matthew 22:39.

22. See Hebrews 12:1–2.
23. Matthew 3:17.
24. See Ephesians 1:4–14.
25. James 3:10.
26. See Romans 4:17.
27. See Jeremiah 1:4–9.
28. Philemon 1:6.
29. 1 Corinthians 13:4.
30. 1 Corinthians 13:5.
31. See Romans 12:16.
32. See James 4:17.
33. See Proverbs 31:28.
34. See Hebrews 3:13.
35. Galatians 6:10.
36. See Luke 6:43–45.
37. See Matthew 25:40.
38. See 2 Timothy 3:1–5.
39. See 1 Corinthians 10:13.
40. Philippians 4:8.
41. See Matthew 26:41.
42. 1 Thessalonians 5:16.
43. Matthew 10:14.
44. Isaiah 54:17.
45. Song of Solomon 1:6.
46. Psalm 46:10.
47. Hebrews 4:3.
48. Romans 8:28 NKJV.
49. Proverbs 3:5–6.
50. Psalm 30:5.
51. Psalm 77:11.

52. 1 Thessalonians 2:13.
53. Psalm 30:5.
54. Luke 12:48.
55. 1 John 4:4.
56. Psalm 91:7.
57. See 2 Corinthians 5:20.
58. See Hebrews 13:15.
59. See James 5:7.
60. See James 2:17.
61. 2 Corinthians 5:7.
62. Isaiah 40:31.
63. Mark 5:36.
64. Romans 12:11.
65. Isaiah 1:19.
66. See Colossians 3:2.

ABOUT THE AUTHOR

Joel Osteen is the pastor of a new generation. Called by many "America's voice of hope," Joel has been recognized as one of the 10 Most Fascinating People by Barbara Walters.

Joel Osteen reaches a huge audience in the United States and across the globe. Tens of millions of people in more than a hundred nations worldwide are inspired through his weekly television broadcasts, his *New York Times* bestselling books, his sold-out international speaking tours, and his weekly top-ten podcasts.

Joel and his wife, Victoria, are the pastors of America's largest church — Lakewood Church in Houston, Texas.